Youth and Employment

Yosuke Uchiyama • Fumitaka Furuoka

Youth and Employment

Creating a Productive and Dynamic Society

Springer

Yosuke Uchiyama
Transportation Institute
Chulalongkorn University
Bangkok, Thailand

Fumitaka Furuoka
Asia-Europe Institute
University of Malaya
Kuala Lumpur, Malaysia

ISBN 978-981-95-3256-8 ISBN 978-981-95-3257-5 (eBook)
https://doi.org/10.1007/978-981-95-3257-5

This Springer imprint is published by the registered company Springer Nature Singapore Pte Ltd.
The registered company address is: 152 Beach Road, #21-01/04 Gateway East, Singapore 189721, Singapore

To Noemie, for your enduring love, grace, and quiet strength, and to my parents for your steadfast support and love that knew no distance.
Yosuke Uchiyama

To my better half and cahaya mata, *Dr Larisa Nikitina*
Fumitaka Furuoka

Preface

What does it mean to be young in a world where work is increasingly precarious and where institutions are more likely to reproduce exclusion than to offer support? This book, *Youth and Employment: Creating a Productive and Dynamic Society*, begins with that question. It explores the structural forces that shape how young people enter, navigate, and reshape the labour market today. Precarity, institutional exclusion, and unequal access to knowledge are not personal shortcomings but manifestations of deeper, systemic conditions. These are not incidental or fleeting; they are intricately entangled with the transformation of the state, corporations, education systems, and the expanding reach of platform capitalism. This book integrates theoretical inquiry with empirical depth to examine how these forces are experienced, negotiated, and, at times, quietly resisted by youth themselves. It is not only a study of employment conditions but also a search for institutional forms through which a more inclusive and generative society might emerge.

My engagement with this theme stems from a series of life transitions across four cities: Tokyo, Kuala Lumpur, Bangkok, and London. These experiences reshaped how I understood career formation—not as an individual trajectory, but as one regulated and constrained by institutional and social contexts. Comparing educational systems, labour practices, and welfare regimes across regions made clear to me how profoundly institutions condition experience and choice—and how young people are not merely recipients of institutional design but also agents of transformation.

My journey began in Tokyo. Although Japanese universities ostensibly uphold academic freedom, I often felt that they functioned more as a rite of passage into society. The job-hunting season, beginning in the last year of university, was less a time of reflection than a synchronised ritual pressuring students into selecting an ostensibly "suitable" path. I, too, was swept into that current. However, a turning point came when I enrolled—alone—in a course where the professor said: *"You must design and carry out your own six-month learning plan. If you succeed, you will receive the highest grade."* It was my first real experience of learning not as something to be received but something to be constructed. It taught me the value of active, self-directed inquiry—an approach that has only grown more essential in today's global society. Building on this experience, I independently planned and undertook fieldwork in Pune, India, visiting the Japanese language department at a local university. I observed classes and delivered a special lecture. Engaging with motivated students there made me acutely aware of how the Japanese ethos of invisibility and non-disruption, cultivated through education, severely limits the scope of possibility. From this moment, my interest in Southeast Asia began to crystallise. Initiated by several visits to the region and a short-term programme in Singapore, I became fascinated by the region's economic dynamism, cultural complexity, and the political logic of the ASEAN Way. This intellectual curiosity led me to pursue graduate studies at the Universiti Malaya in Malaysia, a leading hub for ASEAN studies.

Living in Kuala Lumpur through my master's and doctoral studies meant navigating daily the intersections of institutional design, cultural politics, and social hierarchy. In a multi-ethnic society composed of Malays, Chinese, and Indians, access to education and employment is profoundly shaped by ethno-political considerations. Unlike in Japan, where I benefited from implicit social legibility, as a foreign student in Malaysia, I confronted my outsider status directly. In this multicultural, competitive, and collaborative environment, I learned to assert myself and to make visible the hidden labour often overlooked by institutions. At the Universiti Malaya, I met Professor Fumitaka Furuoka—my supervisor and co-author of this book. A prominent Japanese economist who has lived and worked in Malaysia for over 30 years, he introduced me to the emerging field of gig work in Southeast Asia. He encouraged me to approach questions of labour insecurity and institutional exclusion through theoretical analysis and comparative fieldwork. With his guidance, I conducted research across 11 Malaysian states and interviewed over 100 gig workers—delivery riders, ride-hailing drivers, and hybrid workers. Their accounts revealed the institutional voids, unstable incomes, and social isolation that accompany "flexibility." Among them, 55 young workers formed the empirical backbone of Chapter 6, grounding the book's broader argument for rethinking labour institutions in Asia.

After completing my doctorate, I had the opportunity to join the Chulalongkorn University Transportation Institute in Bangkok, Thailand. Though rooted in civil engineering and transport studies, this research environment offered fertile ground for interdisciplinary work. It allowed me to link labour and infrastructure, especially in relation to informal urban mobility. I investigated how young people sustain livelihoods in grey zones—motorcycle taxis, food delivery, informal transport—and how their everyday practices reconfigure urban space and challenge institutional boundaries. These themes form a critical thread in the book's analysis of informality and legitimacy.

In 2025, I was appointed as a visiting research fellow at the Department of Digital Humanities, Faculty of Arts and Humanities, King's College London. This opportunity marked a pivotal moment: a transition from regional specialisation to comparative institutional research. Through daily conversations with scholars from around the world, I deepened my understanding of youth employment and gig work as global phenomena with locally specific challenges. A formative experience during this period was my engagement with the Independent Workers' Union of Great Britain (IWGB). Hearing from members—delivery riders, ride-share drivers—who were asserting their rights through lawsuits, workshops, and campaigns, I witnessed how individual experiences of precarity can evolve into collective institutional challenges. It revealed to me that young people are not just adapting to institutional constraints—they are actively contesting and transforming them.

These experiences also led me to revisit theories of learning and institutional design. Drawing on Kajita Eiichi's classification of educational goals and Nonaka Ikujiro's SECI model of knowledge creation, this book theorises learning as a process of observation, experimentation, understanding, and internalisation. Youth, in this formulation, are not passive recipients but dynamic participants—acquiring knowledge, challenging systems, and, in doing so, helping to build new institutional forms. The holistic policy and learning framework proposed in Chapter 7 reflects this synthesis of theoretical and empirical insight.

This book is both a personal record of movement and a collective account of how young people live and contest labour precarity. As a young researcher, their experiences resonate with my own—they are not just subjects of inquiry, but mirrors. Institutions are never neutral. Yet it is precisely the voices of youth who confront these structures, and the scholarly efforts to amplify those voices, that may illuminate paths forward. I hope this book offers a modest contribution to that effort.

Bangkok, Thailand
June 2025

Yosuke Uchiyama

Competing Interests The authors have no competing interests to declare that are relevant to the content of this manuscript.

Contents

Chapter 1
Introduction

Chapter 1 introduces the book and its contents. It begins with background that explains how youth unemployment has become a major obstacle to achieving the United Nations Sustainable Development Goal (SDG) of "employment for all." It then presents the theoretical linkages between youth and employment through three perspectives: the two-sector job search theory, a holistic taxonomy of knowledge and skill development for youth, and a two-layer model of platform capitalism. The chapter concludes by outlining the book's overall structure and clarifying how the subsequent empirical and case-study chapters build toward the theoretical contributions and policy implications proposed in this study on youth unemployment.

1.1 Background: Thorny Issue of High Youth Unemployment

We are living in an intriguing time when the world economy is becoming more sustainable and inclusive. In this process, everyone, including young people, may need to make their contribution to their countries to create a sustainable future. This tremendous economic and societal transformation officially began in the 2010s when world leaders discussed it and eventually adopted the Sustainable Development Goals (SDGs). In June 2012, the United Nations Conference on Sustainable Development (UNCSD) suggested the basic ideas and framework for the SDGs in Rio de Janeiro, Brazil. In September 2015, more than 150 political leaders around the world officially approved bold and ambitious SDGs by launching the 2030 Agenda for Sustainable Development in New York City, the United States. The SDGs systematically incorporate seventeen critical global agendas, such as no poverty, zero hunger, excellent health, quality education, and full employment for all, including youth (United Nations, 2024).

Y. Uchiyama, F. Furuoka, *Youth and Employment*,
https://doi.org/10.1007/978-981-95-3257-5_1

Among the 17 goals in the SDGs, there are four that have close links with young people. Firstly, the first goal (SDG1), or the "*no poverty*" goal, aims to eradicate extreme poverty for all, including young people. The provision of decent work for youth could contribute to eliminating their extreme poverty. Secondly, the fourth goal (SDG4), or the "*quality education*" goal, aims to ensure equal access to technical and tertiary education for all, including young people. The provision of quality education and training for youth could serve as an important stepping stone for them to obtain decent work. Thirdly, the tenth goal (SDG10), or the "*reduced inequality*" goal, aims to reduce socioeconomic inequality by promoting universal social, economic, and political inclusion, including young people. A key remedy for alleviating income inequality based on age is to promote decent work for youth. Finally, among these four goals, the eighth goal (SDG8), or the "*decent work and economic growth*" goal, has the closest linkage and the most crucial implication for young people. This connection is primarily due to the explicit mention of youth employment as a key priority in achieving this important goal. In other words, we cannot achieve the fundamental goal of SDG8, or sustained and inclusive full employment, without promoting job opportunities for young people. This goal also implies that providing decent work for youth is a crucial step towards achieving sustainable inclusion, as it addresses an urgent and persistent economic and social issue of youth unemployment (United Nations, 2024).

More specifically, SDG Target 8.5 stipulates that it aims to achieve full employment for all women and men, including young people, by 2030 (United Nations, 2024). However, a question remains: what is full employment? According to economic theory, full employment does not refer to a situation in which everyone has a job. Keynes (1936) famously defined "full employment" as a labour market situation where nobody is involuntarily unemployed. Based on this definition, Beveridge (1944) defined full employment as a labour market condition where the number of vacancies is greater than the number of unemployed workers. In other words, full employment could be considered a labour market condition where job seekers can find employment within a reasonable amount of time (Dornbusch & Fischer, 1990). In this context, full employment for youth is a labour market condition where any young job seeker can find employment within a reasonable time.

Despite this seemingly clear definition, the "ambiguity" of job seekers may make it difficult for researchers to pinpoint the precise level of full employment for youth. More specifically, there are two main reasons for this problem, namely the proliferation of informal job searches and the heterogeneity of job seekers. Firstly, job seekers may use different approaches to job search, namely formal job search and informal job search. A formal job search is a direct method to find a job through contacting employers, collecting information from employment services, and reading newspaper advertisements. By contrast, the informal job search is an indirect method of finding a job through collecting information from friends, relatives, and neighbours. More importantly, young people prefer to use the informal job-search method. (Wielgosz & Carpenter, 1987). From a methodological perspective, job seekers are workers who are actively seeking employment opportunities. In other words, a labour agency may classify "passive" job seekers who prefer to use informal job search methods as "not in the labour force" (US Bureau of Labour Statistics, 2025a). It means that the proliferation of informal job search methods among youths could cause a methodological problem in estimating the exact number of young job seekers in the labour market.

Secondly and more fundamentally, there exists a heterogeneity of job seekers, or a mutually exclusive dichotomy, which includes employed job seekers (i.e., workers who are currently employed but actively seek new job opportunities) and unemployed job seekers (i.e., unemployed workers actively seeking new job opportunities). Employers tend to favour employed job seekers over unemployed ones due to their inability to estimate job productivity accurately, and they often perceive current employment as a sign of high productivity. In other words, the likelihood of unemployment is higher for unemployed job seekers compared to those who are employed (Longhi & Taylor, 2014). Young job seekers tend to have no job experience or current employment. It means that young unemployed job seekers could not find any employment in a labour market condition when "full employment" is achieved for employed job seekers.

In this sense, the unemployment rate, rather than the employment rate, could be considered a more straightforward and better indicator to measure the policy goals of SDG8. This advantage is primarily because unemployment is based on a more concise classification of unemployed workers, specifically those job seekers who have conducted a job search within 4 weeks. The US Bureau of Labour Statistics (2025a) meticulously estimates the unemployment rate by considering the "activeness" of job seekers and calculating the ratio of unemployed workers to the labour force, which includes both employed and unemployed workers. Therefore, we could use the SDG Indicator 8.5.2, which measures the unemployment rate by gender, age, and persons with disabilities, to monitor the progress of SDG8 towards full employment. Figure 1.1 shows that the global youth unemployment rate was around 14% in

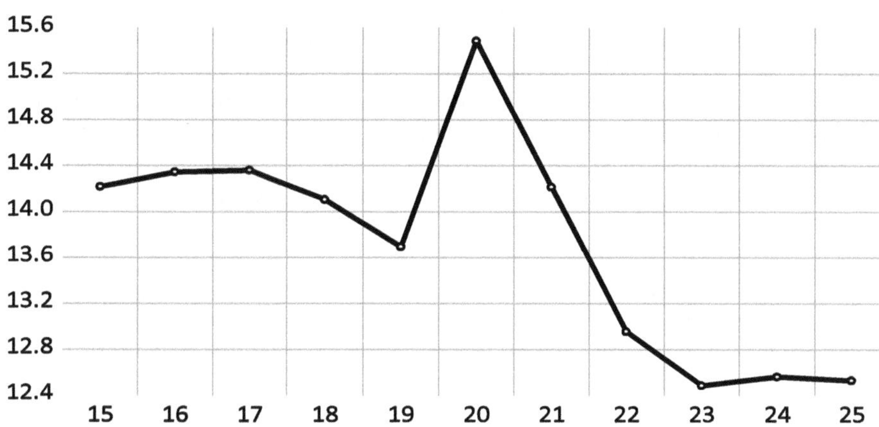

Fig. 1.1 Global youth unemployment rate from 2015 to 2025. Source: International Labour Organisation (2025)

the second half of the 2010s, according to a comprehensive labour market dataset, or ILOSTAT, compiled by the International Labour Organisation. During the COVID-19 pandemic period, it spiked up to 15%. After the end of the pandemic, it was reduced to around 12% (International Labour Organisation, 2025).

The figure indicates that global youth unemployment decreased from 14% in the 2010s to 12% in the 2020s. However, it appears that global youth unemployment will not reach zero. Does this statistic imply that the SDG Target 8.5 will not reach its intended goal? As mentioned previously, the unemployment rate would not reach zero in the labour market even if the economy achieved full employment. There are two alternative schools of thought in the field of macroeconomics that provide contradictory interpretations of the unemployment rate under full employment, namely Keynesian economics and new classical economics. According to the Keynesian definition, the unemployment rate under full employment is the labour market situation where there is an absence of involuntary unemployment (i.e., workers are willing to work, but they are unemployed).[1] However, there would still be a possibility that frictional unemployment (i.e., temporary unemployment due to the transition from an old job to a new job) and voluntary unemployment (i.e., unemployed workers who are unwilling to work) would exist under full employment (Keynes, 1936).[2] Under this Keynesian interpretation, researchers could measure the progress of SDG8 by examining whether there is no "involuntary" unemployment among youth in the labour market. However, it is difficult for them to understand concisely what a measurable difference there is between "voluntary" and "involuntary" unemployment.

Therefore, we may need to use an alternative school of thought or the new classical economics to interpret the unemployment rate under full employment. According to this interpretation, the unemployment rate under full unemployment would be equal to the natural rate of unemployment, also known as the non-accelerating inflation rate of unemployment (NAIRU), which could be considered a steady state of unemployment (Rissman, 1986). The idea of the natural rate of unemployment is suggested by two prominent scholars, namely Phelps (1967) and Friedman (1968). They claimed that the actual unemployment rate would approach its natural rate, which would depend on the labour and commodity markets, such as market imperfections, stochastic volatility of demand and supply, costs of information, and so on (Phelps, 1967; Friedman, 1968). In this alternative interpretation, we can assess the progress of SDG8 by analysing whether youth unemployment worldwide aligns with the natural rate of unemployment or the NAIRU.

[1] Keynes strongly denied the classical economists' assumption that the source of unemployment is "voluntary" unemployment. In other words, classical economists claimed that all workers would be unemployed if the real wage rate exceeded their preference for leisure over work (Keynes, 1936; Tobin, 1972).

[2] Before the Keynesian revolution in the field of macroeconomics, classical economists made a strong assumption that, without government intervention, full employment could be achieved in the labour market, which would automatically adjust labour supply and demand (Keynes, 1936; Tobin, 1972).

This chapter estimates the level of the natural rate of youth unemployment using an estimation method suggested by Ball and Mankiw (2002). Appendix 1.1 offers a detailed explanation of this estimation method. There is a two-step procedure for estimating the natural rate of unemployment for youth. In the first step of estimation, the change in the inflation rate would be regressed by a constant and the unemployment rate. In the second step of estimation, the natural rate of unemployment could be obtained by dividing the intercept by the absolute value of the regression coefficient. In this estimation, the data period is from 2001 to 2023, and the number of observations is 23. The data source for the youth unemployment rate is the International Labour Organisation (2025), and the data source for the inflation rate is the World Bank (2025). Using this method, the change in the inflation rate could be estimated as:

$$\widehat{\Delta p_t} = 10.14 - 0.725 U_t \tag{1.1}$$

where $\widehat{\Delta p_t}$ is the estimated value of the inflation change, and U_t is the unemployment rate. Using this estimation, the natural rate of unemployment for youth could be estimated as 13.95. According to the International Labour Organisation (2025), 94 countries provide data on youth unemployment. Of these 94 countries, 52 have youth unemployment rates that are lower than the estimated natural rate of global unemployment. By contrast, 42 countries have youth unemployment rates which are greater than the natural rate. Based on this estimation, the policy focus of SDG8 should be on how to reduce youth unemployment in these 42 countries where their unemployment rates are greater than the global youth unemployment rate.

1.2 Linking Youth with Employment

This book uses three theoretical perspectives to create a linkage between youth and employment: the two-sector search model for young workers, the taxonomy of holistic knowledge and skill acquisition for youth, and the two-layer model of platform capitalism. Firstly, persistently high levels of youth unemployment may be regarded as the most challenging issue in promoting full employment for everyone. The seriousness of high youth unemployment could be captured by examining patterns of unemployment rates among disadvantaged workers in the United States. Figure 1.2 depicts unemployment rates among disadvantaged workers. These five types of unemployment rates among disadvantaged workers could be separated into three distinctive groups, namely the "low unemployment" group, the "middle unemployment" group, and the "high unemployment" group. Firstly, there is a co-movement between the total unemployment rate and women's unemployment rates. These two unemployment rates are relatively lower among the five unemployment rates. This indicates that gender minorities do not pose a barrier to achieving full employment. Secondly, unemployment rates among Black or African

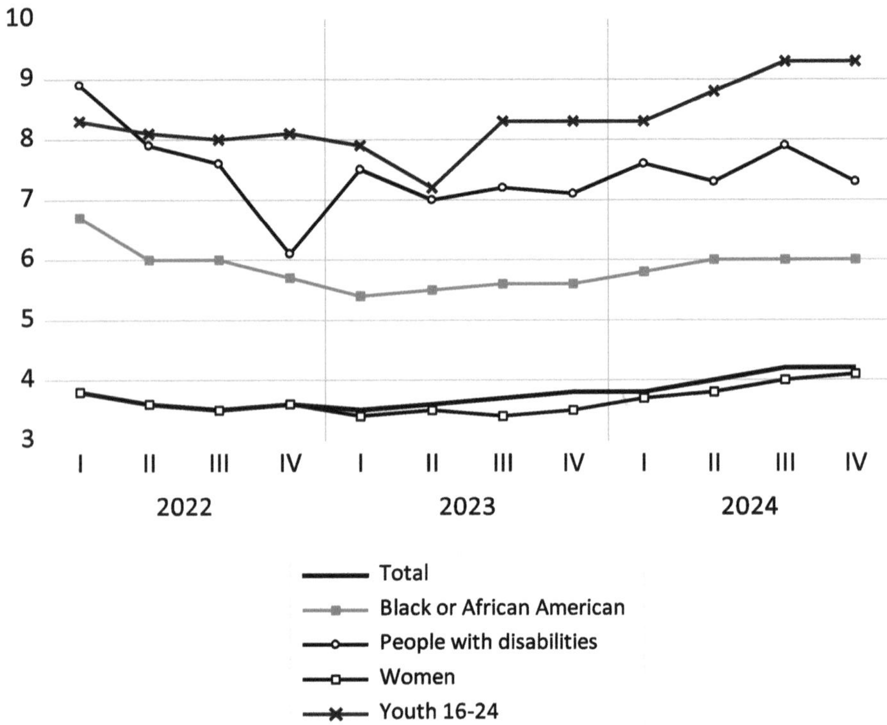

Fig. 1.2 Unemployment Rates among Disadvantaged Workers in the United States from 2022 to 2024. Source: US Bureau of Labour Statistics (2025b)

Americans are between two extreme groups, namely the "low unemployment" group and the "high unemployment" group. This indicates that the ethnic minority is not a major issue; however, measures are needed to reduce unemployment rates to match those of the "low unemployment" group. More importantly, unemployment rates among youth and people with disabilities are relatively higher among these five types of unemployment. The unemployment rates among youth and people with disabilities can be viewed as the "twin challenges" for promoting full employment (Furuoka, 2024a). Especially, there was a decrease in the unemployment rate among people with disabilities in 2022. In 2024, on the other hand, the youth unemployment rate increased. It means that there emerged a wider gap in the unemployment rate between youth and people with disabilities.

Furthermore, Table 1.1 reports the main characteristics of the unemployment rate among disadvantaged workers in the United States. Basically, the findings in this table confirmed the pattern of unemployment rates, as depicted in Fig. 1.2. Firstly, the mean values, standard deviations, maximum values, and minimum values of total unemployment and women's unemployment are approximately identical. These facts confirm the co-movement of these two unemployment rates. Secondly, the mean value of the unemployment rate among Black or African Americans is 56%

Table 1.1 Main characteristics of the unemployment rate among disadvantaged workers in the United States from 2022 to 2024

	Total	Black or African American	People with disabilities	Women	Youth aged 16–24
Mean	3.7	5.8	7.4	3.6	8.3
Standard deviation	0.2	0.2	0.6	0.2	0.5
Maximum	4.2	6.7	8.9	4.1	9.3
Minimum	3.5	5.4	6.1	3.4	7.2

Source: US Bureau of Labour Statistics (2025b)

higher than that of total unemployment. At the same time, the mean value is 43% lower than that of unemployment among youth. These facts also confirm that relatively high unemployment among Black or African American people is an issue, but not a major one. More importantly, the mean value of youth unemployment is 12% higher than that of the unemployment rate among people with disabilities. The fact reveals that high youth unemployment could be considered the greatest challenge to achieving full employment for all.

From a theoretical perspective, the canonical search model could be used to explain the reason why the youth unemployment rate is persistently high. The canonical search model is also known as the Mortensen–Pissarides (MP) search model (Mortensen & Pissarides, 1994; Pissarides, 2000). Particularly, the two-sector model for people with disabilities (Furuoka, 2024b) could be applied to the analysis of high youth unemployment. This specified model for disadvantaged workers is based on extensions of the two-sector model (Acemoglu, 2001). Appendix 1.2 offers a detailed explanation of the two-sector search model for young workers. This model is based on three conditions: the zero-profit condition, the surplus-sharing condition, and the flow-equilibrium condition. However, there is a similarity in the labour market between workers with disabilities and young workers. This section elucidates the unique problem of youth unemployment by focusing on the first condition only.

The deep-seated cause of high unemployment among disadvantaged workers, such as young workers and workers with disabilities, could be that the business cycle has a stronger negative impact on their employment compared to the rest of the population. Under this "procyclical" assumption, disadvantaged workers would face two distinctive problems in the labour market. Firstly, at the downturn phase of the business cycle, disadvantaged workers would lose their employment in the earlier stage of this economic crisis. This characteristic is known as the "first-to-be-fired" aspect in the pattern of disadvantaged workers' employment. Secondly, at the upturn phase of the business cycle, disadvantaged workers would obtain their employment in the later stage of the economic recovery. This characteristic is known as the "last-to-be-hired" aspect (Furuoka, 2024b). In this two-sector search model for young workers, the subscript is used as follows: y denotes young workers aged 16–24, and p denotes older workers aged 25–64. Using these subscripts, the "procyclical" assumption for young workers could be captured by the following inequality (Furuoka, 2024b):

$$\lambda_y > \lambda_p \tag{1.2}$$

for $\beta = y, p$,where λ is the job destruction rate. In other words, young workers are more likely than prime-aged workers to lose their jobs due to an economic shock, resulting in a transition from employment to unemployment. The distinctive feature of young unemployment could be understood by applying this "procyclical" assumption with the "zero-profit" condition, which would be determined by four Bellman equations. The first Bellman equation (Eq. 1.8) indicates that maximising surplus value, or the difference between revenue and cost, is the fundamental force in the industrial relationship between employers and employees. In recent years, traditional capitalism has been transformed into new forms of capitalism, such as post-industrial capitalism and platform capitalism, due to rapid advances in information and communication technologies (ICT) and artificial intelligence (Amorim et al., 2023). However, employers may apply the same business logic of "buying to sell dearer" in these new forms of capitalism. Using this business principle, employers would employ only workers with an abundance of knowledge and skills (Furuoka, 2024b). In other words, employers would not provide sufficient employment opportunities to youth who lack useful knowledge and desirable skills. This is because employers tend to consider that youth would not contribute to the creation of high values in the process of surplus-value maximisation.

The second Bellman equation (Eq. 1.9) indicates that the main component of the value of vacant job value or the search cost (i.e., γ) tends to be proportional to the productivity of a potential employee to fill the vacant job (Pissarides, 2000; Acemoglu, 2001; Furuoka, 2024b). In other words, employers are willing to bear the high cost of finding suitable candidates for seasoned financial professionals or highly specialised IT experts. However, it is less likely that employers will pay additional search costs to find a young worker with less experience. Like workers with disabilities, young workers could be "invisible" in the eyes of job recruiters (Furuoka, 2024b). This "invisibility" of youth could be the main source of prolonged youth unemployment. There is a need for policy intervention to overcome this problem in the labour market.

The third Bellman equation (Eq. 1.10) indicates that the main component of the value of employed workers is their wages. Economic theory assumes that there is a proportionality between wage rate and productivity (Kandori, 2023). Under this assumption, young workers tend to receive relatively lower wages than prime-aged workers due to a lack of experience and skill among young workers. It means that this Ballman equation captures the problem of low wages for young workers. In the labour market, the only available economic incentive for workers to obtain employment is earning a wage from that employment. However, young workers will not be willing to enter the labour market because they expect to obtain employment with only a low wage. There is a structural problem in the labour market where a readily available economic incentive could be too weak to induce and encourage youth to get a job in the labour market.

The fourth Bellman equation (Eq. 1.11) indicates that the main component of the value of unemployed workers is the "utility" of unemployed workers. Economic theory assumes that there is a proportionality between wage rate and marginal utility of leisure (Kandori, 2023). This theory of labour-leisure choice also assumes that the disutility of additional labour is equal to the utility of leisure (Borjas, 2013). If workers dislike increasing their work, the employers may need to pay a higher wage to induce them to work. It also means that this Ballman equation captures a problem of high utility of unemployment for young workers. Some young workers may have a high utility of unemployment or leisure. For example, their parents are willing to provide them with accommodation, food and some money even if they do not have any employment. To maintain their comfortable status quo, these youths would be unwilling to "exchange" their leisure time for working time. Under this situation, employers must pay higher wages to attract these "reluctant" young workers. There is another structural problem in the labour market where some young workers may have a higher utility of being unemployed, which becomes a stumbling block for them to obtain employment.

Under this first condition of the zero-profit in the labour market, the interaction between two types of jobs (i.e., filled jobs and vacant jobs) and two types of workers (i.e., employed and unemployed workers) would determine the equilibrium level of the wage rate. This two-sector search model assumes that any firm could freely enter the market if there are profit-making opportunities. Under this "free-entry" assumption, the asset value of a vacant job would be equal to zero. This assumption simplifies the matches between jobs and workers in the labour market into a combined Bellman equation (i.e., Eq. 1.12). This equation indicates that the expected profit of a filled job would be equal to the expected cost of a vacant job. It also means that there would be equality of revenue and cost in the equilibrium level of wage rate, which is the zero-profit condition.

More importantly, the job-creation (JC) curve (i.e., Eq. 1.13) implies that employers would create a vacant job, which would balance costs and revenue. If employers created a job match between young workers and a less stable job with a high separation rate, the wage rate would be lower because the expected costs of these vacancies would be high. By contrast, a job match between prime-aged workers and more stable jobs with a lower separation rate and wage rate would be higher due to the low expected costs of these vacancies. Two figures in Furuoka's book on disability and employment, namely Fig. 6.1 (page 153) and Fig. 6.2 (page 154), could be used to understand how a low wage rate for young workers would cause a high unemployment rate for them. More precisely, the interactions between the JC curves and a common wage-setting mechanism would determine lower wage rates for young workers than prime-aged workers. In turn, this lower vacancy-unemployment ratio would cause a higher unemployment rate in the negative relationship between vacancy and unemployment. A fundamental question is why younger workers suffer from the "procyclical" tendency to have risky jobs with a high likelihood of destruction. During an economic shock, employers tend to eliminate jobs where productivity is below a certain threshold value, known as reservation productivity (Mortensen & Pissarides, 1994; Pissarides, 2000). This means that younger workers tend to have a higher possibility of losing their jobs because they tend to create a match with low-productivity jobs. It also means that the solution for young unemployment is that they need to upgrade their skills and knowledge so that they would have "better" and less risky jobs, which would not be destroyed by these shocks.

Secondly, another thorny issue of youth unemployment is the lack of work experience among young people. Many young people prefer to enter higher learning institutions, such as universities or colleges. However, the knowledge which could be obtained in universities is not practical enough to obtain employment opportunities in the labour market. On the other hand, employers are not willing to employ workers who have no work experience (Kolesnikova et al., 2015). As was mentioned above, the lack of skills and knowledge could be a root cause of the higher job destruction for young workers. In this context, how do young people obtain the necessary knowledge and skills to obtain employment in the labour market and prevent losing this employment in the economic downturn?

For this purpose, employers may need to provide appropriate training and learning opportunities for youth to acquire certain skills and knowledge. From a theoretical perspective, there is a need to develop a systematic taxonomy, which could be used to develop a lifelong learning process to transform young people into real experts in their workplace. There is a famous taxonomy for educational objectives, as suggested by Bloom et al. (1956). This taxonomy became a fundamental classification for creating curricula in higher learning institutions (Lau et al., 2018). However, Bloom's taxonomy could not be used directly to develop a curriculum for a youth training program. This is mainly because Bloom's taxonomy could not fully incorporate the business practices in its classifications.

To overcome this problem, this book reconstructs a holistic framework for the systematic acquisition of knowledge and skills by young people to develop fully their potential. Specifically, it proposes a new taxonomy that can connect both goal setting in the educational field and knowledge formation in the company. This framework is constructed by integrating Eiichi Kajita's taxonomy of educational objectives (Kajita, 2014), which is based on teaching practices in school education, and Ikujiro Nonaka's knowledge management theory (Nonaka, 1991), which focuses on the knowledge creation process in companies. By connecting both theories, it is possible to overcome the disconnect between education and practice and construct a knowledge system that contributes to career development, especially for youths. The rationale for this proposal and the details of the integrated theory are discussed in Chap. 2. Furthermore, Chap. 2 builds on this integrative taxonomy and presents an educational framework with more international applicability by incorporating the four learning stages and their corresponding educational philosophies.

In the proposed taxonomy, the first stage, the "opening", represents the initial phase of knowledge acquisition. Within modern capitalist systems, companies function as repositories of accumulated knowledge, and young individuals require access to this accumulation through apprenticeships or other employment opportunities. At this stage, experiential knowledge must be identified, visualised, and rebuilt; failing to do so may render subsequent knowledge acquisition processes superficial and incomplete. Moreover, cultivating an orientation toward self-realisation is a critical foundation for sustained learning. The second stage, the "showing", involves the absorption of practical knowledge through the imitation of physical actions and evaluative criteria demonstrated by senior workers. This stage facilitates the transfer of experiential knowledge that cannot be fully captured through formalised instructions or standardised procedures. In the third stage, the "awakening", the cumulative effects of imitation and experiential learning reach a critical threshold, giving rise to sudden insights, structural understanding, or what is often described as an "aha" experience. At this stage, knowledge deepens through the reciprocal transformation and integration of tacit and formal knowledge systems. Finally, the fourth stage, the "entering", represents the application of new knowledge to practical business contexts and the integration between knowledge and value creation. At this point, knowledge is socially reproduced as young workers emerge as autonomous carriers of expertise capable of generating new value within society.

Thirdly, the incidence of youth unemployment is not isolated. In other words, a persistently high level of youth unemployment has taken place in the new form of capitalism under the rapid development of information and communications technology (ICT) and artificial intelligence (AI). This new capitalism could be called "platform capitalism". In the context of the Asian digital and platform economy, Yosuke Uchiyama of Chulalongkorn University made a significant contribution to the existing literature on digital capitalism in the region by publishing three prominent articles (Uchiyama et al., 2024; Uchiyama & Furuoka, 2025; Uchiyama, 2025). Uchiyama claimed that the rapid expansion of platform economic transactions and the proliferation of gig work represented the rise of platform capitalism, which emerged from neoliberal capitalism. There are two prominent features of capital accumulation in this new capitalism that differ from conventional capitalism. The first feature is that gig workers could be considered as the main contributors to profit maximisation. The second feature is that the platform owners would bear the least risk when conducting the business transaction. In other words, platform owners controlled the means of production using algorithms and metrics in this explorative structure of business transactions and commodified the labour-power of gig workers with the cheapest possible labour cost (Uchiyama et al., 2024; Uchiyama & Furuoka, 2025; Uchiyama, 2025).

Furthermore, Uchiyama claims the presence of a dual-layer exploration mechanism to control gig workers in digital capitalism. In the first layer of this exploration mechanism, platform owners would exploit legal loopholes in the employment laws to justify their crude "cost-saving" practice. In this tripartite structure of digital capitalism, the two main parties involved in the power concentration and profit-maximisation mechanism—platform owners and consumers—would align with each other to form a strong alliance that isolates gig workers. In the second layer of this mechanism, platform owners would buy possibly the "cheapest" labour power from gig workers by commoditising them through a "black box" of algorithms and metrics. In this explorative commodification process, gig workers would often be deprived of receiving minimum wage and social protection because of their "legal" status as independent contractors rather than "regular" employees in the firms (Uchiyama et al., 2024; Uchiyama & Furuoka, 2025; Uchiyama, 2025).

Nevertheless, the dominant assumption in previous debates around the platform economy has been that the lack of institutions and the absence of regulation are central to the problem-setting of gig-worker vulnerability and that platform companies are located outside the system and are evaders of its regulation (Srnicek, 2017; Stewart & Stanford, 2017). However, recent studies have pointed out that platform firms are not merely subject to regulation but are rather involved in the design of the system itself, strategically restructuring existing institutional resources (Leonardi & Pirina, 2020; Uchiyama et al., 2024). Therefore, it is now imperative to move beyond the discourse of institutional absence and to articulate a new structural perspective whereby platform companies embed themselves within existing institutional frameworks and actively reconfigure them to serve their strategic interests.

Building on this critical perspective, the present study brings together two existing theoretical frameworks: platform capitalism, which conceptualises capital accumulation in digital spaces as a mediating structure of labour (Srnicek, 2017), and regulatory capitalism, which understands regulatory restructuring itself as constitutive of capitalism (Levi-Faur, 2005). The institutional configuration that emerges at the intersection of these frameworks is theorised herein as a strategically embedded form of institutional restructuring, whereby platform firms reshape existing governance arrangements to align with their economic and operational logics. This new conceptual foundation shows that platform companies are not entities external to institutions but rather cleverly embedded within them, selectively reorganising and redefining existing institutional frameworks and public infrastructure while restructuring them in line with their profit structures. From this perspective, it becomes possible to go beyond the traditional unitary understanding of the enterprise as a regulated entity and to identify the mechanism by which the industry functions as a co-constituent of the system.

Furthermore, by integrating the above conceptual perspective with Eiichi Kajita's classification of educational objectives and Ikujiro Nonaka's theory of knowledge creation (SECI model), this book proposes a comprehensive educational and institutional solution to the disconnect in knowledge formation and lack of institutional support that youths face in a platform working environment. This integrated model—Youth Labour Knowledge Formation under structurally embedded institutional constraints—reconceptualises knowledge acquisition as a visible and institutionally embedded process. It ensures that youths are not marginalised or excluded from the system but are instead positioned as active bearers of knowledge and co-constructors of institutional design.

1.3 Structure of the Book

Following this introductory chapter, the second chapter is a literature review chapter, which offers detailed explanations of the theoretical perspective and conceptual framework of this study. This chapter introduced two interrelated but distinctive constructs for the underlying theoretical perspectives, namely platform capitalism and regulatory capitalism. Firstly, platform capitalism is a new form of capitalism that has emerged in the twenty-first century. The characteristic of this twenty-first-century capitalism is the use of digital and network technology to exploit workers through the mediation of services and workers. The main problem with this form of capitalism is that it makes workers more fluid and vulnerable. In this context, the main challenge in industrial relations in the twenty-first century is how to protect young people from the exploitation of a new form of capitalism. Secondly, regulatory capitalism emphasises the crucial role of regulation in the development and transformation of all forms of capitalism. In other words, this perspective would provide an institutionalist perspective to reformulate the relationship between states, corporations, workers and consumers. From this perspective, the market would not function properly without rules and regulations. In other words, this perspective could be used to justify the active labour market policies (ALMPs) that provide some legal protection for youth. Thirdly, this book reconceptualises platform firms not as external disruptors but as strategically embedded actors that operate from within institutional frameworks. Rather than bypassing existing systems, these firms actively participate in the reorganisation of governance structures, leveraging public infrastructure and institutional ambiguity to enhance their competitive positioning. In doing so, they internalise and reconfigure institutional mechanisms in line with profit-maximising logic. Under these dynamics, the precariousness of youth employment has intensified. In response, this chapter presents a conceptual framework aimed at supporting holistic knowledge and skill development among young people. This framework synthesises two theoretical models: Eiichi Kajita's taxonomy of educational objectives (Kajita, 2014) and Ikujiro Nonaka's knowledge management theory (Nonaka, 1991), enabling a rethinking of youth education and labour formation under platform-mediated employment conditions.

The third chapter is the first analytical chapter, which uses several advanced statistical methods to examine the validity of the first assumption of the Law of One Unemployment Rates. According to this assumption, there would be "uniformity" among the patterns of unemployment rates among different demographic groups. For this purpose, this chapter used four kinds of the ADF-type unit root test, namely the augmented Dickey-Fuller (ADF) test (Dickey & Fuller, 1979, 1981), the Fourier ADF (FADF) test (Enders & Lee, 2012), the ADF with a structural break (ADF–SB) test (Perron & Vogelsang, 1992, 1993) and the FADF with a structural break (FADF–SB) test (Furuoka, 2017). These tests were used to examine whether the unemployment rates are unit root processes or not. Additionally, this chapter also used four kinds of KPSS-type stationarity tests, namely the KPSS test (Kwiatkowski et al., 1992), the Fourier KPSS (FKPSS) test (Becker et al., 2006), the KPSS with structural break (KPSS-SB) test (Kurozumi, 2002) and the Fourier KPSS with structural break (FKPSS-SB) test (Furuoka, 2017). The findings from these stationarity tests could be used to confirm the findings from the ADF-type tests.

The fourth chapter serves as the second analytical chapter and employs a specific statistical procedure to test the validity of the LOUR's second assumption. The second assumption stipulates that there would be no persistence in the unemployment gaps, which are differentiated by gender (i.e., the gender unemployment gap), disability (i.e., the disability unemployment gap), and age (i.e., the age unemployment gap). This chapter focuses on the age unemployment gap, which is the unemployment difference between young workers and prime-age workers. For empirical analysis, this chapter considered two types of young workers, namely teenage workers aged 16–19 and young workers aged 20–24. It also considered five types of elderly workers, namely the lower prime-age workers aged 25–34, the middle prime-aged workers aged 35–44, the upper prime-aged workers aged 45–54, and the older workers aged 55–64. This paper also used two kinds of ADF-type unit root tests, namely, the ADF test (Dickey & Fuller, 1979, 1981) and the Yaya–Ogbonna–Furuoka–Alana (YOFA) test (Yaya et al., 2021) and two kinds of KPSS-type stationarity tests, namely, the KPSS test (Kwiatkowski et al., 1992) and the KPSS-YOFA test. Among these four tests, the KPSS-YOFA test is a new stationarity test that synthesises the methodologies of the YOFA test and the KPSS test.

The fifth chapter is the third analytical chapter that examines "high-end" gig work, particularly crowdwork and online freelancing in Thailand. There is a wealth of literature on "low-end" gig workers, such as delivery workers and e-hailing workers. However, there is a lack of systematic research on high-paid gig work, which may require higher knowledge and skills. Especially, there is little systematic research on the "high-end" gig workers in developing countries. So, this chapter aims to fill this important gap by conducting systematic interviews with high-end gig workers in Thailand. Crowdwork could be defined as "micro task-based" gig work which are distributed to a "crowd" of numerous gig workers through the platform. On the other hand, online freelancing could be defined as a "project-based" gig work where clients would offer a contract to freelancers through the platform. For data collection, nine high-end gig workers were selected, and in-depth interviews were conducted with each of these nine. Furthermore, for data analysis, thematic analysis is used to identify the main themes of interview scripts.

The sixth chapter is the final key analytical chapter in this book. Low-end gig work has emerged as the primary source of employment for young workers, particularly in developing countries, following the decline of manufacturing sectors. For example, the Malaysian government estimated that there were more than 300,000 micro-workers and gig workers in 2020, and this gig work contributed to 40% of the livelihoods of poor people in the country. Particularly, it is estimated that more than 90% of delivery workers are young people. Despite the increase in the number of empirical studies on this crucial topic, there is still a lack of systematic empirical findings regarding "low-end" gig work in developing countries. This study is the first of its kind to conduct a comprehensive nationwide interview for gig workers, which covered over eleven states out of the thirteen states in the country. For data collection, twenty e-hailing gig workers and thirty-five food delivery gig workers were selected for the in-depth interview. For data analysis, a systematic and detailed thematic analysis is used to examine the contents of the interview manuscript.

The seventh chapter is the concluding chapter, which consists of four sections. The first section summarised the main findings of four analytical chapters, from Chapter Three to Chapter Six. The second section in the conclusion chapter is the theoretical contribution. It examines whether empirical findings would give some additional insights into the existing literature on youth employment. The third section aims to outline practical implications derived from the empirical findings. The final section offers a holistic taxonomy for knowledge and skill development for youth as a remedy to mitigate the thorny issue of youth unemployment.

Appendix 1.1 Estimation of the Non-accelerating Inflation Rate of Unemployment Among Global Youth

The mainstream economic theories seem to assume that the level of unemployment under full employment would converge to the non-accelerating inflation rate of unemployment (NAIRU) rather than zero. For example, the US government uses NAIRU to measure whether full employment is achieved. This is because the government considers it a useful policy tool to ensure the lowest unemployment rate and stable unemployment (Friedman, 1968; Rissman, 1986; Michaillat & Saez, 2024). However, a practical and methodological question remains: how to estimate the NAIRU. A simple method to estimate the NAIRU is suggested by Ball and Mankiw. Their estimation is based on the trade-off between inflation and unemployment. Under this assumption, the impact of monetary policy would move the inflation rate in the opposite direction of the unemployment rate (Ball and Mankiw, 2002). For example, an increase in the money supply would cause an increase in inflationary pressure, but it would contribute to reducing the unemployment rate. By contrast, a decrease in the money supply would increase unemployment and decrease the inflation rate.

Under the theoretical assumption of the traditional Phillips curve (Phillips, 1958), the trade-off relationship between unemployment and inflation could be formulated as (Ball and Mankiw, 2002; Gordon, 2011; Furuoka et al., 2023):

$$p_t = \gamma + \alpha U_t + \varepsilon_t \tag{1.3}$$

where p_t is the inflation rate, U_t is the unemployment rate, ε_t is an error term, γ is an intercept, and α is the slope coefficient, which is used to capture the strength of the trade-off relationship between inflation and unemployment rate. In the downward Phillips curve relationship between inflation and unemployment, α is less than zero (i.e., $\alpha < 0$).

However, some new classical economists criticised a theoretical block of the traditional Phillips curve or the co-movement of the inflation rate with unemployment rates by stressing the importance of expectations (Lucas & Rapping, 1969; Lucas, 1972; Lucas, 1973; Sargent & Wallace, 1975). For example, Lucas and Rapping (1969) claimed that there is a proportional co-movement between the expected inflation rate (p^*) and actual inflation rate (p). Under this hypothesis, a downward-sloping Phillips curve would exist only if the elasticity of inflation expectations concerning inflation or the ratio of the change in expected inflation (Δp^*) to change in actual inflation (Δp) is less than unity. Furthermore, Lucas (1972) strongly denied the notion of the "money illusion", where economic agents tend to fail to differentiate between nominal and real money (Fisher, 1928; Keynes, 1936).[3] The money illusion could be used to explain the traditional Phillips curve relationship between inflation and unemployment.[4] Instead, Lucas claimed that all economic agents are rational, and their expectations would be optimal. In the absence of the "money illusion", Lucas assumed that any negative relationship between unemployment and inflation could be caused by imperfect information on whether inflation is caused by a change in aggregate demand or money supply (Lucas, 1972). Furthermore, Lucas (1973) pointed out that the difference between the actual inflation rate and expected inflation, which is conditioned on the available information I_t or $p_t - E_t[p_t| I_t]$ would have an impact on the cyclical component of aggregate supply. Similarly, Sargent and Wallace (1975) claimed that the difference between the actual inflation rate and expected inflation or $p_t - E_{t-1}(p_t)$ would have an impact on

[3]The notion of "money illusion" has also been harshly criticised by some prominent Keynesian economists, such as James Tobin. For example, Tobin famously claimed that there is no bigger crime than the assumption of "money illusion", which could be committed by theoretical economists (Tobin, 1972). Consequently, the notion of "money illusion" has become an anathema among theoretical economists (Fehr & Tyran, 2001). However, after another revolution in behavioural economics, the "money illusion" is accepted as a basic assumption for understanding human behaviour (Erber, 2012).

[4]Before the advent of rational expectations theory, some prominent economists used this concept in their theories. For example, Friedman (1968) proclaimed a theory of monetary non-neutrality. According to him, this new macroeconomic theory is based on a misperception or "money illusion" among workers. If there were an increase in the money supply, there would be an increase in the nominal wage. Thus, workers are willing to provide more labour services because they tend to focus on the nominal wage and have a misperception that their "reward" for work has increased (Fehr & Tyran, 2005). At that time, macroeconomists believed that the government could use economic policy to manipulate the inflation rate and the unemployment rate. More precisely, a monetary policy could be used to create "artificially" a desirable equilibrium point Z with a relatively high unemployment rate of U_Z and relatively low inflation of P_Z. If U_Z would be higher than the unemployment rate in the labour market equilibrium $\overline{U}$, workers may need to provide the amount of labour E_Z which is greater than the labour supply at the labour market equilibrium $\overline{E}$. However, the problem with this idea is that there is a gap between the "artificially" induced labour supply and the actual labour supply $\left(E_Z - \overline{E}\right)$. The presence of this unfilled gap was justified and explained by the notion of "money illusion" among workers. In this interpretation, workers would make "irrational" decisions that would increase their labour supply by interpreting the nominal inflation of money wage induced by an increase in money supply as an increase in real wage (Carlin & Soskice, 1990).

aggregate supply. They also asserted that the difference between expected future inflation and expected current inflation in the future or $E_{t-1}(p_{t+1}) - E_{t-1}(p_t)$ would have an impact on aggregate supply.

Under these alternative assumptions of the "rational expectations",[5] the trade-off relationship between unemployment and inflation could be reformulated by incorporating expected inflation (Ball and Mankiw, 2002; Gordon, 2011; Furuoka et al., 2023):

$$p_t = E_{t-1}(p_t) + \alpha U_t + \varepsilon_t \tag{1.4}$$

where $E_{t-1}(p_t)$ is the expected inflation rate. Furthermore, the available proxy for the expected inflation rate is the lagged value of the inflation rate. Under this assumption of adaptive expectation, the trade-off relationship between inflation and unemployment could be expressed as a backwards-looking Philipps curve (Ball and Mankiw, 2002; Gordon, 2011; Furuoka et al., 2023):

$$p_t = p_{t-1} + \alpha U_t + \varepsilon_t \tag{1.5}$$

where p_{t-1} is the lagged value of the inflation rate.

However, the natural rate revolution transformed the fundamental assumption of the Phillips curve type of trade-off relationship between inflation and unemployment. The natural rate of unemployment, or equilibrium unemployment, is the unemployment rate at which inflation remains unchanged. In other words, the natural rate of unemployment is consistent with a consistent and stable level of unemployment. In other words, if the government uses a monetary policy to reduce the unemployment rate below its natural rate, it will cause upward pressure on the inflation rate. It means that this monetary policy would reduce the unemployment rate but increase the inflation rate (Phelps, 1967; Friedman, 1968; Gordon, 2011). In this context, there is no trade-off between the inflation rate and unemployment, but there is a negative association between the inflation rate and the unemployment gap between the actual unemployment rate and its natural rate or the NAIRU. By taking account of the natural rate of unemployment, the natural rate-augmented Phillips curve can be expressed as (Ball and Mankiw, 2002; Gordon, 2011; Furuoka et al., 2023):

---

[5]The rational expectations hypothesis was first formulated by Muth (1961). Muth defined it as a rationality assumption that the average of expectations is accurate, which is expressed as $E_{t-1}(p_t) = E(p_t | I_{t-1})$. It means that "subjective" expectation of price level (i.e., $E_{t-1}(p_t)$) would be equal to the "objective" expectation of price level (i.e., $E(p_t | I_{t-1})$). In other words, the rational expectations hypothesis is basically based on the assumption of the equality of the "subjective" and "objective" expectations. However, mainstream economists did not pay due attention to this interesting and innovative idea for more than a decade. It started transforming basic assumptions of macroeconomic theories and their estimation methods only after the publication of three seminal papers by Robert Lucas (1972, 1973, 1983). In other words, Lucas initiated this revolution of rational expectations in the field of macroeconomics by using this largely ignored hypothesis (Mishkin, 1995).

$$p_t = p_{t-1} + \alpha(U_t - U^*) + \varepsilon_t \tag{1.6}$$

where U^* is the natural rate of unemployment. For the estimation of the natural rate of unemployment, the natural rate-augmented Phillips curve could be further reformulated (Ball and Mankiw, 2002; Gordon, 2011; Furuoka et al., 2023):

$$\Delta p_t = p_t - p_{t-1} = \alpha U_t - \alpha U^* + \varepsilon_t \tag{1.7}$$

Using this formulation, the value of the natural rate of unemployment or the NAIRU for youth (YU^*) could be estimated by regressing the inflation change (Δp_t) on a constant ($\alpha \times YU^*$) and the unemployment rate of the youth (YU_t).

Appendix 1.2 The Two-Sector Search Model for Youth

The persistently high level of youth unemployment rate emerged as the main challenge to achieving full employment for all, which is stipulated in SDG Target 8.5. The two-sector search model for youth could be used to examine the main reason why young people tend to suffer from high unemployment. This model is extended from the two-sector search model, which is suggested by Acemoglu (2001). He created a sophisticated conceptual model to understand the problem of a "bad" job. Furuoka (2024b) extended this two-sector search model to examine the issues of employment among people with disabilities. In this appendix, the two-sector search model for people with disabilities is adjusted and modified for the analysis of youth unemployment.

Following the theoretical foundation of the Mortensen–Pissarides (MP) search model (Mortensen & Pissarides, 1994; Pissarides, 2000), the two-sector search model for youth is also based on three conditions, namely the zero-profit condition, the surplus-sharing condition and the flow-equilibrium condition. However, the basic problem of the high unemployment rate could be understood by examining the first condition of the zero-profit. This zero-profit condition is determined by the interaction of four asset values: the asset value of the filled job (i.e., J^F), the asset value of a vacant job (i.e., J^V), the asset value of the employed worker (i.e., J^E) and the asset value of unemployed workers (i.e., J^U). These asset values could be formally described by four Bellman equations (Pissarides, 2000). Using the first Bellman equation, the asset value of the filled job (i.e., J^F) could be expressed as (Mortensen & Pissarides, 1994; Pissarides, 2000; Acemoglu, 2001; Heijdra & van der Ploeg, 2002; Furuoka, 2024b):

$$rJ_\beta^F = (o - w) - \lambda_\beta \left(J_\beta^F - J_\beta^V \right) \tag{1.8}$$

for $\beta = y, p$, where o is the revenue or output of the filled job, w is the cost or wage of the filled job, and λ is the Poisson arrival rate of a shock to separate workers from the filled job. This job separation rate or job destruction rate is considered an "exogenous" rate which governs the flow from employment to unemployment in the labour market. In this sense, $(J^F - J^V)$ is considered the net loss for employers when the shock arrives and destroys the filled jobs. More importantly, $(o - w)$ is considered the surplus value, which is the difference between revenue and cost. The basic objective of employers is to produce as much surplus value as possible in their business transactions. More precisely, there are two separate movements in this process of surplus-value maximisation. In the first movement, employers would buy the labour force at a price w from employees in the labour market. Employers would buy the cheapest labour force (i.e., the lowest value of w) to decrease the cost. In the second movement, employers would sell products at a price o to buyers in the product market. Employers would sell their products at the most expensive price (i.e., the highest value of o) to increase revenue. In other words, the value creation of "buying in order to sell dearer" is the basic principle in merchant capitalism as well as industrial capitalism (Marx, 1986).

Regarding the second Bellman equation, the asset value of a vacant job (i.e., J^V) could be expressed as (Mortensen & Pissarides, 1994; Pissarides, 2000; Acemoglu, 2001; Heijdra & van der Ploeg, 2002; Furuoka, 2024b):

$$rJ_\beta^V = -\gamma + q(\theta)\left(J_\beta^F - J_\beta^V\right) \tag{1.9}$$

for $\beta = y, p$, where γ is the search cost to find a suitable worker to fill the vacant job, $q(\theta)$ is the Poisson arrival rate of the match for the vacant job to "meet" with the well-suited worker. In this context, $(J^F - J^V)$ is considered the net gain for employers if they can find suitable workers to fill their vacant jobs. Furthermore, this job-filling rate or $q(\theta)$ is the function of θ, which is a ratio of the vacancy rate to the unemployment rate or $\theta = v/u$. This vacancy-unemployment ratio could be used to capture the "tightness" of the labour market. In the "tight" labour market, the number of vacant jobs is relatively higher than the number of unemployed workers. In these labour market conditions, employers may face more difficulties in finding suitable workers. By contrast, the number of job seekers is relatively higher than the number of job openings in the "loose" labour market. In these labour market conditions, employers may find it easier to employ well-suited workers.

With regard to the third Bellman equation, the asset value of the employed worker (i.e., J^E) could be expressed as (Mortensen & Pissarides, 1994; Pissarides, 2000; Acemoglu, 2001; Heijdra & van der Ploeg, 2002; Furuoka, 2024b):

$$rJ_\beta^E = w - \lambda_\beta\left(J_\beta^E - J_\beta^U\right) \tag{1.10}$$

for $\beta = y, p$, where w is the wage rate for employed workers and λ is the Poisson arrival rate of a shock to separate or destroy jobs from employed workers. In this context, $(J^E - J^U)$ is considered the net loss for the employed worker if they were to lose their employment. More importantly, there is a proportional relationship between the wages of employed workers and their productivity. This is because the marginal productivity of labour should be equal to the wage rate at the profit-maximising point (Kandori, 2023). This means that workers with high productivity would receive higher wages in the process of profit maximisation.

Regarding the fourth Bellman equation, the asset value of the unemployed (i.e., J^U) could be expressed as (Mortensen & Pissarides, 1994; Pissarides, 2000; Acemoglu, 2001; Heijdra & van der Ploeg, 2002; Furuoka, 2024b):

$$rJ^U_\beta = z + \theta q(\theta)\left(J^E_\beta - J^U_\beta\right) \tag{1.11}$$

for $\beta = y, p$, where z is the net utility of the unemployed worker, $\theta q(\theta)$ is the Poisson arrival rate of the match for unemployed workers to "meet" with vacant jobs. In this context, (J^E – J^U) is the net gain for unemployed workers to find a suitable employment opportunity. The main component of the value of unemployed workers is the "utility" of unemployment, including income from unemployment insurance and the value of unpaid household work. If unemployed workers received generous payments under the unemployment insurance scheme, they would not be keen to find new employment until the end of the insurance payment. More importantly, if employed workers did many useful household works, such as cooking, child-caring, cleaning, laundering and shopping and would get unpaid but high utility, they would also not be keen to seek employment opportunities.

By combining these Bellman equations, the zero-profit condition could be expressed as (Mortensen & Pissarides, 1994; Pissarides, 2000; Acemoglu, 2001; Heijdra & van der Ploeg, 2002; Furuoka, 2024b):

$$(o - w) - \left(r + \lambda_\beta\right)\gamma/q(\theta) = 0 \tag{1.12}$$

for $\beta = y, p$, where (o – w) is the surplus value or expected revenue of a filled job and $(r+\lambda_\beta)\lambda/q(\theta)$ is the expected cost of a vacant job (Heijdra & van der Ploeg, 2002; Furuoka, 2024b). This cost is expressed as the product of the discounted job separation rate (r + λ_β) and relative search cost ($\lambda/q(\theta)$). This equation for the "zero-profit" condition could be reformulated as the job-creating (JC) curve (Mortensen & Pissarides, 1994; Pissarides, 2000; Acemoglu, 2001; Heijdra & van der Ploeg, 2002; Furuoka, 2024b):

$$w_\beta = o - \left(r + \lambda_\beta\right)\gamma/q(\theta) \tag{1.13}$$

for β = y, p. The right side of the equation is the difference between the expected revenue of a filled job and the expected cost of the vacant job. From the employers' perspective, wage payment (i.e., w) is an important component of total cost (w+(r + λ_β)$\gamma/q(\theta)$) which should balance with the total revenue (o = w+(r+λ_β)$\gamma/q(\theta)$). Under this delicate cost-revenue balance, employers would set a low wage for a vacant job with a higher separation rate.

References

Acemoglu, D. (2001). Good jobs and bad jobs. *Journal of Labour Economics, 19*, 1–21.

Amorim, H., Cardoso, A. C. M., & Bridi, M. A. (2023). Industrial platform capitalism. *Work Organisation, Labour & Globalisation, 17*(2), 27–46.

Ball, L., & Mankiw, N. G. (2002). The NAIRU in theory and practice. *Journal of Economic Perspectives, 16*(4), 115–136.

Becker, R., Enders, W., & Lee, J. (2006). A stationarity test in the presence of an unknown number of smooth breaks. *Journal of Time Series Analysis, 27*(3), 381–409.

Beveridge, W. H. (1944). *Full employment in a free society*. Routledge.

Bloom, B. S., Engelhart, M. D., Furst, E. J., Hill, W. H., & Krathwohl, D. R. (1956). Taxonomy of educational objectives: The classification of educational goals. In *Handbook 1: Cognitive domain*. Longman.

Borjas, G. J. (2013). *Labour economics*. McGraw-Hill.

Carlin, W., & Soskice, D. W. (1990). *Macroeconomics and wage bargain*. Oxford University Press.

Dickey, D. A., & Fuller, W. A. (1979). Distribution of the estimators for autoregressive time series with a unit root. *Journal of the American Statistical Association, 74*, 427–431.

Dickey, D. A., & Fuller, W. A. (1981). Likelihood ratio statistics for autoregressive time series with a unit root. *Econometrica, 49*, 1057–1072.

Dornbusch, R., & Fischer, S. (1990). *Macroeconomics*. McGraw-Hill.

Enders, W., & Lee, J. (2012). The flexible Fourier form and Dickey-Fuller type unit root tests. *Economic Letters, 117*, 196–199.

Erber, G. (2012). Problem of money illusion in economics. In H. M. Krämer, H. M. Trautwein, H. D. Kurz, H. M. Trautwein, H. D. Kurz, H. Kramer, & H. Hagemann (Eds.), *Macroeconomics and the history of economic thought* (pp. 251–266). Taylor & Francis.

Fehr, E., & Tyran, J. R. (2001). Does money illusion matter? *American Economic Review, 91*(5), 1239–1262.

Fehr, E., & Tyran, J. R. (2005). Expectations and the effects of money illusion. In B. Agarwal & A. Vercelli (Eds.), *Psychology, rationality and economic behaviour: Challenging standard assumptions* (pp. 155–180). Palgrave Macmillan UK.

Fisher, I. (1928). *Money illusion*. Adelphi.

Friedman, M. (1968). Role of monetary policy. *American Economic Review, 58*(1), 1–17.

Furuoka, F. (2017). A new approach to testing unemployment hysteresis. *Empirical Economics, 53*(3), 1253–1280.

Furuoka, F. (2024a). Patterns and convergence of unemployment rate among people with disabilities: Testing the law of one unemployment rate. In *Disability and employment: Towards a humanistic economy* (pp. 69–109). Springer Nature Singapore.

Furuoka, F. (2024b). Labour market interventions to reduce the disability unemployment gap. In *Disability and employment: Towards a humanistic economy* (pp. 147–176). Springer Nature Singapore.

Furuoka, F., Pui, K. L., Chomar, M. T., & Nikitina, L. (2023). Trade openness and the Phillips curve: Evidence from ASEAN countries. *Singapore Economic Review, 68*(6), 1891–1915.

Gordon, R. J. (2011). The history of the Phillips curve: Consensus and bifurcation. *Economica, 78*(309), 10–50.

Kandori, M. (2023). *Mighty microeconomics: A guide to thinking like an economist*. Cambridge University Press.

Kurozumi, E. (2002). Testing for stationarity with a break. *Journal of Econometrics, 108*(1), 63–99.

Kwiatkowski, D., Phillips, P. C. B., Schmidt, P., & Shin, Y. (1992). Testing the null hypothesis of stationarity against the alternative of a unit root. *Journal of Econometrics, 54*, 159–178.

Heijdra, B. J., & van der Ploeg, F. (2002). *Foundations of modern macroeconomics*. Oxford University Press.

International Labour Organisation. (2025). *ILOSTAT data explorer*. Accessed Jan 02, 2025, from Available at https://ilostat.ilo.org/data/

Keynes, J. M. (1936). *General theory of employment, interest and money*. Macmillan.
Kolesnikova, J., Kamasheva, A., & Fakhrutdinova, A. (2015). Higher education demands of the labour market. *Procedia–Social and Behavioural Sciences, 191*, 1183–1186.
Kajita, E. (2014). "Kai-Ji-Go-Nyu" no kyoiku-shiso to jissenka [Educational philosophy of "Kai-Ji-Go-Nyu" and its application], *Journal of Humanistic Education*, 2, 1–8. Available at https://momokyo.repo.nii.ac.jp/records/75
Lau, K. H., Lam, T. K., Kam, B. H., Nkhoma, M., & Richardson, J. (2018). Benchmarking higher education programs through alignment analysis based on the revised Bloom's taxonomy. *Benchmarking: An International Journal, 25*(8), 2828–2849.
Leonardi, E., & Pirina, G. (2020). Uber in the Portuguese gig economy: A laboratory for platform capitalism. *Work Organisation, Labour & Globalisation, 14*(2), 46–63.
Levi-Faur, D. (2005). The global diffusion of regulatory capitalism. *The Annals of the American Academy of Political and Social Science, 598*(1), 12–32.
Longhi, S., & Taylor, M. (2014). Employed and unemployed job seekers and the business cycle. *Oxford Bulletin of Economics and Statistics, 76*(4), 463–483.
Lucas, R. E., & Rapping, L. A. (1969). Price expectations and the Phillips curve. *American Economic Review, 59*(3), 342–350.
Lucas, R. E. (1972). Expectations and the neutrality of money. *Journal of Economic Theory, 4*(2), 103–124.
Lucas, R. E. (1973). Some international evidence on the output-inflation trade-off. *American Economic Review, 63*(3), 326–334.
Lucas, R. E. (1983). Econometric policy evaluation: A critique. In K. Brunner & A. Meltzer (Eds.), *Carnegie-Rochester conference series on public policy* (pp. 19–46). Elsevier.
Marx, K. (1986). *Capital: A critique of political economy*. Progress Publishers.
Mishkin, F. S. (1995). The rational expectations revolution: A review article. *NBER working paper., No. 5043.*
Michaillat, P., & Saez, E. (2024). The full-employment rate of unemployment in the United States. *Brookings Papers on Economic Activity, 55*(2), 1–55.
Nonaka, I. (1991). The knowledge-creating company. *Harvard Business Review., 69*(6), 96–104.
Mortensen, D. T., & Pissarides, C. A. (1994). Job creation and job destruction in the theory of unemployment. *Review of Economic Studies, 61*, 397–415.
Muth, J. F. (1961). Rational expectations and the theory of price movements. *Econometrica, 29*(3), 315–335.
Perron, P., & Vogelsang, T. J. (1992). Testing for a unit root in a time series with a changing mean: Corrections and extensions. *Journal of Business & Economic Statistics, 10*(4), 467–470.
Perron, P., & Vogelsang, T. J. (1993). A note on the asymptotic distributions of unit root tests in the additive outlier model with breaks. *Brazilian Review of Econometrics, 13*(2), 18–20.
Pissarides, C. A. (2000). *Equilibrium unemployment theory*. MIT Press.
Phelps, E. S. (1967). Phillips curves, expectations of inflation and optimal unemployment over time. *Economica, 34*(3), 254–281.
Phillips, A. W. (1958). The relation between unemployment and the rate of change of money wage rates in the United Kingdom, 1861-1957. *Economica, 25*(100), 283–299.
Rissman, E. R. (1986). What is the natural rate of unemployment? *Federal Reserve Bank of Chicago Economic Perspectives, 10*(5), 3–17.
Sargent, T. J., & Wallace, N. (1975). Rational expectations, the optimal monetary instrument, and the optimal money supply rule. *Journal of Political Economy, 83*(2), 241–254.
Srnicek, N. (2017). *Platform capitalism*. John Wiley & Sons.
Stewart, A., & Stanford, J. (2017). Regulating work in the gig economy: What are the options? *The Economic Labour Relations Review, 28*(3), 420–437.
Tobin, J. (1972). Inflation and unemployment. *American Economic Review, 62*(1), 1–18.
Uchiyama, Y., Furuoka, F., & Omar, S. A. (2024). The rise and contestation of platform capitalism: Evidence from two food delivery blackouts in Malaysia. *Journal of Industrial Relations, 00221856241294107.*

Uchiyama, Y., & Furuoka, F. (2025). Uberisation and resistance to online food delivery gig work in Asia: Lessons from Malaysia. *Journal of Contemporary Asia*, 1–18.

Uchiyama, Y. (2025). Cosmolocalism against platform capitalism: Evidence from ridesharing. *tripleC: Communication, Capitalism & Critique. Open Access Journal for a Global Sustainable Information Society, 23*(1), 23–39.

United Nations. (2024). *United Nations summit on sustainable development*, 25–27 September 2015, Accessed Nov 18, 2024, from https://www.un.org/en/conferences/environment/newyork2015

US Bureau of Labour Statistics. (2025a). *Concepts and definitions*. Accessed Jan 02, 2025, from https://www.bls.gov/cps/definitions.htm

US Bureau of Labour Statistics. (2025b). *BLS Data Finder 1.1*. Accessed Jan 02, 2025, from https://data.bls.gov/dataQuery/search

Wielgosz, J. B., & Carpenter, S. (1987). The effectiveness of alternative methods of searching for jobs and finding them: An exploratory analysis of the data bearing upon the ways of coping with joblessness. *American Journal of Economics and Sociology, 46*(2), 151–164.

World Bank. (2025). *"World development indicators"*. Accessed Jan 02, 2025, from https://databank.worldbank.org/source/world-development-indicators

Yaya, O. S., Ogbonna, A. E., Furuoka, F., & Gil-Alana, L. A. (2021). A new unit root test for unemployment hysteresis based on the autoregressive neural network. *Oxford Bulletin of Economics and Statistics, 83*(4), 960–981.

Chapter 2
Theorising a New Taxonomy and Ecosystem of Youth Employment in the Contemporary Labour Market

Chapter 2 reviews and extends scholarship to theorise a new taxonomy and ecosystem for youth employment in digitally mediated labour markets. It begins by orienting the reader to the chapter's aims and scope, then introduces two lenses on the employment ecosystem: platform capitalism, which emphasises the intermediation of work by platform firms, and regulatory capitalism, which highlights how rules, standards, and enforcement shape opportunities and risks. Building on this, the ensuing discussion presents Kajita's taxonomy of educational objectives and clarifies its theoretical underpinnings before introducing Nonaka's knowledge management theory. The chapter synthesises Kajita's and Nonaka's models into a holistic framework for capability formation, applies this theoretical synthesis to platform-mediated capitalism, and highlights its implications for analysing youth employment pathways, governance gaps, and skill development across formal and informal work settings.

2.1 Introduction

Since the 2000s, labour markets have increasingly expanded beyond traditional full-time or office-based employment, embracing socially flexible working arrangements that transcend geographic constraints (Judy & d'Amico, 1997; Lee & Joseph Sirgy, 2019). In particular, the development of digitalisation and the rise of ICTs have facilitated the proliferation of online platforms, enabling place- and time-independent ways of working (Kässi & Lehdonvirta, 2018). Another factor behind this expansion of jobs is the problem of youth unemployment. Although the issue of youth unemployment has been addressed since the 1980s, especially in the context of the worsening job insecurity since the global financial crisis, this type of employment plays an important role as a receptacle for young people (Churchill & Craig, 2019; Daud et al., 2024). Based on these background, self-discretionary workstyles and portfolio-based employment have become attractive career options for many

Y. Uchiyama, F. Furuoka, *Youth and Employment*,
https://doi.org/10.1007/978-981-95-3257-5_2

youths' population (Myhill et al., 2023; Uchiyama & Furuoka, 2025). At the same time, autonomous knowledge acquisition, problem-solving skills and practical adaptability are essential for the sustainability of these new working possibilities (Ravenelle, 2019).

However, despite the growing trend towards more flexible forms of work, it is underpinned by structural instability and an institutional void. Notably, emerging forms of employment favoured by younger generations, such as platform-based gig work, often fall outside the scope of employment contracts and statutory protections, thereby exposing workers to isolation under the guise of individual responsibility (Uchiyama & Furuoka, 2025). As a result, workers internalise various risks in engaging in such work. For example, key features include income insecurity, the absence of social protection and career advancement opportunities, and the lack of trade union representation (Behrendt et al., 2019; Cini et al., 2022; Uchiyama et al., 2022). From the perspective of contemporary capitalism and labour in neoliberalism, such precariousness faced by workers is internalised in platform capitalism (McKenzie, 2022). Platform capitalism is a new structure of capital accumulation that organises labour through its intermediary role in digital space and accumulates value by forming political alliances with investors and consumers while shifting social risks to workers, utilising algorithmic control and legal ambiguity (Srnicek, 2017; Uchiyama et al., 2024). Platform capitalism masquerades as technological neutrality and free choice for this new way of working, but forms an institutional structure that minimises risks for companies and allows them to avoid legal and social guarantees for workers (Stewart & Stanford, 2017).

This situation can be in the context of a broader institutional transformation. Namely, it can be traced back to regulatory capitalism as a concept that symbolises the structural changes in the state and capitalist system that have emerged since the 1980s (Levi-Faur, 2005, 2017). Regulatory capitalism sees regulation as playing an essential role in the process of expansion, adaptation and transformation of capitalism, not merely as an external constraint but as its institutional component. This differs from the common belief of neoliberalism, which advocates liberalisation, privatisation and deregulation, but rather has the paradoxical feature that the creation and strengthening of regulation is a continuous development (Braithwaite, 2005). The responsibility for regulation is no longer confined to the state. It is now characterised by an institutional structure in which a diverse array of actors, such as corporations, NGOs, international organisations and professional networks, participate in the formation and implementation of regulatory frameworks. Platform firms provide a clear example of this shift.

Under these structures, young workers are particularly torn between the expectations of work flexibility and skill building and the reality of social exclusion. To address this, there has been much discussion about self-organisation and the development of legislation at the governmental level for empowerment in their enclosure in platform capitalism (Todolí-Signes, 2017; Woodcock, 2021). However, the key problem overlooked here is not only social resistance and regulation but also the lack of institutional guarantees of opportunities to acquire knowledge and skills that support young workers. The current education system and vocational training are not sufficiently adapted to significantly shifting labour market changes, making young people even more vulnerable to "non-employment", "informal", and "precarious" situations (MacDonald & Giazitzoglu, 2019). Achieving genuine decent and sustainable work akin to traditional lifetime employment within the flexible context of gig and platform labour requires a critical discourse on the development of institutional frameworks and the cultivation of knowledge capable of challenging the prevailing imbalance of power between workers and platform companies.

As a theoretical tool for clarifying that these power structures are not merely the consequence of institutional absence but are strategically constructed from within, this chapter reconceptualises platform firms not as actors that bypass regulatory frameworks but as entities embedded within and actively shaping existing governance arrangements. These firms operate by subordinating and reconfiguring institutional mechanisms to align with their own profit-maximising logic. This perspective utilises two previously discrete theoretical domains: platform capitalism and regulatory capitalism. It provides a conceptual lens through which to analyse how platform firms structure control and domination. Crucially, institutional fragmentation and legal ambiguity are not seen as failures of governance but as resources strategically exploited by platforms to reinforce their dominance while avoiding institutional accountability.

This book offers both a theoretical and institutional response to these structural challenges. Specifically, it proposes a framework that enables young people to progressively acquire and internalise knowledge and skills, thereby cultivating autonomous professional subjectivities within precarious work environments. Central to this effort is the development of a new taxonomy that spans the domains of education and employment. Accordingly, this chapter formulates an innovative conceptual framework for institutional design in youth knowledge formation under platform-mediated labour conditions. It integrates two advanced theoretical perspectives: a taxonomy for holistic knowledge and skill acquisition in the platform era, combining Eiichi Kajita's classification of educational goals with Ikujiro Nonaka's theory of knowledge creation (Kajita, 2014; Nonaka, 1991).

This model does not aim merely to redesign educational processes. Rather, it seeks to render visible and re-institutionalise the learning trajectories that have been systematically obscured under the macro-ecosystem of platform capitalism. It provides a knowledge-based foundation for repositioning young workers as sustainable, system-embedded agents through continuous learning rather than as expendable labour within an increasingly fluid and stratified labour market.

2.2 Platform Capitalism

A new phase characterising twenty-first-century capitalism is the rise of platform capitalism. This is an accumulation regime that uses digital technologies and networks to create and extract value through the mediation of services and labour (Srnicek, 2017). While traditional industrial capitalism was based on ownership of the means of production and direct control of labour, platform companies are innovative in that they create markets and generate profits through mediation rather than ownership (Howson et al., 2022; Papadimitropoulos, 2021; Uchiyama et al., 2024). These platform-based accumulation models build on technological developments in ICT and algorithms to advance data-driven market construction while also reconfiguring firm-worker relations, as well as markets and norms (Kenney & Zysman, 2020; Langley & Leyshon, 2017; Stewart & Stanford, 2017). Under forms of domination such as algorithmic labour management and black-boxing of evaluation and reward systems, workers are given nominal freedom as self-employed workers but are effectively bound by algorithms and evaluation mechanisms (Griesbach et al., 2019; Jarrahi et al., 2021).

Platform companies make labour more fluid and low-paid while colluding with investors and consumers to enclose the market and establish a monopoly position (Pasquale, 2016; Schor & Attwood-Charles, 2017). In the process, workers' flexibility and autonomy are emphasised, while precarious performance-linked evaluation systems and individual competition place them in high-risk, low-security work situations (Haidar & Keune, 2021; Uchiyama et al., 2022). By being legally classified as independent contractors and excluded from employment protection, companies cleverly avoid employment liability (Cherry & Aloisi, 2016; Roy-Mukherjee & Harrison, 2020). Within this institutional exclusion, companies control and stratify workers based on algorithms and data to encourage internal competition while reinforcing the domination of performance criteria through the visibility of evaluations on the platform (Van Dijck et al., 2019; Van Doorn & Badger, 2020) Uchiyama et al. (2024) organise the domination structure of such platforms as a two-tier structure of (1) capital concentration through linkages with investors and consumers, and (2) institutional and technological exclusion of workers (Uchiyama et al., 2024).

In this context, the absence of regulation is not just a lack of governance but the very strategy by which companies strategically utilise existing institutional and normative frameworks and restructure labour management power relations (Leonardi & Pirina, 2020; Rahman & Thelen, 2019). This greater institutional flexibility promotes disconnection of skill accumulation and increased competition between workers, making it difficult to build collective solidarity (Chan, 2023; Uchiyama & Furuoka, 2025; Woodcock & Graham, 2020).

2.3 Regulatory Capitalism

Regulatory capitalism is positioned as a framework that represents the restructuring of the relationship between the state and capitalism since the 1980s (Levi-Faur, 2005, 2017). The concept focuses on the constitutive role of regulation in the expansion, transformation and adaptation of capitalism and provides a perspective for an institutionalist reinterpretation of the relationship between capitalism, the state and society (Levi-Faur, 2005, 2017). What distinguishes this concept from neoliberal deregulation and privatisation is its paradoxical feature of increasing institutional complexity through the relocation and restructuring of regulations rather than their reduction (Braithwaite, 2005; Levi-Faur, 2005). In other words, regulatory capitalism does not free markets from state interference but rather recalls the role of regulation as a device to sustainably reconfigure capitalism by actively reorganising the institutional relationships between market, state and society. In this framework, regulation is not limited to direct command and control by the state but operates institutionally through a variety of instruments and actors, including soft law and algorithmic governance, self-disciplined contracts, third-party monitoring regimes and industry certification systems (Schmidt & Scott, 2021; Scott, 2015). Regulatory actors also extend beyond the state to include companies, international organisations, civil society and professional associations, allowing regulatory networks to function as multi-layered governance.

Levi-Faur (2017) categorises regulatory functions into three types: restrictive, empowering and constitutive, and contends that constitutive regulation, which establishes the very institutional foundations of capitalism, is of particular significance. This type of regulation functions to create and maintain the institutional premises of capitalism, such as markets, firms, contracts, ownership, legal personality and intellectual property. This mechanism negates the traditional view of the market as an institutionally autonomous entity and makes clear that the market itself is an institutionally constituted subject. Based on this understanding, Levi-Faur (2017) introduces a distinction between the regulation of capitalism and the regulatory capitalism. While the former plays the role of correcting the negative externalities created by capitalism, such as labour protection, environmental standards and fair competition, the latter performs the more fundamental function of designing and constructing the very institutional conditions that allow markets to exist. In particular, the latter regulation is regarded as the institutional basis for the capitalist system as an essential element of capitalist legitimacy and reproduction (Levi-Faur, 2017).

In this structure, the state is no longer a mere market interventionist but an institutional designer. In other words, there is an ongoing functional differentiation in which the state designs and oversees the institutional framework while companies innovate and provide services within it (Levi-Faur & Jordana, 2005). Within this framework, businesses and civil society are expected to operate autonomously, while a multi-layered regulatory regime emerges through the interplay between these self-organising dynamics and the institutional design initiated by the state (Levi-Faur, 2009). Such regulatory regimes have evolved into a mode of governance in which the multiple functions of institutional design, enforcement and compliance are shared by diverse actors, including the state, the private sector and professional networks. The expansion of regulatory capitalism has proceeded through a complex interplay of top-down institutional introduction by states and international organisations, bottom-up demands from business and civil society, and horizontal processes of institutional imitation and mutual learning. Among these, the social emulation of institutional forms mediated by expert knowledge stands out as a particularly significant mechanism (Jordana & Levi-Faur, 2005).

As described above, regulatory capitalism emerges as a third model of capitalism in which the state's ability to design institutions and the self-organising nature of markets are linked, different from both nineteenth-century laissez-faire capitalism and twentieth-century welfare state coordinated capitalism (Levi-Faur, 2009). Although the state remains at the helm, governance structures that jointly build institutional order with business and civil society are becoming dominant. This structure has led to increased regulation in areas such as labour, environment and information protection, which has become the basis for the institutional stability and legitimacy of contemporary capitalism (Levi-Faur, 2005).

Furthermore, Farrand and Carrapico (2018) advocate the concept of Networked Regulatory Capitalism, in which the state, the private sector, and independent institutions are all involved in institution-building. This emphasises the point that institutional design is no longer a state monopoly but takes place in a multi-layered process of negotiation and legitimation (Farrand & Carrapico, 2018). Regulatory capitalism goes beyond traditional notions of the regulatory state and regulatory governance and focuses theoretically on structural aspects of capitalism itself. Therefore, it is essential for this framework to have a perspective that captures the multi-layered power structures at the intersection of state, market and professional knowledge and the mechanisms of cross-institutional diffusion (Levi-Faur, 2017).

2.4 Kajita's Educational Taxonomy and its Buddhist Foundations

Eiichi Kajita is a leading expert on educational psychology in Japan. Born in 1941, Kajita is a devout catholic and president of five universities, including a famous Catholic University, Kyoto Notre Dame University in Kyoto, and a prominent Christian university, St. Andrew's University of Education in Osaka. Notably, Kajita's taxonomy is based on the Buddhist concept of "Kai-Ji-Go-Nyu" (开示悟入 in Chinese), which is explained in the second volume of the *Lotus Sutra* (Kajita, 2014). In this sutra, the Buddha explained the following four reasons why the Buddha appeared in this world, namely: *Kai* or the "opening" the door of the Buddha's wisdom, *Ji* or the "showing" the Buddha's wisdom, *Go* or the "awakening to the Buddha's wisdom and *Nyu* or the "entering" to the Buddha wisdom (Watson, 2004).

Kajita's four-step taxonomy stems from the "five steps of teaching method" put forward by Tsunesaburo Makiguchi (1871–1944). Makiguchi's teaching method identified five phases: evaluation, intuition, reflection, re-evaluation, and application. Table 2.1 was created by Makiguchi to compare his teaching method with the Buddhist concept of "Kai-Ji-Go-Nyu" and other educational philosophies. As the table shows, the "evaluation" and the "intuition" steps, in Makiguchi's method, correspond to the "opening" and "showing" phases, while the final "application"

Table 2.1 Comparison of different educational philosophies

Kajita (1941-)	Opening	Showing	Awakening	Entering
Rein (1847–1929)	Preparation	Presentation	Comparison Systemisation	Application
Dörpfeld (1824–1893)	Intuition		Reflection	Application
Makiguchi (1871–1944)	Evaluation Intuition		Reflection Evaluation	Application

Source: Kajita (2014)

step corresponds to the "entering" phase. The third and fourth steps closely align with the"awakening" phases (Kajita, 2014).

Makiguchi considered the "opening" phase crucial for the mental and emotional preparation for successful education and learning (Makiguchi, 2015). According to Makiguchi's student, Shigetake Arishima, the "opening" phase aims to "open the eyes" to one's own potential. The following phases, from "showing" to "entering", are set to actualise one's potential (Kajita, 2014).

2.5 A Comparison of Pedagogical Traditions: Rein, Dörpfeld, and Makiguchi

Makiguchi's five-step method draws on two prominent educational philosophies, namely, Rein's five-step method and Dörpfeld's three-step method. Rein identified the following five steps in the educational process: preparation, presentation, comparison, systematisation and application (Noss, 1898). In 1893, Rein developed his five-step method by modifying the Herbartian pedagogical theory of the four steps of instruction that included clearness, association, system and method (Ellerton & Clements, 2005). More precisely, Rein made a notable contribution to the understanding of Herbartian pedagogy by separating clearness into "preparation" and "presentation" and adding the final step of the "application" (Westfall, 1975). As Table 2.1 shows, the first step, "preparation", in Rein's method corresponds to the "opening" phase; the second step, the "presentation", corresponds to the "showing" phase. In line with Makiguchi's method, the last step, the "application", in Rein's method, corresponds to the "entering" phase. The "comparison" and "generalisation" steps are closely aligned with the "awakening" phase (Kajita, 2014). In the Herbartian pedagogical tradition, education acts as yeast "hidden" in flour, which causes fermentation. In other words, the effect of education might not be immediately recognised, but it does "quicken" students' minds and spirits (Noss, 1898).

Dörpfeld identified the following three phases in the process of education: intuition, reflection, and application. As Table 2.1 shows, the final phase, "application", in Dörpfeld's method corresponds to the "entering" phase in Kajita's taxonomy. In line with Makiguchi's method, the first two steps, "intuition" and "reflection", approximately coincide with three phases from the "opening" to the "awakening" phase (Kajita, 2014). Despite similarities between Makiguchi's and Dörpfeld's methods, the former has additional elements of the "double evaluation" phases. This is because the aim of Makiguchi's educational philosophy or the system of value-creation pedagogy is to make students happy (Ikeda et al., 2000). Initially, in the "first evaluation" phase, students appraise their current states using their own knowledge and understanding gained from previous "studying-by-living" experiences. Later on in the "second evaluation" phase, knowledge and skills students acquired during the earlier phases, namely from "opening" to "awakening", are evaluated again in order to determine whether the process of education had contributed to the creation of students' happiness (Tanaka et al., 2025). In other words, the core of Makiguchi's educational philosophy is the "value-creation" in the students' lives, which would take place in the final "application" phase following the second "evaluation". In Dörpfeld's philosophy, the first phase, "intuition", is important because without it, any educational effort could not be considered successful (Heidelberger & Neurath, 2024).

Kajita identified the first phase, "opening", as the most crucial among the four phases in his taxonomy. This is a different view from the predominant Japanese conceptions of education that place emphasis on the second phase, "showing". There has been a robust discussion among educational experts in Japan about the best ways to teach and educate students. However, these discussions do not consider the importance of helping students to 'open their eyes' or develop awareness of their own potential. Therefore, in the first phase, the "opening", teachers need to help students develop a "growth" mindset and remove their misconceptions, if any, about learning and acquiring knowledge. In the second phase, the "showing", teachers need to help students actualise their potential by introducing new knowledge and giving new skills, and by providing explanations in clear and accessible terms to students. In the third phase, the "awakening", teachers should aim to bring students to having sudden insights or the "aha" moments in their learning and knowledge discoveries. Finally, in the "entering" phase, students need to become able to use knowledge in practical ways and in their daily lives (Omiya, 2024). The discussion presented in this section is important for establishing a theoretical linkage between Kajita's taxonomy of educational objectives and Nonaka's knowledge management theory. It will also aid in developing a taxonomy for holistic knowledge and skill acquisition for youth.

2.6 Nonaka's Theory of Knowledge Creation: The SECI Model

Ikujiro Nonaka (1935–2025) is a leading expert in business studies. He is also known as the "father of knowledge management". From 1977 to 1983, Nonaka taught knowledge management at Harvard Business School; he was also a Professor

Table 2.2 Four phases of knowledge creation

Phases	The first phase of SECI	The second phase of SECI	The third phase of SECI	The fourth phase of SECI
Modes	Socialisation	Externalisation	Combination	Internalisation
Conversion	Tacit to tacit	Tacit to explicit	Explicit to explicit	Explicit to tacit

Source: Nonaka and Takeuchi (1995)

at Hitotsubashi University from 1998 to 2010. Nonaka has made a major contribution to business studies by differentiating between two kinds of organisational knowledge, namely tacit knowledge and explicit knowledge.

According to Nonaka, tacit knowledge is unarticulated knowledge and is tied to human senses. Some prominent examples of tacit knowledge are intuition, implicit rules, and movement skills. In contrast, explicit knowledge is well-articulated and documented knowledge; it includes technical specifications, numbers, figures and so forth. From the perspective of training and learning in an organisation, tacit knowledge is personalised knowledge which is difficult to transfer from one person to another. Explicit knowledge is generalised knowledge, and it can be easily shared among individuals (Nonaka, 1991; Nonaka, 1994; Nonaka & Von Krogh, 2009).

Nonaka and his colleague at Harvard Business School, Hirotaka Takeuchi, developed a thought-provoking model of the creation of knowledge. They proposed that new knowledge is created through dynamic interaction between tacit knowledge and explicit knowledge. This model proposes four distinct phases in which tacit knowledge and explicit knowledge are transformed into new organisational knowledge. These phases include socialisation, externalisation, combination, and internalisation (SECI) (Nonaka & Takeuchi, 1995). Table 2.2 shows the phases in the SECI model.

According to Nonaka and Takeuchi, in the first phase, "socialisation", tacit knowledge is shared among colleagues through imitation and observation. For example, a senior staff member becomes a mentor to a junior staff member, who acquires tacit knowledge from the mentor by imitating and observing their actions and practices. In the second phase, "externalisation", personal tacit knowledge transforms into explicit knowledge of the staff, provided the personal knowledge is well-defined and has a clear structure so that it can be understood by others. In the third phase, "combination", the explicit knowledge can be collected and combined. This synthesised new knowledge is shared among all members of the organisation. In the final stage, "internalisation", the explicit knowledge is internalised and converted into personal knowledge through the whole learning-by-doing process (Nonaka & Takeuchi, 1995).

2.7 Synthesising Kajita's and Nonaka's Models: Toward a New Integrated Taxonomy

Based on the existing models, this book proposes a new taxonomy that can be used to develop a curriculum that enables young people and learners to gain the necessary skills and knowledge, particularly in job settings. This taxonomy builds on a pedagogical model that incorporates actual practices in educational institutions and the management of knowledge and skills model that takes account of actual practice in business corporations. Thus, it integrates the taxonomy of educational objectives developed by Eiichi Kajita and the knowledge management model proposed by Ikujiro Nonaka. The following discussion highlights the theoretical linkage between Kajita's taxonomy and Nonaka's knowledge management. As shown in Table 2.3, the proposed global taxonomy combines the phases from prior educational philosophies discussed in Sect. 2.6 with the process of knowledge acquisition.

The first phase, the "opening", is critical in the process of knowledge acquisition. In the modern capitalist economy, firms are 'storehouses' of knowledge and skills. In other words, young people need to have access to this stored, extensive knowledge through internships or other forms of employment, such as a short-term contract. In other words, firms must open their doors to young people and give them some initial employment opportunities. In this phase, it is important for young workers to systematise the tacit knowledge that they have acquired through past experiences. Without this step, there is a danger of failing to acquire new knowledge and skills offered by the firms. Developing and maintaining a "growth" mindset is also critical in the efforts to expand one's knowledge and practical skills. In the second phase, the "showing", senior staff members share with young workers their personal tacit knowledge. Young workers acquire new knowledge through imitating and observing their seniors. In this process, mentorship provided by senior staff facilitates knowledge acquisition. In the third phase, the "awakening", young workers come to a stage where they experience a realisation of sudden discoveries and insights or the "aha" moments. This is achieved by the systemisation of tacit knowledge obtained through imitation and observation, combination and synthesis of explicit knowledge, and eventual internalisation of the explicit knowledge into personal tacit knowledge. In the final phase, the "entering", young workers master the tacit and explicit knowledge so that they can apply it in practice.

Table 2.3 Taxonomy for holistic knowledge and skill acquisition

Phases	Opening	Showing	Awakening	Entering
Mode	Preparation	Socialisation	Externalisation Combination Internalisation	Application
Knowledge management	Systemisation of personal tacit knowledge	Tacit to tacit	Tacit to tacit, through explicit	Application of new knowledge

Source: Authors

2.8 Youth Labour Knowledge Formation in Digital-Mediated Labour Environments

This section addresses the formation of youth labour knowledge by integrating three key dimensions: educational development, knowledge creation and transmission, and institutional control structures in the context of digital-mediated labour environment. It aims to make visible and institutionalise the recognition and assessment of informal and often invisible learning processes among young people who are structurally marginalised within the digital economy.

The theoretical foundation is constructed by integrating three distinct yet interrelated perspectives. The first is Eiichi Kajita's four-stage cognitive learning model of educational goals (Kai, Ji, Go and Nyu), which conceptualises knowledge not simply as information but as a process of ontological transformation. The second is Ikujiro Nonaka's SECI model of knowledge creation, which consists of the phases of socialisation, externalisation, combination and internalisation. Together, these two frameworks enable the development of a taxonomy for holistic knowledge and skill acquisition, highlighting the dynamic nature of knowledge as it flows between individuals and organisations and between practical experience and theoretical understanding. Thirdly, the analysis considers the structural conditions under which knowledge formation takes place, particularly the way in which digital platform-based labour arrangements intersect with broader institutional systems. Rather than treating platform companies as external to institutional environments, this perspective views them as strategically embedded actors that influence governance structures by selectively utilising and reshaping existing public infrastructure and institutional arrangements. This approach enables a nuanced theorisation of the difficulties young workers face in acquiring and applying knowledge within such fragmented and precarious labour contexts, and it informs the direction of necessary institutional responses. The following discussion provides a theoretical organisation of youth labour knowledge formation processes, along with the surrounding mechanisms of institutional support and obstruction, as summarised in Table 2.4.

The first phase corresponds to 'Kai' (the "opening") and 'Socialisation'. This is the phase in which the conditions for the possibility of connection to labour knowledge are questioned, as this is where young people's agency is institutionally constituted for the first time. In this phase, the focus is on the learning entry point where young people realise their own potential and enter the world of knowledge and experience. Although socialisation in the SECI model is a process in which tacit knowledge is transmitted through mimetic learning with others and physical communal acts, such initial learning opportunities are themselves systematically absent in the context of platform labour. Companies utilise public infrastructure and policy resources to mobilise young labour while avoiding employment responsibilities. As a result, youths are placed in a structure where they are thrown into the market outside the system. At this stage, explicit guarantees of introductory learning opportunities such as mandatory internship schemes and institutionalised vocational training programmes would be essential.

Table 2.4 Mechanism of youth labour knowledge formation under platform-based labour contexts

Knowledge formation stage	Kajita's classification of education	Nonaka's SECI model	Institutional barriers to youth knowledge formation	Institutional reconfiguration
Stage 1: Introduction and contact	Opening (Kai): Realising the potential of the self	Socialisation: Mimetic acquisition of tacit knowledge	– Uninstitutionalised opportunities for youths to come into contact with knowledge and labour practices – Companies mobilise using public resources while denying employment responsibilities	Institutional guarantees of initial contact opportunities
Stage 2: Presentation of knowledge and observation	Showing (Ji): Encountering knowledge	Externalisation: Formalisation of tacit knowledge	– Lack of mentoring schemes and peer learning support – Unsupported knowledge-sharing institutions – Concealment by competitive structures	Public development of mentoring and peer learning systems, and making them subject to evaluation
Stage 3: Insight and integration	Awakening (Go): Integration and awareness of knowledge	Combination: Structural reconstruction of knowledge	– Dependence on fragmented evaluation of labour outcomes – Difficulties with semantic integration and reflection – Systematisation of internalised knowledge	Introduction of portfolio systems, reflective evaluation systems, and knowledge-based performance indicators
Stage 4: Application and reproduction	Entering (Nyu): Practising and establishing knowledge	Internalisation: Transformation into practical knowledge	– Institutional unrecognition of the acquisition of practical knowledge – Devalorisation of learning not linked to careers and rewards	Visualisation and certification systems for practical skills

Source: Authors

The second stage corresponds to 'Ji' (the "showing") and externalisation. This is the process by which knowledge is presented visibly by others to youths, and the learners accept and reconstruct it. While the SECI model was originally conceptualised as a framework for knowledge management within business organisations, this study reinterprets it as a model of knowledge formation among youths across the domains of education and labour. It offers a perspective that positions platform labour as a site where the formation of a community of knowledge is obstructed. Indeed, in platform labour, the lack of mentoring systems and the algorithm-driven competitive environment make knowledge sharing and transfer institutionally difficult. The reality is that even the very basic learning opportunity for youths to learn from their seniors is not guaranteed. At this stage, there is an urgent need to institutionalise peer review and mentoring systems and to introduce a mechanism to make the presentation and sharing of knowledge subject to evaluation.

The third stage relates to 'Go' (the "awakening") and combination. This is the stage where young people integrate the knowledge and experiences they have acquired and make sense of them in their own context. In the SECI model, consolidation is the process of creating organisational knowledge through the combination and reconfiguration of formal knowledge. It is reinterpreted as an integrated process of self-understanding and learning for young workers. However, the fragmentation of knowledge and the emphasis on performance-based assessment in platform work make it difficult to reconstruct meaning. Youths acquire skills and experiences, but these do not lead to a coherent job function or career, thus inhibiting the systematisation of knowledge. At this stage, systems to encourage reflection in the workplace and the visualisation of learning outcomes through portfolio-based assessment play an important role.

The fourth stage corresponds to 'Nyu' (the "entering") and internalisation. This is the process where the knowledge gained is deeply internalised into the youths' own behaviour patterns and decision-making, and used as practical knowledge. At this stage, knowledge is not mere information but is reproduced as value judgements and social action. In particular, it is of critical importance for young workers that such internalised knowledge is systematically acknowledged and connected to their career trajectories and broader social recognition. However, there is little institutional recording or qualification of this practical knowledge, and young people's learning is unlikely to be reflected in their remuneration or job performance. This situation creates a fundamental contradiction in which learning is not recognised. To address this, the implementation of micro-credentialing and practice-based accreditation systems is strongly recommended as a means of enhancing the social recognition of knowledge.

Although each stage of knowledge formation is part of a continuous process, it is often fragmented by the prevailing institutional arrangements associated with platform-mediated labour. Youths engage in learning through work, yet this learning remains disconnected from formal systems, compelling them to assume full responsibility within a disjointed and unsupported learning trajectory. This framework seeks to serve as both an institutional and theoretical blueprint for reconstructing these disrupted circuits of learning, enabling youths to acquire knowledge autonomously and to develop into socially recognised and legitimised actors in the context of digital-mediated labour environment.

2.9 Conclusion

This chapter presents a multi-layered theoretical framework for reconceptualising the challenges of youth employment in the modern era from institutional and epistemological perspectives. From a macro perspective, it reveals how, with the spread of digitalisation in employment, platform companies are acting not from outside but from within the system, strategically utilising public resources to reorganise governance structures and reproduce asymmetrical power relations. This perspective transcends the traditional dichotomy of regulation versus liberalisation, theoretically capturing the co-constructive relationship between platform capitalism and regulatory institutions. From a micro perspective, this chapter proposes a new classification framework for knowledge and skill formation by integrating Kajita Eiichi's classification of educational goals and Nonaka and Takeuchi's SECI model. This framework is structured around four stages: disclosure, presentation, awakening, and acquisition and clarifies how fragmented and often invisible learning processes unfold in the unstable labour environment faced by young people. It theoretically organises how institutional gaps at each stage hinder youths' acquisition, integration, and application of knowledge. The theoretical framework of this chapter does not merely criticise the current institutional shortcomings but provides an institutional and theoretical blueprint for reconstructing fragmented learning circuits. This requires the institutionalisation of informal learning, the visualisation and evaluation of tacit knowledge, and the establishment of mechanisms to socially recognise young people's autonomous knowledge formation. This perspective makes it possible to rethink young people not as consumable labour in traditional employment or emerging forms of work such as platform work and gig work, but as subjects of knowledge and co-creators of institutional change. Furthermore, this chapter emphasises the need for a paradigm shift from governance structures that marginalise young people to institutional designs that focus on their potential. There is a need to transition from learning trajectories lacking structural cognition to institutionally recognised frameworks and from the privatisation of institutions by platform companies to institutional design based on shared social values. By theorising the potential for knowledge formation among youths in the modern era, where spatial and temporal constraints have been dismantled, this chapter points toward a comprehensive institutional response to the broader theme of "youths and employment."

References

Behrendt, C., Nguyen, Q. A., & Rani, U. (2019). Social protection systems and the future of work: Ensuring social security for digital platform workers. *International Social Security Review, 72*(3), 17–41.

Braithwaite, J. (2005). Neoliberalism or regulatory capitalism. *RegNet Occasional Paper, 5*.

Chan, J. (2023). Class, labour conflict, and workers' organisation. *The Economic Labour Relations Review, 34*(3), 383–394.
Cherry, M. A., & Aloisi, A. (2016). Dependent contractors in the gig economy: A comparative approach. *American University Law Review, 66*, 635–690.
Churchill, B., & Craig, L. (2019). Gender in the gig economy: Men and women using digital platforms to secure work in Australia. *Journal of Sociology, 55*(4), 741–761.
Cini, L., Maccarrone, V., & Tassinari, A. (2022). With or without U (nions)? Understanding the diversity of gig workers' organising practices in Italy and the UK. *European Journal of Industrial Relations, 28*(3), 341–362.
Daud, S. N. M., Osman, Z., Samsudin, S., & Phang, I. G. (2024). Adapting to the gig economy: Determinants of financial resilience among "Giggers". *Economic Analysis and Policy, 81*, 756–771. https://doi.org/10.1016/j.eap.2024.01.002
Ellerton, N. F., & Clements, M. A. (2005). A mathematics education ghost story: Herbartianism and school mathematics. In Clarkson, P.C. (ed.) Proceedings of the Annual Conference of the Mathematics Education Group, Melbourne, 7th-9th July 2005, (pp. 313–321). Melbourne: Royal Melbourne Institute of Technology.
Farrand, B., & Carrapico, H. (2018). *Blurring public and private: Cybersecurity in the age of regulatory capitalism.* Security privatisation: How non-security-related private businesses shape security governance, 197–217.
Griesbach, K., Reich, A., Elliott-Negri, L., & Milkman, R. (2019). Algorithmic control in platform food delivery work. *Socius, 5*, 2378023119870041.
Haidar, J., & Keune, M. (2021). *Work and labour relations in global platform capitalism.* Edward Elgar Publishing.
Heidelberger, M. J. W. o. t. s. w. c. R. C., & Neurath, O. (2024). *Between Pietism and Herbartianism: Archaeological vestiges in Carnap's thought.* 19–75.
Howson, K., Ferrari, F., Ustek-Spilda, F., Salem, N., Johnston, H., & Katta, S.,…Graham, M. (2022). Driving the digital value network: Economic geographies of global platform capitalism. *Global Networks, 22*(4), 631–648. https://doi.org/10.1111/glob.12358
Ikeda, D., Saito, K., Endo, T., & Suda, H. (2000). *The wisdom of the lotus sutra* (Vol. II). CA: World Tribune Press.
Jarrahi, M. H., Newlands, G., Lee, M. K., Wolf, C. T., Kinder, E., & Sutherland, W. (2021). Algorithmic management in a work context. *Big Data & Society, 8*(2), 20539517211020332.
Jordana, J., & Levi-Faur, D. (2005). The diffusion of regulatory capitalism in Latin America: Sectoral and national channels in the making of a new order. *The Annals of the American Academy of Political and Social Science, 598*(1), 102–124.
Judy, R. W., & d'Amico, C. (1997). *Workforce 2020: Work and workers in the 21st century.* Hudson Institute.
Kajita, E. (2014). "Kai-Ji-go-Nyu" no kyoiku-shiso to jissenka [Educational philosophy of "Kai-Ji-go-Nyu" and its application]. *Journal of Humanistic Education, 2*, 1–8.
Kässi, O., & Lehdonvirta, V. (2018). Online labour index: Measuring the online gig economy for policy and research. *Technological Forecasting and Social Change, 137*, 241–248. https://doi.org/10.1016/j.techfore.2018.07.056
Kenney, M., & Zysman, J. (2020). The platform economy: Restructuring the space of capitalist accumulation. *Cambridge Journal of Regions, Economy and Society, 13*(1), 55–76. https://doi.org/10.1093/cjres/rsaa001
Langley, P., & Leyshon, A. (2017). Platform capitalism: The intermediation and capitalisation of digital economic circulation. *Finance and Society, 3*(1), 11–31.
Lee, D.-J., & Joseph Sirgy, M. (2019). Work-life balance in the digital workplace: The impact of schedule flexibility and telecommuting on work-life balance and overall life satisfaction. In M. Coetzee (Ed.), *Thriving in digital workspaces: Emerging issues for research and practice* (pp. 355–384). Springer. https://doi.org/10.1007/978-3-030-24463-7_18

Leonardi, E., & Pirina, G. (2020). Uber in the Portuguese gig economy: A laboratory for platform capitalism. *Work Organisation, Labour & Globalisation, 14*(2), 46–63. https://doi.org/10.13169/workorgalaboglob.14.2.0046
Levi-Faur, D. (2005). The global diffusion of regulatory capitalism. *The Annals of the American Academy of Political and Social Science, 598*(1), 12–32.
Levi-Faur, D. (2009). Regulatory capitalism and the reassertion of the public interest. *Policy Society, 27*(3), 181–191.
Levi-Faur, D. (2017). *Regulatory capitalism* (pp. 289–302). Foundations, Applications.
Levi-Faur, D., & Jordana, J. (2005). The rise of regulatory capitalism: The global diffusion of a new order. *The Annals of the American Academy of Political and Social Science, 598*(1), 200–217.
MacDonald, R., & Giazitzoglu, A. (2019). Youth, enterprise and precarity: Or, what is, and what is wrong with, the 'gig economy'? *Journal of Sociology, 55*(4), 724–740.
Makiguchi, T. J. S. (2015). *On attitudes toward education: The attitude toward guiding learning and the attitude toward learning [1936]. 12*(2), 244–251.
McKenzie, M. D. J. (2022). Micro-assets and portfolio management in the new platform economy. *Distinktion: Journal of Social Theory, 23*(1), 94–113.
Myhill, K., Richards, J., & Sang, K. (2023). Job quality, fair work and gig work: The lived experience of gig workers. In *Technologically mediated human resource management* (pp. 116–141). Routledge.
Nonaka, I. (1991). The knowledge-creating company. *Harvard Business Review, 69*(6), 96–104.
Nonaka, I. (1994). A dynamic theory of organisational knowledge creation. *Organisation Science, 5*(1), 14–37.
Nonaka, I., & Takeuchi, H. (1995). *The knowledge-creating company: How Japanese companies create the dynamics of innovation*. Oxford University Press. https://doi.org/10.1093/oso/9780195092691.001.0001
Nonaka, I., & Von Krogh, G. (2009). Perspective—Tacit knowledge and knowledge conversion: Controversy and advancement in organisational knowledge creation theory. *Organisation Science, 20*(3), 635–652.
Noss, T. B. (1898). The best of Herbartianism. *Journal of Education, 47*(17 (1176)), 261–261.
Omiya, M. (2024). Interview with Eiichi Kajita. *Seikyo Online*. https://www.seikyoonline.com/article/C3C7B16124470926299974BBFCC81774
Papadimitropoulos, E. (2021). Platform capitalism, platform cooperativism, and the commons. *Rethinking Marxism, 33*(2), 246–262.
Pasquale, F. (2016). Two narratives of platform capitalism. *Yale Law & Policy Review, 35*, 309–320.
Rahman, K. S., & Thelen, K. (2019). The rise of the platform business model and the transformation of twenty-first-century capitalism. *Politics and Society, 47*(2), 177–204. https://doi.org/10.1177/0032329219838932
Ravenelle, A. (2019). "We're not Uber:" control, autonomy, and entrepreneurship in the gig economy. *Journal of Managerial Psychology, 34*(4), 269–285.
Roy-Mukherjee, S., & Harrison, M. (2020). The shifting boundaries of capitalism and the conflict of surplus value appropriation within the gig economy. In *Conflict and shifting boundaries in the gig economy: An interdisciplinary analysis* (pp. 45–62). Emerald Publishing Limited.
Schmidt, R., & Scott, C. (2021). Regulatory discretion: Structuring power in the era of regulatory capitalism. *Legal Studies, 41*(3), 454–473.
Schor, J. B., & Attwood-Charles, W. (2017). The "sharing" economy: Labour, inequality, and social connection on for-profit platforms. *Sociology Compass, 11*(8), e12493.
Scott, C. (2015). Regulatory capitalism, accountability and democracy. In *Accountability and regulatory governance: Audiences, controls and responsibilities in the politics of regulation* (pp. 189–208). Springer.
Srnicek, N. (2017). *Platform capitalism*. John Wiley & Sons.
Stewart, A., & Stanford, J. (2017). Regulating work in the gig economy: What are the options? *The Economic Labour Relations Review, 28*(3), 420–437.

Tanaka, K., Tomioka, H., & Minei, Y. (2025). Tsunesaburo Makiguchi's perspective on morality and its significance: Based on moral education aimed at "Reiwa-style school education in Japan." Journal of Educational Studies, 77, 239–253.
Todolí-Signes, A. (2017). The end of the subordinate worker? The on-demand economy, the gig economy, and the need for protection for crowdworkers. *International Journal of Comparative Labour Law Industrial Relations, 33*(2), 241–268.
Uchiyama, Y., & Furuoka, F. (2025). Uberisation and resistance to online food delivery gig work in Asia: Lessons from Malaysia. *Journal of Contemporary Asia, 1-18*. https://doi.org/10.1080/00472336.2024.2449081
Uchiyama, Y., Furuoka, F., & Akhir, M. N. M. (2022). Gig workers, social protection and labour market inequality: Lessons from Malaysia. *Jurnal Ekonomi Malaysia, 56*(3), 165–184.
Uchiyama, Y., Furuoka, F., & Omar, S. A. (2024). The rise and contestation of platform capitalism: Evidence from two food delivery blackouts in Malaysia. *Journal of Industrial Relations, 00221856241294107*. https://doi.org/10.1177/00221856241294107
Van Dijck, J., Nieborg, D., & Poell, T. (2019). Reframing platform power. *Internet Policy Review, 8*(2), 1–18.
Van Doorn, N., & Badger, A. (2020). Platform capitalism's hidden abode: Producing data assets in the gig economy. *Antipode, 52*(5), 1475–1495.
Westfall, B. H. (1975). German educational thought adapted to American schools: Herbartian influence on American teacher education through selected publications of Charles De Garmo and Charles and Frank McMurry. Ph.D. thesis submitted to Northern Illinois University.
Watson, B. (2004). T*he record of the orally transmitted teachings*.
Woodcock, J. (2021). *The fight against platform capitalism: An inquiry into the global struggles of the gig economy*. University of Westminster Press.
Woodcock, J., & Graham, M. (2020). The gig economy. *Polity*.

Chapter 3
Patterns of Youth Unemployment Rate: Empirical Analysis of the First Assumption of the Law of One Unemployment Rate (LOUR)

Chapter 3 is the first analytical chapter of the book. It examines patterns and variations in youth unemployment rates. The chapter then introduces the first assumption of the Law of One Unemployment Rate (LOUR), which posits the "uniformity" of unemployment patterns across demographic groups. To contextualise this assumption, the chapter presents a literature review that summarises major empirical findings on youth unemployment rates and highlights both consistencies and divergences reported in previous studies. It then details the methodology of this study and specifies the data sources and research design used for the empirical analysis of LOUR's first assumption. The chapter concludes by synthesising the evidence on the uniformity of unemployment rates.

3.1 Introduction

The high unemployment rate among young people has been a major social problem for decades (O'Higgins, 1997, O'Higgins, 2017; Olubusoye et al., 2023). For example, O'Higgins (1997) pointed out that there was an increasing awareness of the youth unemployment problem among the Organisation for Economic Co-operation and Development (OECD) countries since the 1990s. Among 38 OECD countries, youth unemployment rates were greater than 30% in three countries, Spain, Italy and Ireland, in 1993. The Spanish government successfully reduced youth unemployment by increasing the minimum wage. By the beginning of the 2000s, the high level of youth unemployment had become a global concern. Among developed countries, the average value of total unemployment rates in the OECD countries is around 5%. By contrast, the average value of youth unemployment was around 13% in these countries in 1998. In other words, approximately 10 million youth could not find any appropriate employment in these developed countries. In developing countries, young people also cannot find decent work. The

Y. Uchiyama, F. Furuoka, *Youth and Employment*,
https://doi.org/10.1007/978-981-95-3257-5_3

youth unemployment rate is around 16% in Brazil and approximately 19% in Chile in 1998 (O'Higgins, 2001).

Furthermore, O'Higgins (2016) claimed that youth unemployment rates in the European Union (EU) countries continued to increase during the 2000s and the 2010s. Interestingly, the economic recession in the EU region during the 2000s had a stronger negative impact on prime-aged workers than on young workers. Unemployment rates among prime-aged workers increased by 53% for the period of 2007–2014. By contrast, the unemployment rate among young workers increased by only 41% during the same period. According to the International Labour Organisation (ILO), the global youth unemployment rate in 2016 was around 13%. However, the number of unemployed youths around the world decreased from around 76 million in 2009 to around 70 million in 2016 (O'Higgins, 2017). More recently, Olubusoye et al. (2023) claimed that youth unemployment remains a serious issue around the world. Around 40% of youth who lacked working experience suffered from prolonged unemployment around the world. In the case of Nigeria, the youth unemployment rate was 8.4% in 1991 and increased to 20.7% in 2016 (Olubusoye et al., 2023).

Against this background, this chapter used some advanced statistical methods to examine the patterns of youth unemployment. As Furuoka (2024a) claimed, the main objective of economic sciences is to examine and identify the *patterns* of economic data, which are determined by the interaction of supply and demand in the market. However, there is still a lack of systematic inquiry into the pattern of youth unemployment. More importantly, there is no consensus on the pattern of youth unemployment rates. Some researchers claimed the stationary process of the youth unemployment rate (Zimmermann, 1991; Li et al., 2021), while others pointed to the unit root process. (Zimmermann, 1991; Altuzarra, 2015; Cheratian et al., 2023). For example, Zimmermann (1991) claimed that there were gender differences in the pattern of youth unemployment. In other words, the female youth unemployment rate is a unit root process, and the male youth unemployment rate is a stationary process. However, Altuzarra (2015) claimed that both female and male youth unemployment rates have the same pattern, and these unemployment rates are unit root processes. On the other hand, Li et al. (2021) pointed out that the young female unemployment rate is a stationary process. By contrast, Cheratian et al. (2023) claimed that the youth unemployment rate is a unit root process.

Furthermore, there are two main hypotheses to define the patterns in the time-series data of unemployment rates, namely the natural rate hypothesis and the hysteresis hypothesis. According to the natural rate hypothesis, the unemployment rate would have a propensity for "mean-reversion", in which unemployment rates would return to the natural rate of unemployment (Furuoka, 2024b). Friedman (1968) defined this proposition of the "natural" rate of the unemployment rate time series. He claimed that a lower unemployment rate or an unemployment rate below the natural rate may indicate the excess demand for labour in the market. This excess demand would create upward pressure on the wage level. On the other hand, a higher unemployment rate or an unemployment rate above the natural rate may indicate an excess supply of labour. This excess supply would create downward pressure on the wage rate. Thus, the unemployment rate would eventually return to the natural rate or equilibrium level of unemployment, which is determined by the Walrasian system of general equilibrium equations. Furthermore, he asserted that the natural rate of unemployment would be determined by the structural characteristics of the labour market, such as market imperfection, stochastic fluctuations of product demands and supplies in the commodity market, cost of information and the cost of mobility (Friedman, 1968).

However, there are some prominent economists who opposed the idea that unemployment rates would return to the Walrasian equilibrium level of unemployment. For example, Karl Polanyi claimed that persistent unemployment is an example of market failure (Block & Somers, 2014). Polanyi believed that economic fluctuation could have a negative impact on employees in the labour market. In the stochastic process of economic fluctuations, economic booms may create new jobs, while economic recessions may destroy them. However, the problem is that job destruction during the recession would often be greater than the job creation during the boom (Polanyi, 1944). Similarly, Joseph Stiglitz also claimed that the persistently high unemployment rate could be indicative of the malfunction of the labour market (Stiglitz, 2009). On the other hand, Olivier Blanchard and Lawrence Summers defined the unemployment hysteresis hypothesis (Blanchard & Summers, 1986a, 1986b, 1987). They claimed that the unemployment rate would not return to the equilibrium level of unemployment. This is because the equilibrium level of unemployment would be equal to the actual level of unemployment in the past. In other words, insiders or current employees in the firms may have no intention to reduce their wage rate in the economic recession. As a result, the "excess" supply or number of unemployed workers in the labour market would not decrease due to wage inflexibility (Blanchard & Summers, 1986a, 1986b, 1987).

For the purpose of empirical analysis, the current study employs four different ADF-type unit root tests, namely the augmented Dickey–Fuller (ADF) test (Dickey & Fuller, 1979, 1981), the Fourier ADF (FADF) test (Enders & Lee, 2012), the ADF with a structural break (ADF–SB) test (Perron & Vogelsang, 1992, 1993) and the FADF with a structural break (FADF–SB) test (Furuoka, 2017), and four different KPSS-type of stationarity tests, namely the KPSS test (Kwiatkowski et al., 1992), the Fourier KPSS (FKPSS) test (Becker et al., 2006), the KPSS with structural break (KPSS-SB) test (Kurozumi, 2002) and the Fourier KPSS with structural break (FKPSS-SB) test (Furuoka, 2017), to examines the patterns of youth unemployment.

The theoretical foundation for the analysis of patterns in youth unemployment is the first assumption of the Law of One Unemployment Rates (LOUR). This assumption can be defined as uniformity in the patterns in the unemployment rates of different demographic groups, which are separated by some demographic characteristics, such as gender, ethnic group, age and disability status. More precisely, there would be a uniformity of unemployment patterns in the absence of labour market frictions, mobility costs, information costs, and discrimination under a competitive labour market with a perfectly flexible wage rate. The validity of the first assumption of the LOUR could be tested empirically by examining whether there are any differences in the pattern of unemployment rates among different demographic groups (Furuoka, 2024a; Furuoka et al., 2025). For example, the US Bureau of Labour Statistics (2025) compiled data on unemployment rates among different age cohorts, such as the unemployment rate among young workers and the unemployment rate among prime-aged workers. Under the first assumption of the LOUR, there would be uniformity in the pattern of unemployment rates among these two demographic groups.

This chapter consists of five sections. Following this introductory chapter, the second section reviews prominent research which examined the pattern of youth unemployment rates. The third section explains the data and methods used to examine the pattern of the youth unemployment rate. The fourth section reports the empirical findings on the pattern and convergence of youth unemployment rates. The fifth section is the conclusion.

3.2 Literature Review

There is a wealth of literature on the patterns of youth unemployment rates since the beginning of the 1990s (Zimmermann, 1991; Koustas & Veloce, 1996; Tolvi, 2003; Wu, 2009). Table 3.1 summarises prominent research on the systematic empirical analysis of this topic. For example, Zimmermann (1991) used the augmented Dicky-Fuller (ADF) test for the persistence of unemployment in seven different age cohorts, namely workers aged 16–19, workers aged 20–24, workers aged 25–34, workers aged 35–44, workers aged 45–54, workers aged 55–59 and workers aged 60 and above, in Germany for the period of 1950–1987. The findings indicated that the ADF test failed to reject the null hypothesis of unit root for female workers in all seven age cohorts, except workers aged 35–44 and workers aged 60 and above. The unit root test also failed to reject the null hypothesis for male workers in all age cohorts, except workers aged 16–19, workers aged 20–24 and workers aged 60 and above. This means that there are minor differences in the pattern of unemployment between young and prime-aged workers. Among female workers, the unemployment rates of prime-aged workers are relatively less persistent than the unemployment rates of young workers. By contrast, among male workers, youth unemployment is less persistent than the unemployment rate of prime-aged workers. Koustas and Veloce (1996) used the Geweke-Porter-Hudak (GPH) method to examine the persistence of unemployment rates among young and prime-aged workers in Canada for the period of 1947–1992. Their findings claimed that the estimated fractional integration coefficient for prime-aged male workers is 1.04, while the coefficient for prime-aged female workers is 0.92. By contrast, the fractional integration coefficient for young workers is only 0.60. This means that there is a higher level of unemployment persistence among prime-aged workers than young workers in Canada. Tolvi (2003) employed the autoregressive fractionally integrated moving average (ARFIMA) method to examine the persistence of the unemployment rate among young workers in Finland for the period of 1989–2002. The findings indicated that the estimated fractional integration coefficient for young

Table 3.1 Summary of empirical analysis on the pattern of youth unemployment rates

Authors (Year)	Country	Data (Source of data)	Methods	Results
Zimmermann (1991)	Germany	Annual data 1950–1987 Young female and male, prime-aged female and male, (German Statistical Office)	ADF test	Minor difference in the pattern of unemployment between young and prime-aged workers
Koustas and Veloce (1996)	Canada	Quarterly data 1947Q1–1992Q4 Prime-aged females and males, young (Statistics Canada)	GPH test	Lower persistence for youth unemployment in comparison to prime-aged worker unemployment Fractional integration parameter Prime-aged male: 1.02 Prime-aged female: 0.92 Youth: 0.60
Tolvi (2003)	Finland	Monthly data 1989 M1-2002 M1 Young female and young male (Statistics Finland)	ARFIMA method	Lower persistence for young female and male unemployment in comparison to those of all ages Fractional integration parameter Young female: 0.69 Young male: 0.57 Female (in all ages): 0.93 Male (in all ages): 0.97
Wu (2009)	29 provinces in China	Yearly data 1989–1998 Young and total	AR (1) model	Lower persistence for youth unemployment in comparison to the total unemployment rate
Caporale and Gil-Alana (2014)	15 EU countries	Annual data 1980–2005 Youth (World Development Indicators)	Robinson test	Persistence of youth unemployment rate in five countries: Finland, the Netherlands, Portugal, and Spain Fractional integration parameter Finland: 1.96 Netherlands: 1.79 Portugal: 1.69 Spain: 1.62
Altuzarra (2015)	Spain	Quarterly data 1976Q1-2012Q4	ZA test and GPH test	Lower persistence for youth unemployment

(continued)

Table 3.1 (continued)

Authors (Year)	Country	Data (Source of data)	Methods	Results
		Prime-aged female and male, young female and male, young, prime-aged (National Statistics Institute of Spain)		in comparison to prime-aged worker unemployment Fractional integration parameter Young male: 0.775 Young female: 0.770 Prime-aged male: 0.685 Prime-aged female: 1.036
Gil-Alana et al. (2019)	Turkey	Quarterly data 1988Q3-2013Q4 Young female and young male (TURKSTAT database)	Robinson test	Lower persistence for youth workers in comparison to workers of all ages Fractional integration parameter Young male: 0.778 Young female: 0.846
Li et al. (2021)	12 Asian countries	Annual data 1991–2020 Young and prime-aged female (World Development Indicators)	Fourier KSS test	Minor difference in the pattern of unemployment between young and prime-aged female workers
Cheratian et al. (2023)	Iran	Quarterly data 2001Q2-2020Q1 Workers aged 15–24, workers aged 25–29, workers aged 30 and over (Statistical Centre of Iran)	GARCH unit root tests	No difference in the pattern of unemployment rate between young and prime-aged workers
Torun et al. (2023)	Turkey, Azerbaijan, Turkmenistan, Kyrgyzstan, Kazakhstan, Uzbekistan	Annual data 1991–2019 Young workers and workers of all ages (World Income Inequality Database)	Panel stationarity test	No difference in the pattern of unemployment rate between young workers and workers of all ages
Nnyanzi et al. (2024)	47 countries in SSA	Annual data 1991–2020 Young female and male workers (World Development Indicators)	Panel unit root test with a structural break	The unemployment rate of young workers is a unit root process

(continued)

Table 3.1 (continued)

Authors (Year)	Country	Data (Source of data)	Methods	Results
Yilanci et al. (2024)	5 countries in the Nordic region	Monthly data 1983 M1-2022M5 Young female and male, prime-aged female and male (Eurostat)	Fourier KSS test	No difference in the pattern of unemployment rate between young workers and workers of all ages
Cat and Kirca (2024)	Turkey	Monthly data 2005 M1-2023M10 Young females and males aged 15–24, older females and males aged 25–74 (OECD database)	Wavelet-based unit root tests	Minor difference in the pattern of unemployment rate between young workers and workers in all age groups
Yavuz et al. (2024)	27 countries in the European Union	Annual data 1991–2023 Youth (World Bank database)	Factorial PANIC unit root test	The unemployment rate of young workers is a unit root process
Furuoka (2024b)	United States	Monthly data 2008 M6-2022M6 Youth aged 16–19 (US Bureau of Labour Statistics)	YOFA unit root tests	Minor difference in the pattern of unemployment rate between young workers and workers in all age groups
Balci (2025)	Turkey	Monthly data 2005 M1-2024M6 Youth (Turkish Statistical Institute)	ADF-GARCH with level break and trend break	Youth unemployment is a root process

female workers aged 15–24 is 0.69, which is lower than that coefficient for overall female workers aged 15–64 (i.e., 0.93). Similarly, the estimated fractional integration coefficient for young male workers aged 15–24 is 0.75, which is lower than that coefficient for overall male workers aged 15–64 (i.e., 0.97). These findings are in line with those from the previous study (Koustas & Veloce, 1996) that youth unemployment is less persistent than the unemployment rates of prime-aged workers. Wu (2009) also used the first-order autoregressive (i.e. AR(1)) model to examine the persistence of youth unemployment in 29 provinces in China for the period of 1989–1998. The researcher claimed that youth unemployment rates are less persistent than the total unemployment rates.

In the 2010s, some researchers used advanced statistical methods, such as the Robinson test, the Zivot and Andrews (ZA) test and the semiparametric fractional integration method, for the analysis of the pattern of youth unemployment rates

(Caporale & Gil-Alana, 2014; Altuzarra, 2015; Gil-Alana et al., 2019). For example, Caporale and Gil-Alana (2014) used the Robinson test to examine the persistence of the youth unemployment rate in 15 European Union (EU) countries for the period of 1980–2005. They claimed that the Robinson test failed to reject the null hypothesis that the fractional integration parameter is not greater than 1 for all these EU countries except Finland, the Netherlands, Portugal and Spain. In other words, these findings indicated the higher level of youth unemployment persistence in these four EU countries. Altuzarra (2015) also pointed out three main reasons for high youth unemployment rates, namely low human capital accumulation, lack of experience and the difference between the skills of young people at the time of completion of education and those required in the labour market. This researcher also used the ZA test and the GPH method to examine the persistence of nine different demographic types of unemployment rates, namely total unemployment, male unemployment, female unemployment, prime-aged worker unemployment, young worker unemployment, young male unemployment, young female unemployment, prime-aged male unemployment, and prime-aged female unemployment. The researcher claimed that the ZA test failed to reject the null hypothesis of a unit root for all these nine demographic groups. On the other hand, the findings from the GPH test could be summarised into three main points. The first point is that the fractional integration (FI) parameter of young workers is 0.759, which is lower than that of prime-aged workers (i.e., 0.837). The second point is that the FI parameter of young males is 0.775, which is lower than that of males in all ages (i.e., 0.821), while the FI parameter of young females is 0.770, which is lower than that of females in all ages (i.e., 0.998). The third point is that the least persistent unemployment among these nine demographic groups is prime-aged males, whose FI parameter is 0.685, while the most persistent unemployment is prime-aged females, whose FI parameter is 1.036. In other words, the findings of the first and second points are in line with previous research (Koustas & Veloce, 1996; Tolvi, 2003). By contrast, the findings of the third point that young male unemployment is more persistent than prime-aged male unemployment are contradictory to these studies. Gil-Alana et al. (2019) employed the semiparametric fractional integration method to examine the dynamics of youth unemployment in Turkey for the period 1988–2012. They pointed out that the semiparametric estimation of the FI parameter for young female workers is 0.846, which is lower than that for female workers of all ages (i.e., 0.868). These findings are in line with previous studies (Koustas & Veloce, 1996; Tolvi, 2003). By contrast, the semiparametric estimation of the FI parameter for young male workers is 0.778, which is higher than for male workers of all ages (i.e., 0.733). These findings are in line with previous research (Altuzarra, 2015).

In the 2020s, experts in applied economics used some sophisticated statistical methods, such as the Fourier Kapetanios-Snell-Shin (KSS) test, the GARCH unit root test and the panel stationarity test, for the analysis of youth unemployment dynamics (Li et al., 2021; Cheratian et al., 2023; Torun et al., 2023). For example, Li et al. (2021) used the Fourier KSS test to examine the dynamics of young and prime-aged female workers in 12 Asian countries for the period of 1991–2020. Their findings indicated that the Fourier KSS test could reject the null hypothesis of a unit root for young female workers in all Asian countries. However, the same test failed to reject the null hypothesis for prime-aged female workers in Nepal and Pakistan. It means that there is a minor difference in the pattern of unemployment between young and prime-aged female workers in Asia. They also provided an interesting explanation of the unit root process of prime-aged female workers in Nepal and Pakistan. They pointed out that prime-aged female workers tend to obtain employment in the manufacturing sector to earn extra income. However, prime-aged female workers are discriminated against in their workplace, so economic shocks tend to permanently destroy their employment opportunities in the manufacturing sector. Furthermore, human capital endowments of prime-aged female workers are lower than those of young female workers in Pakistan. Thus, economic shocks tend to destroy permanently employment opportunities for prime-aged female workers. Cheratian et al. (2023) employed the generalised autoregressive conditional heteroskedasticity (GARCH) unit root test to examine the unemployment dynamics of three different age groups, namely workers aged 15–24, workers aged 25–29, and workers aged 30 and over, in Iran for the period of 2001–2020. They pointed out that there is a huge mismatch between the skills of young workers and those required in the labour market in Iran. Employers in Iran tend to consider university graduates as "unskilled" young workers. As a consequence, there is a very high unemployment rate among university graduates, especially among graduates of private universities in Iran. They used the four types of the GARCH unit root tests, namely the ADF-GARCH test (Cook, 2008), the ADF-GARCH test with level break and trend break (Narayan & Popp, 2010), the ADF-GARCH test with trend break (Narayan & Liu, 2015) and the ADF-GARCH test with two trend breaks (Narayan et al., 2016). They pointed out that these four GARCH unit root tests failed to reject the null hypothesis of unit root for the young workers aged 15–24. They also pointed out that these GARCH tests failed to reject the null hypothesis for the prime-aged workers aged 25–29. They also claimed that these tests could not reject the null hypothesis for the prime-aged worker aged 30 and over. In other words, they concluded that there is no difference in the pattern of unemployment rate between young and prime-aged workers in Iran. Torun et al. (2023) used the panel stationarity test to examine the dynamics of youth unemployment rates in six countries whose majority of the population speaks the Turkish language, namely Turkey, Azerbaijan, Turkmenistan, Kyrgyzstan, Kazakhstan, and Uzbekistan, for the period of 1991–2019. They claimed that the panel stationarity test failed to reject the null hypothesis of the stationary process for young workers. They also asserted that the panel stationarity test failed to reject the null hypothesis for workers of all ages. It means that there is no difference in the unemployment pattern between young workers and workers of all ages.

More recently, the empirical analysis of young unemployment and the age unemployment gap is still a very popular topic among experts in applied economics. Researchers employed some sophisticated statistical methods, such as panel unit root test with structural break, Fourier KSS test, wavelet-based unit root test, the factorial PANIC unit root tests and the fractional integration test, for their empirical analysis (Nnyanzi et al., 2024; Yilanci et al., 2024; Cat & Kirca, 2024; Yavuz et al., 2024;

Furuoka, 2024b). For instance, Nnyanzi et al. (2024) used the panel unit root test with a structural break for the empirical analysis of young unemployment rates in 47 countries in Sub-Saharan Africa (SSA) for the period of 1991–2021. They claimed that there are around 18 million young job seekers per year in the SSA. However, there were around 3 million job creations for young workers per year. In other words, around 15 million young people would not find a job match in the labour market in SSA. In order to increase the job match between job vacancies and young job seekers, policymakers in SSA countries have implemented various active labour market policies (ALMPs), such as the School Leavers Industrial Fund (SLIF), Youth Venture Fund (YVF) and Youth Livelihood Fund (YLF). They claimed that the panel unit root test with structural break failed to reject the null hypothesis of unit root for young female workers. They also pointed out that the panel unit root test could not reject the null hypothesis for young male workers. It implied that the unemployment rates among young workers in SSA could be considered a unit root process. Yilanci et al. (2024) used four types of unit root tests, including the Fourier KSS test, to examine the dynamics of young unemployment rates in the five countries in the Nordic regions, namely Denmark, Finland, Iceland, Norway and Sweden, for the period of 1983–2022. They claimed that these Nordic countries are considered welfare states in which the government plays a significant role in maintaining economic growth and stability. As a consequence, unemployment rates in this region tend to be relatively lower than in other European states. Among these five Nordic countries, youth unemployment rates in three countries, namely Denmark, Iceland and Norway, are relatively lower. Among them, youth unemployment is the highest in Finland. They examined the four types of workers, namely young female workers, young male workers, female workers of all ages and male workers of all ages. They claimed that these four types of unit root tests failed to reject the null hypothesis of unit root for all four types of workers in Denmark. By contrast, these tests could not reject the null hypothesis for all four types of workers, except the male workers of all ages in Finland. Similarly, these tests also could not reject the null hypothesis for all workers, except young female workers, in Iceland. In the case of Norway and Sweden, these tests failed to reject the null hypothesis for all four types of workers. It means that there is no difference in unemployment persistence between young workers and workers of all ages. Cat and Kirca (2024) employed the wavelet-based unit root tests to examine the dynamics of unemployment rates in four different demographic groups, namely young female workers aged 15–24, older female workers aged 25–74, young male workers aged 15–24, and older male workers aged 25–74, in Turkey for the period of 2005–2023. They claimed that a high unemployment rate, or around 10.5%, has become a critical economic issue in the country. Young female workers suffered from a relatively higher unemployment rate of around 22.3%, which is a serious problem. They also pointed out that the wavelet-based unit root test could reject the null hypothesis of a unit root in the short-run employment for all these four demographic groups, except older male workers. On the other hand, the wavelet-based test could reject the null hypothesis of a unit root in the medium-run employment for all four groups. They also claimed that the wavelet test could reject the null hypothesis in the long run for only older female workers and old male workers. Despite its minor discrepancy. Their findings indicated that there is a minor difference in the pattern of unemployment among young and prime-aged workers. Yavuz et al. (2024) used the factorial PANIC unit root tests to examine the dynamics of young unemployment in 27 countries in the European Union for the period of 1991–2023. They claimed the factorial Panic test with two-level breaks failed to reject the null hypothesis of unit root for all these 27 EU countries, except Germany, Finland, Croatia and Spain. On the other hand, the factorial Panic test with two-trend breaks failed to reject the null hypothesis for all 27 EU countries except Hungary and Poland. These findings may indicate that youth unemployment rates are a unit root process. Furuoka (2024b) used the fractional integration test and the Yaya-Ogbonna-Furuoka–Alana (YOFA) test (Yaya et al., 2021) to examine the age unemployment gap in the United States for the period of 2008–2022. He claimed that the pattern of youth unemployment rates is different from the pattern of total unemployment. The findings from the Geweke-Porter-Hudak (GPH) test (Geweke & Porter-Hudak, 1983) indicated there is no persistence in total unemployment in line with the natural rate hypothesis. By contrast, there is persistence in youth unemployment in line with the hysteresis hypothesis. These findings are confirmed by the YOFA test, which indicated no convergence of the unemployment gap between youth unemployment and total unemployment. Balci (2025) employed the ADF-GARCH test with level break and trend break (Narayan & Popp, 2010) to examine the dynamics of youth unemployment in Turkey for the period of 2005–2024. The researcher pointed out that the ADF-GARCH test failed to reject the null hypothesis of a unit root in youth unemployment in the country. In other words, the empirical findings indicated that youth unemployment could be considered a non-stationary process.

3.3 Data and Methods

This study uses the time-series data on the unemployment rates from the US Bureau of Labour Statistics. This is because the US statistics office has the most sophisticated and detailed data on each different demographic group. This study examines unemployment rates among six different age cohorts. The young workers aged 16–24 are separated into two demographic groups, namely teenage workers aged 16–19 and young workers aged 20–24. The prime-aged workers aged 25–54 are separated into three demographic groups, namely the lower prime-aged workers aged 25–34, the middle prime-aged workers aged 35–44 and the upper prime-aged workers aged 45–54. The remaining demographic group is the eldest demographic group among these six groups, or older workers aged 55–64 (US Bureau of Labour Statistics, 2025).

As O'Higgins (1997) clearly mentioned, some young people may suffer from some disabilities. In other words, disability status could be an additional factor that could prevent young people from obtaining employment. This study duly takes account of this issue. Thus, six demographic groups with different age cohorts are

Table 3.2 Variables on Twelve Demographic Groups

Name of variable	Description	Code name	Data course
PWD16–19	Unemployment rate among people with disabilities aged 16–19	LNU0407–4600	US Bureau of Labour Statistics, 2025
PWD20–24	Unemployment rate among people with disabilities aged 20–24	LNU0407–5570	US Bureau of Labour Statistics, 2025
PWD25–34	Unemployment rate among people with disabilities aged 25–34	LNU0407–5580	US Bureau of Labour Statistics, 2025
PWD35–44	Unemployment rate among people with disabilities aged 35–44	LNU0407–5585	US Bureau of Labour Statistics, 2025
PWD45–54	Unemployment rate among people with disabilities aged 45–54	LNU0407–5590	US Bureau of Labour Statistics, 2025
PWD55–64	Unemployment rate among people with disabilities aged 55–64	LNU0407–5595	US Bureau of Labour Statistics, 2025
PND16–19	Unemployment rate among people without disabilities aged 16–19	LNU0407–4896	US Bureau of Labour Statistics, 2025
PND20–24	Unemployment rate among people without disabilities aged 20–24	LNU0407–5349	US Bureau of Labour Statistics, 2025
PND25–34	Unemployment rate among people without disabilities aged 25–34	LNU0407–5359	US Bureau of Labour Statistics, 2025
PND35–44	Unemployment rate among people without disabilities aged 35–44	LNU0407–5364	US Bureau of Labour Statistics, 2025
PND45–54	Unemployment rate among people without disabilities aged 45–54	LNU0407–5369	US Bureau of Labour Statistics, 2025
PND55–64	Unemployment rate among people without disabilities aged 55–64	LNU0407–5374	US Bureau of Labour Statistics, 2025

further separated by disability status. In other words, there would be twelve different demographic groups in this study of youth unemployment dynamics. The names of variables and sources of data on the unemployment rate in these twelve demographic groups are reported in Table 3.2.

In order to examine the pattern and convergence of youth unemployment, this study will conduct two stages of empirical analysis. In the first stage of empirical analysis, this study examines the patterns of youth unemployment using four types of ADF-type tests, namely the augmented Dickey-Fuller (ADF) test (Dickey & Fuller, 1979, 1981), the Fourier ADF (FADF) test (Enders & Lee, 2012), the ADF with a structural break (ADF–SB) test (Perron & Vogelsang, 1992, 1993) and the FADF with a structural break (FADF–SB) test (Furuoka, 2017). If these unit root tests identify uniformity in the pattern of the twelve unemployment rates or whether these unemployment rates are a unit root process or not, these findings are in line with the LOUR (For a more detailed explanation of these ADF tests, please refer to Appendix 3.1).

In the second stage of empirical analysis, the empirical findings from these ADF-type tests are confirmed by the four types of KPSS-type stationarity tests, namely the KPSS test (Kwiatkowski et al., 1992), the Fourier KPSS (FKPSS) test

(Becker et al., 2006), the KPSS with structural break (KPSS-SB) test (Kurozumi, 2002) and the Fourier KPSS with structural break (FKPSS-SB) test (Furuoka, 2017). If these stationarity tests identify uniformity in the pattern of the twelve unemployment rates or whether these unemployment rates are stationary processes or not, these findings are in line with the LOUR (For a more detailed explanation of these KPSS tests, please refer to Appendix 1 in Chap 4.).

3.4 Empirical Evidence

In the first stage of empirical analysis, four different kinds of ADF-type unit root tests are used to examine the time-series data of 12 different demographic groups. Table 3.3 reports the empirical findings from the ADF test and the FADF test. As the findings in the table indicate, the ADF test failed to reject the null hypothesis of unit root for all these twelve unemployment rates, except *PND25–34*. This means that unemployment for people without disability aged 25–34 could be considered as a stationary process, while the remaining eleven unemployment rates are unit root processes. Similarly, the FADF test confirmed the findings from the ADF test. In other words, the FADF test indicates that unemployment rates among eleven different demographic groups are a unit root process, except the unemployment rate of the people without disability aged 25–34 (i.e., a stationary process).

Table 3.4 reports the empirical findings from the ADF-SB test. As the findings in the table indicate, the ADF-SB test could reject the null hypothesis of a unit root for all six unemployment rates among people with disabilities, except *PWD16–19*. This

Table 3.3 Empirical findings from the ADF test and FADF test

Variable	ADF statistics	Frequency	FADF statistics
PWD16–19	−1.609	1	−2.912
PWD20–24	−2.148	1	−2.916
PWD25–34	−2.144	1	−3.339
PWD35–44	−2.145	1	−3.613
PWD45–54	−2.216	1	−3.256
PWD55–64	−2.324	1	−3.234
PND16–19	−2.559	1	−2.682
PND20–24	−2.297	2	−3.152
PND25–34	−3.850*	2	−4.512*
PND35–44	−2.393	2	−2.432
PND45–54	−3.053	1	−4.444
PND55–64	−2.803	2	−3.294

Notes: * denotes the significance of 0.05%; 1% and 5% critical values for the ADF test are −4.191 and − 3.547 (see Table 3.12); 1% and 5% critical values for the FADF test with $k = 1$ are −5.165 and − 4.456; 1% and 5% critical values for the FADF test with $k = 2$ are −4.899 and − 4.198 (see Table 3.14)

Table 3.4 Empirical findings from the ADF-SB test

Variable	Breakpoint (year)	Break-position (percentage)	ADF-SB statistics
PWD16–19	2019	68.7	−3.372
PWD20–24	2019	68.7	−13.293**
PWD25–34	2019	68.7	−12.203**
PWD35–44	2019	68.7	−9.757**
PWD45–54	2019	68.7	−10.735**
PWD55–64	2019	68.7	−13.146**
PND16–19	2016	50.0	−3.737
PND20–24	2019	68.7	−4.035*
PND25–34	2019	68.7	−10.191**
PND35–44	2019	68.7	−8.878**
PND45–54	2019	68.7	−8.228**
PND55–64	2019	68.7	−13.359**

Notes: ** denotes the significance of 5%; * denotes the significance of 0.05%, 1% and 5% critical values for the ADF-SB test with break-position in the interval of $\{0.50 < \lambda \leq 0.75\}$ are −4.664 and − 3.852; 1% and 5% critical values for the ADF-SB test with break-position in the interval of $\{0.25 < \lambda \leq 0.50\}$ are −4.585 and − 3.906 (see Table 3.16)

means that unemployment for people with disabilities aged 16–19 could be considered as the unit root process, while the remaining five unemployment rates among people with disabilities are stationary processes. Similarly, the ADF-SB test could reject the null hypothesis of a unit root for all six unemployment rates among people without disabilities, except *PND16–19*. This means that unemployment for people without disability aged 16–19 could be considered as a stationary process, while the remaining five unemployment rates among people without disabilities are unit root processes. In other words, the ADF-SB test indicated that there is a difference or no uniformity in the pattern of unemployment rate among teenage workers with or without disabilities, namely *PWD16–19, PND16–19,* and the remaining ten demographic groups.

Table 3.5 reports the empirical findings from the FADF-SB test. As the findings in the table indicate, the FADF-SB test could reject the null hypothesis of a unit root for all six unemployment rates among people with disabilities. This means that all six unemployment rates among people with disabilities are stationary processes. It means that there is a uniformity in the pattern of unemployment rates among people with disabilities. However, the FADF-SB test confirmed the empirical evidence from the ADF-SB test that all six unemployment rates among people without disabilities, except *PND16–19,* are stationary processes.

The findings from four different kinds of the ADF-type unit root test are summarised in Table 3.6. As the summary table indicates, the unemployment rate of teenage workers without disabilities aged 16–19 could be considered as the unit root process because all four kinds of unit root tests failed to reject the null hypothesis of the unit root process. Similarly, the unemployment rate of teenage workers with disabilities aged 16–19 could also be considered as the unit root

Table 3.5 Empirical findings from the FADF-SB test

Variable	Frequency	Breakpoint (year)	Break-position (percentage)	FADF-SB statistics
PWD16–19	1	2019	68.7	−5.910**
PWD20–24	1	2019	68.7	−12.689**
PWD25–34	1	2019	68.7	−14.839**
PWD35–44	1	2019	68.7	−12.362**
PWD45–54	2	2019	68.7	−14.375**
PWD55–64	2	2019	68.7	−22.544**
PND16–19	1	2019	68.7	−4.180
PND20–24	1	2019	68.7	−5.571**
PND25–34	2	2019	68.7	−10.639**
PND35–44	1	2023	93.7	−7.554**
PND45–54	1	2019	68.7	−9.069**
PND55–64	1	2019	68.7	−12.199**

Notes: ** denotes the significance of 1%; * denotes the significance of 5%; 1% and 5% critical values for the FADF-SB test with $k = 1$ and break-position in the interval of $\{0.50 < \lambda \leq 0.75\}$ are −5.474 and − 4.752; 1% and 5% critical values for the FADF-SB test with $k = 2$ and break-position in the interval of $\{0.50 < \lambda \leq 0.75\}$ are −5.228 and − 4.414; 1% and 5% critical values for the FADF-SB test with $k = 1$ and break-position in the interval of $\{0.75 < \lambda \leq 1.00\}$ are −5.471 and − 4.670 (see Table 3.18)

Table 3.6 Summary of the ADF-type unit root tests

Variable	ADF test	FADF test	ADF-SB test	ADF-SB test
PWD16–19	Unit root	Unit root	Unit root	Stationarity
PWD20–24	Unit root	Unit root	Stationarity	Stationarity
PWD25–34	Unit root	Unit root	Stationarity	Stationarity
PWD35–44	Unit root	Unit root	Stationarity	Stationarity
PWD45–54	Unit root	Unit root	Stationarity	Stationarity
PWD55–64	Unit root	Unit root	Stationarity	Stationarity
PND16–19	Unit root	Unit root	Unit root	Unit root
PND20–24	Unit root	Unit root	Stationarity	Stationarity
PND25–34	Stationarity	Stationarity	Stationarity	Stationarity
PND35–44	Unit root	Unit root	Stationarity	Stationarity
PND45–54	Unit root	Unit root	Stationarity	Stationarity
PND55–64	Unit root	Unit root	Stationarity	Stationarity

process because three kinds of unit root tests failed to reject the null hypothesis. On the other hand, unemployment rates of lower prime-aged workers without disabilities aged 25–34 could be considered as a stationary process. The remaining nine unemployment rates are indecisive because two types of unit root tests rejected the null hypothesis of unit root, while the other two types of unit root tests failed to reject the null hypothesis. Despite some ambiguity in the empirical findings, the empirical findings from the ADF-type unit root test indicated two interesting empirical findings. Firstly, the unemployment rate among teenage workers with or without

Table 3.7 Empirical findings from the KPSS test and FKPSS test

Variable	KPSS statistics	Frequency	FKPSS statistics
PWD16–19	0.137	1	0.052
PWD20–24	0.122	1	0.051
PWD25–34	0.140	1	0.048
PWD35–44	0.147	1	0.047
PWD45–54	0.127	1	0.051
PWD55–64	0.113	1	0.050
PND16–19	0.106	1	0.059*
PND20–24	0.082	2	0.094
PND25–34	0.058	2	0.057
PND35–44	0.092	2	0.136
PND45–54	0.099	2	0.119
PND55–64	0.075	2	0.081

Notes: * denotes significance of 5% critical values for the KPSS test are 0.158 and 0.216 (see Table 4.6); 1% and 5% critical values for the FADF test with $k = 1$ are 0.057 and 0.073; 1% and 5% critical values for the FADF test with $k = 2$ are 0.144 and 0.223 (see Table 4.8)

disabilities aged 16–19 tends to be considered as a unit root process in line with the hysteresis hypothesis. It means that this unemployment rate would not have a tendency towards mean-reversion. In other words, these teenage workers would suffer from a prolonged unemployment rate because their unemployment rates would not return to normal levels after the end of the economic crisis. Secondly, the unemployment rate among lower prime-aged workers without disability aged 25–34 tended to be considered as a stationary process in line with the natural rate hypothesis. It means these unemployment rates have a mean-reversion tendency. In other words, these prime-aged teenage workers would not suffer from a prolonged unemployment rate because their unemployment rate would return to a normal level quickly after the end of the economic crisis.

In the second stage of empirical analysis, four different kinds of KPSS-type stationarity tests are used to examine the time-series data of 12 different demographic groups. Table 3.7 reports the empirical findings from the KPSS test and the FKPSS test. As the findings in the table indicate, the KPSS test failed to reject the null hypothesis of stationarity for all twelve unemployment rates. This means that all these twelve different kinds of unemployment rates are stationary processes. Furthermore, the FKPSS test mainly confirmed the findings from the KPSS test. In other words, the FKPSS test also indicated that unemployment rates among twelve different demographic groups are stationary processes, except for *PND16–19*. This means that the unemployment rates of teenage workers without disabilities aged 16–19 could be considered as a unit root process. By contrast, the remaining eleven unemployment rates could be considered as a stationary process.

Table 3.8 reports the empirical findings from the KPSS-SB test. As the findings in the table indicate, the KPSS-SB test failed to reject the null hypothesis of stationarity for all twelve different unemployment rates. In other words, the KPSS-SB test confirmed the findings from the KPSS test and the FKPSS test that all these

Table 3.8 Empirical findings from the KPSS-SB test

Variable	Breakpoint (year)	Break-position (percentage)	KPSS-SB statistics
PWD16–19	2020	75.0	0.095
PWD20–24	2020	75.0	0.075
PWD25–34	2020	75.0	0.074
PWD35–44	2020	75.0	0.076
PWD45–54	2020	75.0	0.071
PWD55–64	2020	75.0	0.063
PND16–19	2015	43.7	0.062
PND20–24	2020	75.0	0.091
PND25–34	2020	75.0	0.064
PND35–44	2019	68.7	0.095
PND45–54	2022	87.5	0.060
PND55–64	2020	75.0	0.067

Notes: ** denotes the significance of 5%, 1% and 5% critical values for the KPSS-SB test with break-position in the interval of $\{0.20 < \lambda \leq 0.50\}$ are 0.126 and 0.178; 1% and 5% critical values for the KPSS-SB test with break-position in the interval of $\{0.50 < \lambda \leq 0.75\}$ are 0.129 and 0.164; 1% and 5% critical values for the KPSS-SB test with break-position in the interval of $\{0.75 < \lambda \leq 1.00\}$ are 0.125 and 0.174 (see Table 4.10)

unemployment rates among different demographic groups could be considered as a stationary process. Furthermore, the breakpoint took place in 2020 for all these twelve different demographic groups, except workers without disabilities aged 16–19, workers without disabilities aged 35–44, and workers without disabilities aged 45–54. In the case of teenage workers without disabilities aged 16–19 and workers without disabilities aged 35–44, the breakpoint took place before 2020. By contrast, in the case of workers without disabilities aged 45–55, the breakpoint took place after 2020.

Table 3.9 reports the empirical findings from the FKPSS-SB test. As the findings in the table indicate, the FKPSS-SB test failed to reject the null hypothesis of stationarity for all six unemployment rates among workers with disabilities, except *PWD16–19* and *PWD20–24*. In other words, the FKPSS-SB test indicated that the unemployment rate among young people with disabilities aged 16–24 could be considered as a unit root process. By contrast, the unemployment rate among prime-aged and older workers with disabilities aged 25–64 could be considered as a stationary process. Moreover, the FKPSS-SB test also failed to reject the null hypothesis of stationarity for all six unemployment rates among workers without disabilities, except *PND16–19* and *PND20–24*. It also means that the unemployment rate among young people without disabilities aged 16–24 could be considered a unit root process. By contrast, the unemployment rate among prime-aged and older workers without disabilities could be considered a stationary process.

The findings from four different kinds of the KPSS-type stationarity test are summarised in Table 3.10. As the summary table indicated, all these tests indicated that all these unemployment rates failed to reject the null hypothesis of stationarity,

Table 3.9 Empirical findings from the FKPSS-SB test

Variable	Frequency	Breakpoint (year)	Break-position (percentage)	FKPSS-SB statistics
PWD16–19	1	2020	75.0	0.060*
PWD20–24	1	2020	75.0	0.057*
PWD25–34	2	2020	75.0	0.081
PWD35–44	2	2020	75.0	0.072
PWD45–54	2	2020	75.0	0.079
PWD55–64	2	2020	75.0	0.075
PND16–19	1	2015	43.7	0.052*
PND20–24	1	2020	75.0	0.053*
PND25–34	1	2020	75.0	0.042
PND35–44	2	2019	68.7	0.064
PND45–54	1	2022	87.5	0.041
PND55–64	1	2020	75.0	0.048

Notes: * denotes the significance of 5%; 1% and 5% critical values for the FKPSS-SB test with $k = 1$ and break-position in the interval of $\{0.50 < \lambda \leq 0.75\}$ are 0.049 and 0.061; 1% and 5% critical values for the FKPSS-SB test with $k = 2$ and break-position in the interval of $\{0.50 < \lambda \leq 0.75\}$ are 0.093 and 0.133; 1% and 5% critical values for the FKPSS-SB test with $k = 1$ and break-position in the interval of $\{0.75 < \lambda \leq 1.00\}$ are 0.048 and 0.061 (see Table 4.12)

Table 3.10 Summary of the KPSS-type stationarity tests

Variable	KPSS test	FKPSS test	KPSS-SB test	FKPSS-SB test
PWD16–19	Stationarity	Stationarity	Stationarity	Unit root
PWD20–24	Stationarity	Stationarity	Stationarity	Unit root
PWD25–34	Stationarity	Stationarity	Stationarity	Stationarity
PWD35–44	Stationarity	Stationarity	Stationarity	Stationarity
PWD45–54	Stationarity	Stationarity	Stationarity	Stationarity
PWD55–64	Stationarity	Stationarity	Stationarity	Stationarity
PND16–19	Stationarity	Unit root	Stationarity	Unit root
PND20–24	Stationarity	Stationarity	Stationarity	Unit root
PND25–34	Stationarity	Stationarity	Stationarity	Stationarity
PND35–44	Stationarity	Stationarity	Stationarity	Stationarity
PND45–54	Stationarity	Stationarity	Stationarity	Stationarity
PND55–64	Stationarity	Stationarity	Stationarity	Stationarity

except for young workers. For example, the FKPSS-SB test indicated that the unemployment rates are a unit root process for three different demographic groups, namely teenage workers with disabilities aged 16–20, young workers with disabilities aged 20–24 and young workers without disabilities aged 20–24. Furthermore, both the FKPSS test and the FKPSS-SB test showed that the unemployment rate among teenage workers without disabilities aged 16–20 could also be considered as a unit root process. Despite these minor discrepancies, these different KPSS tests

Table 3.11 Overall findings on the pattern of unemployment rate

Variable	Statistical tests which indicated a unit root	Statistical tests which indicated stationarity	Number of Statistical tests which indicated stationarity	Overall
PWD16–19	ADF, FADF, ADF-SB, FKPSS-SB	FADF-SB, KPSS, FKPSS, KPSS-SB	4/8	Indecisive
PWD20–24	ADF, FADF, FKPSS-SB	ADF-SB, FADF-SB, KPSS, FKPSS, KPSS-SB	5/8	Stationarity
PWD25–34	ADF, FADF	ADF-SB, FADF-SB, KPSS, FKPSS, KPSS-SB, FKPSS-SB	6/8	Stationarity
PWD35–44	ADF, FADF	ADF-SB, FADF-SB, KPSS, FKPSS, KPSS-SB, FKPSS-SB	6/8	Stationarity
PWD45–54	ADF, FADF	ADF-SB, FADF-SB, KPSS, FKPSS, KPSS-SB, FKPSS-SB	6/8	Stationarity
PWD55–64	ADF, FADF	ADF-SB, FADF-SB, KPSS, FKPSS, KPSS-SB, FKPSS-SB	6/8	Stationarity
PND16–19	ADF, FADF, ADF-SB, FADF-SB, FKPSS, FKPSS-SB	KPSS, KPSS-SB	2/8	Unit root
PND20–24	ADF, FADF, FKPSS-SB	ADF-SB, FADF-SB, KPSS, FKPSS, KPSS-SB	5/8	Stationarity
PND25–34	ADF, FADF	ADF-SB, FADF-SB, KPSS, FKPSS, KPSS-SB, FKPSS-SB	6/8	Stationarity
PND35–44	ADF, FADF	ADF-SB, FADF-SB, KPSS, FKPSS, KPSS-SB, FKPSS-SB	6/8	Stationarity
PND45–54	ADF, FADF	ADF-SB, FADF-SB, KPSS, FKPSS, KPSS-SB, FKPSS-SB	6/8	Stationarity
PND55–64	ADF, FADF	ADF-SB, FADF-SB, KPSS, FKPSS, KPSS-SB, FKPSS-SB	6/8	Stationarity

generally indicated that the unemployment rate among these different demographic groups could be considered as a stationary process.

Table 3.11 reports the overall findings on the pattern of twelve unemployment rates, which are examined by eight different statistical tests (i.e., four kinds of the ADF-type unit root test and four kinds of KPSS-type stationarity test), namely the ADF test, the FADF test, the ADF-SB test, the FADF-SB test, the KPSS test, the FKPSS test, the KPSS-SB test and the FKPSS-SB test. These findings from the

ADF-type tests and the KPSS-type tests could be summarised into four interesting facts. Firstly, six out of eight different statistical tests indicated the stationary process of eight unemployment rates, namely *PWD25–34*, *PWD45–44, PWD45–54, PWD55–64, PND25–34, PND45–44, PND45–54, PND55–64*. It means that unemployment rates among these prime-aged and older workers with or without disabilities aged 25–64 could be considered as a stationary process in line with the natural rate hypothesis. These prime-aged and older workers would not suffer from the prolonged unemployment rate because their unemployment rate would have a mean-reversion propensity. Secondly, five out of eight different statistical tests indicated the stationary process of the two unemployment rates, namely *PWD20–24* and *PND20–24*. It means that unemployment rates among these young workers with or without disabilities aged 20–24 could be considered a stationary process because the majority of statistical tests show stationarity. However, the usage of different significance levels would change this conclusion. For example, as Table 3.7 indicates, the estimated statistic of the FKPSS test for young workers with disabilities aged 20–25 is 0.051, which is less than its 5% critical value of 0.057. Thus, the null hypothesis of stationarity could not be rejected for this demographic group. On the other hand, the 10% critical value of the FKPSS test is 0.049. In other words, the null hypothesis of stationarity could be rejected if the 10% critical values are used for the hypothesis testing. If so, overall findings on the young workers with disabilities aged 20–24 are indecisive because four out of eight statistical tests indicated stationarity.

Thirdly, four out of eight different statistical tests indicated the stationary process of *PWD16–19*. It means that unemployment rates among these teenage workers with disabilities aged 16–19 could be considered as indecisive because half of the statistical tests indicated a stationary process, and the other half of the statistical tests indicated a unit root process. However, the usage of different significance levels would also change this conclusion. For example, as Table 3.7 indicates, the estimated statistic of the FKPSS test for teenage workers with disabilities aged 16–19 is 0.051, which is less than its 5% critical value of 0.057. On the other hand, the 10% critical value of the FKPSS test is 0.049, which is less than the estimated FKPSS statistic for this demographic group. Similarly, as Table 3.7 indicates, the estimated statistic of the KPSS test for teenage workers with disabilities aged 16–19 is 0.137, which is less than its 5% critical value of 0.158. On the other hand, the 10% critical value of the KPSS test is 0.129, which is less than the estimated KPSS statistic for this demographic group. If so, overall findings on the teenage workers with disabilities aged 16–19 are a unit root process because only two out of eight statistical tests indicated stationarity. Fourthly, only two out of eight different statistical tests indicated the stationary process of *PWD16–19*. It means that unemployment rates among teenage workers with disabilities aged 16–19 could be considered a unit root process because less than half of the statistical tests indicated a stationary process. In other words, only two KPSS-type stationarity tests, namely the KPSS test and the KPSS-SB test, indicated the stationary process of unemployment rates among this demographic group. The remaining six statistical tests indicated the unit root process of this unemployment rate.

To put it in a nutshell, overall empirical findings on the pattern of unemployment rates indicate that there is no uniformity among the twelve different unemployment rates. If the 5% significance level is used for hypothesis testing, unemployment rates of teenage workers without disabilities aged 16–19 could be considered as a unit root process, and unemployment rates of teenage workers with disabilities aged 16–19 could be indecisive. However, if the 10% significance level is used, two types of unemployment rates, namely unemployment rates of teenage workers without disabilities aged 16–19 and unemployment rates of teenage workers with disabilities aged 16–19, could be considered as a unit root process, and unemployment rates of young workers with disabilities aged 20–24 could be indecisive. There are some discrepancies in the pattern of unemployment rates among young workers and prime-aged workers. It could be concluded that there are some discrepancies in the pattern of unemployment rates among young workers and prime-aged workers, which is contrary to the Law of One Unemployment Rates (LOUR).

3.5 Conclusion

This chapter used several advanced statistical tests to examine the pattern of youth unemployment rates. The empirical findings could be summarised into two main findings. Firstly, if the 5% significance level is used for hypothesis testing, the unemployment rate of teenage workers without disabilities aged 16–19 could be considered as a unit root process, and the remaining 11 unemployment rates could be a stationary process. Secondly, if the 10% significance level is used for hypothesis testing, two unemployment rates, namely the unemployment rate of teenage workers without disabilities aged 16–19 and the unemployment rate of teenage workers with disabilities aged 16–19, could be considered as a unit root process, and the remaining 10 unemployment rates could be a stationary process.

In conclusion, there are minor discrepancies in the patterns of unemployment rates among different demographic groups. More precisely, the unemployment rates of teenage workers with and without disabilities aged 16–19 could not be considered a stationary process. In other words, these unemployment rates would not return to the "normal" level after the end of the economic crisis. These findings may offer some contradictory evidence on the first assumption of the Law of One Unemployment Rate (LOUR). In this context, policymakers may need to pay due attention to the lack of mean-reversion in unemployment rates of teenage workers aged 16–19. Without appropriate active labour market policies (ALMs), they would suffer from a prolonged unemployment rate.

Appendix 3.1 ADF-type Tests for the Empirical Analysis of the Law of One Unemployment Rate (LOUR)

This study uses the five different ADF-types of unit root tests to test the Law of One Unemployment Rate (LOUR). Firstly, the most fundamental test among these unit root tests is the augmented Dickey-Fuller (ADF) test (Dickey & Fuller, 1979, 1981). They proposed the following autoregressive model for the Dickey-Fuller (DF) unit root test (Dickey & Fuller, 1979, 1981):

$$y_t = \rho y_{t-1} + \varepsilon_t \tag{3.1}$$

where y_t is the variable of interest, $y_0 = 0$, ρ is the autoregressive parameter of interest, which is a real number, ε_t is the sequence of independent Gaussian random variables with mean zero and variance δ^2, $\varepsilon_t \sim NID(0, \delta^2)$. The time-series y_t will converge to a stationary process if $|\rho| < 1$. If $\rho = 1$, this variable could be called a random walk (Dickey & Fuller, 1979, 1981). This autoregressive parameter could be estimated as (Dickey & Fuller, 1979, 1981):

$$\widehat{\rho} = \left(\sum_{t=2}^{n} y_{t-1}^2\right)^{-1} \sum_{t=2}^{n} y_t y_{t-1} \tag{3.2}$$

where n is the number of observations. If $|\rho| < 1$,this estimator is asymptotically normally distributed with mean ρ and variance $(1 - \rho)^2/n$. The estimate of $(\widehat{\rho} - \rho)$ could be expressed as (White, 1958; Dickey & Fuller, 1979, 1981):

$$\widehat{\rho} - \rho = \left(\sum_{t=2}^{n} y_{t-1}^2\right)^{-1} \sum_{t=2}^{n} y_t e_t \tag{3.3}$$

where e_t is residual from Eq. (3.1). The t-statistic for the $\widehat{\rho}$ could be estimated as (White, 1958; Dickey & Fuller, 1979, 1981):

$$\widehat{t}_\rho = \widehat{\rho} / s_\rho \tag{3.4}$$

where s_ρ is the standard error for the autoregressive parameter. The standard error could be estimated as follows (White, 1958; Dickey & Fuller, 1979, 1981):

$$s_\rho^2 = \frac{\sum_{t=2}^{n} e_t}{n-3} \left[\frac{1}{n-1} + \overline{y}_{t-1}^2 \left(\sum_{t=1}^{n} (y_{t-1} - \overline{y}_{t-1})^2 \right)^{-1} \right] \tag{3.5}$$

where $\overline{y}_{t-1}$ is the mean value of y_{t-1}. The t-value of the null hypothesis of $\rho = 1$ can be expressed as (White, 1958; Dickey & Fuller, 1979, 1981; Hayashi, 2000):

$$t = \frac{\frac{1}{n}\sum_{t=2}^{n} \Delta y_t y_{t-1}}{s\sqrt{\frac{1}{\frac{1}{n^2}\sum_{t=2}^{n} y_{t-1}^2}}} \tag{3.6}$$

where Δ is the difference operator, $\Delta y_t = y_t - y_{t-1}$ and s is the standard error of the regression, which can be expressed as (White, 1958; Dickey & Fuller, 1979, 1981; Hayashi, 2000):

$$s = \sqrt{\frac{1}{n-2}\sum_{t=1}^{n} e_t^2} \tag{3.7}$$

where e_t is residual from Eq. (3.1). The numerator of the fraction in Eq. (3.6) would converge in distribution to (White, 1958; Dickey & Fuller, 1979, 1981; Hayashi, 2000):

$$\frac{1}{n}\sum_{t=1}^{n} \Delta y_t y_{t-1} \ {}^{d}\!\rightarrow \frac{\gamma_0}{2}[w(1)]^2 - \frac{\gamma_0}{2} \tag{3.8}$$

where $w(r)$ is a standard Wiener process and γ_o is the variance of Δy_t. The denominator of the fraction in Eq. (3.6) would converge in distribution (White, 1958; Dickey & Fuller, 1979, 1981; Hayashi, 2000):

$$\frac{1}{n^2} y_{t-1}^2 \xrightarrow{d} \gamma_0 \int_0^1 [w(r)]^2 \, dr \tag{3.9}$$

Thus, the t-statistic for the null of $\rho = 1$ could converge in distribution (White, 1958; Dickey & Fuller, 1979, 1981; Hayashi, 2000):

$$t \xrightarrow{d} \frac{\frac{1}{2}\left([w(1)]^2 - 1\right)}{\sqrt{\int_0^1 [w(r)]^2 \, dr}} \tag{3.10}$$

Let $\{\varepsilon_t^\mu\}$ be the demeaned time series, which is created from a random walk time series $\{\varepsilon_t\}$. According to the Proposition 9.2(d) in Hayashi (2000):

$$\frac{1}{n}\sum_{t=1}^{n} \left(\varepsilon_t^\mu - \varepsilon_{t-1}^\mu\right) \times \varepsilon_{t-1}^\mu \xrightarrow{d} \frac{\lambda^2}{2}\left\{[w^\mu(1)]^2 - [w^\mu(0)]^2\right\} - \frac{\gamma_0}{2} \tag{3.11}$$

Table 3.12 Empirical distribution of the ADF test statistics

	0.01	*0.05*	*0.10*	*0.50*	*0.90*	*0.95*	*0.99*
$n = 50$	−4.199	−3.547	−3.230	−2.168	−1.201	−0.891	−0.221
$n = 100$	−4.055	−3.484	−3.158	−2.155	−1.206	−0.845	−0.237
$n = 500$	−3.994	−3.471	−3.160	−2.163	−1.236	−0.941	−0.357
$n = 1000$	−3.906	−3.404	−3.156	−2.178	−1.260	−0.961	−0.369

where λ^2 is the long-run variance of $\{\Delta\varepsilon_t\}$ and $\lambda^2 = \gamma_0$. If $\{\varepsilon_t\}$ is driftless $I(1)$, then $\{\Delta\varepsilon_t\}$ is zero-mean $I(0)$ or white noise. According to the Proposition 9.2(c) in Hayashi (2000):

$$\frac{1}{n^2}\sum\nolimits_{t=1}^{n}\left(\varepsilon_{t-1}^{\mu}\right) \xrightarrow{d} \lambda^2\int_0^1 \left[w^{\mu}(r)\right]^2 dr \tag{3.12}$$

Combining (3.10) and (3.11), the distribution of the t-statistic for the $\widehat{\rho}$ could be expressed as a Wiener Process (White, 1958; Dickey & Fuller, 1979, 1981; Hayashi, 2000):

$$t_{\rho} = \frac{\frac{1}{2}\left(\left[w^{\mu}(1)\right]^2 - \left[w^{\mu}(0)\right]^2 - 1\right)}{\sqrt{\int_0^1 \left[w^{\mu}\mu(r)\right]^2 dr}} \tag{3.13}$$

where $w(r)$ is a standard Wiener process. Equation (3.1) of the Dicky-Fuller (DF) unit root test could be reformulated as the augmented Dicky-Fuller (ADF) test (White, 1958; Dickey & Fuller, 1979, 1981; Hayashi, 2000; Furuoka, 2017):

$$\Delta y_t = \mu + \beta t + \rho y_{t-1} + \sum_{i=1}^{p} \Delta y_{t-i} + \varepsilon_t \tag{3.14}$$

where μ is the intercept, t is a deterministic trend, and β is the slope parameter for the trend, and p is number of lagged differences. Under the null hypothesis of unit root process, the empirical distribution of the ADF test would be estimated using 1000 replications of four different sample sizes, namely $T = 50$, $T = 100$, $T = 500$, $T = 1000$ and two frequencies, namely $k = 1$, $k = 2$,and four break points, namely $\omega = 0.125$, $\omega = 0.375$, $\omega = 0.625$, $\omega = 0.875$ (Cheung et al., 1994; Furuoka, 2017; Yaya et al., 2021). Table 3.12 reports the empirical distribution of the ADF test statistics. As the empirical findings in the table indicate, the 0.01 point of distribution was −4.199 when the number of observations was 50, and it increased to −3.906 when the number of observations increased to 1000. For the comparison, the critical values for the ADF test statistics are reported in Table 3.13. The estimated critical values for the ADF test in the current study are in line with those values estimated by previous studies, namely Fuller (1976) and MacKinnon (1996).

Table 3.13 Critical values for ADF test statistics

	Fuller (1976)		
	1%	*5%*	*10%*
$n = 50$	−4.16	−3.50	−3.18
$n = 100$	−4.05	−3.45	−3.15
$n = 500$	−3.97	−3.42	−3.12
	MacKinnon (1996)		
	1%	*5%*	*10%*
$n = 50$	−4.16	−3.50	−3.18
$n = 100$	−4.05	−3.45	−3.15
$n = 500$	−3.97	−3.41	−3.13
	Current study		
	1%	*5%*	*10%*
$n = 50$	−4.19	−3.54	−3.23
$n = 100$	−4.05	−3.48	−3.15
$n = 500$	−3.99	−3.47	−3.16

However, the seminal paper by Pierre Perron pointed out that the ADF test would suffer from low power if there were structural breaks or nonlinearities in the time series (Perron, 1989). Thus, Enders and Lee (2012) suggested that Fourier approximation functions should be incorporated into the ADF framework. This nonlinear unit root test is known as the Fourier ADF (FADF) test (Enders & Lee, 2012; Furuoka, 2017):

$$\Delta y_t = \mu + \beta t + \rho y_{t-1} + \gamma_1 \, sin \, \frac{2\pi kt}{n} + \gamma_2 \, cos \, \frac{2\pi kt}{n} + \sum_{i=1}^{p} \Delta y_{t-i} + \varepsilon_t \tag{3.15}$$

where *sin* is the sine function, *cos* is the cosine function, $\pi = 3.1416$, k is the frequency for the Fourier approximation function, γ_1 is the slope coefficient for the sine function and γ_2 is the slope coefficient for the cosine function. Under the null hypothesis of the unit root process, the empirical distribution of the ADF test would be estimated using 1000 replications of four different sample sizes, namely $T = 50$, $T = 100$, $T = 500$, $T = 1000$ and two frequencies, namely $k = 1$, $k = 2$ (Cheung et al., 1994; Furuoka, 2017; Yaya et al., 2021). Table 3.14 reports the empirical distribution of the FADF test statistics. As the table indicates, in the case of $k = 1$, the 0.01 point of distribution was −5.165 when the number of observations was 50, and it increased to −3.851 when the number of observations increased to 1000. Similarly, in the case of $k = 2$, the 0.05 point of distribution was −4.198 when the number of observations was 50, and it increased slightly to −3.978 when the number of observations increased to 1000. Interestingly, the range of the empirical distribution of FADF in the case of $k = 2$ is narrower than that of the empirical distribution in the case of $k = 1$. For the comparison, the critical values for the FADF test statistics are reported in Table 3.15. The estimated critical values for the FADF test in the current study are generally in line with those values estimated by Ender and Lee (2012), who suggested this unit root test of the FADF test.

Table 3.14 Empirical distribution of the FADF test statistics

	FADF test ($k = 1$)						
	0.01	*0.05*	*0.10*	*0.50*	*0.90*	*0.95*	*0.99*
$n = 50$	−5.165	−4.456	−4.158	−3.081	−2.181	−1.909	−1.331
$n = 100$	−5.062	−4.397	−4.071	−3.094	−2.200	−1.948	−1.450
$n = 500$	−4.838	−4.264	−3.999	−3.093	−2.248	−2.014	−1.563
$n = 1000$	−4.851	−4.277	−4.011	−3.076	−2.235	−2.001	−1.511
	FADF test ($k = 2$)						
	0.01	*0.05*	*0.10*	*0.50*	*0.90*	*0.95*	*0.99*
$n = 50$	−4.899	−4.198	−3.830	−2.502	−1.120	−0.709	−0.029
$n = 100$	−4.715	−4.068	−3.736	−2.529	−1.268	−0.839	−0.004
$n = 500$	−4.555	−4.021	−3.692	−2.550	−1.302	−0.954	−0.158
$n = 1000$	−4.537	−3.978	−3.686	−2.571	−1.324	−0.954	−0.296

Table 3.15 Critical values for FADF test statistics

	Enders and Lee (2012)		
[$k = 1$]	*1%*	*5%*	*10%*
$n = 100$	−4.95	−4.35	−4.05
$n = 500$	−4.69	−4.05	−3.71
[$k = 2$]	*1%*	*5%*	*10%*
$n = 100$	−4.81	−4.29	−4.07
$n = 500$	−4.57	−3.99	−3.67
	Current study		
[$k = 1$]	*1%*	*5%*	*10%*
$n = 100$	−5.06	−4.39	−4.07
$n = 500$	−4.83	−4.26	−3.99
[$k = 2$]	*1%*	*5%*	*10%*
$n = 100$	−4.71	−4.06	−3.73
$n = 500$	−4.55	−4.02	−3.69

Furthermore, Perron and Vogelsang (1992) suggested that a structural break should be incorporated into the ADF framework. This unit root test with structural break is known as the ADF with structural break (ADF-SB) test (Perron & Vogelsang, 1992, 1993; Furuoka, 2017):

$$\Delta y_t = \mu + \beta t + \rho y_{t-1} + \delta DU_t + \theta D(T_B)_t + \sum_{i=1}^{p} \Delta y_{t-i} + \varepsilon_t \tag{3.16}$$

where δ is the slope parameter for the structural break dummy, $DU_t = 1$ if $T_B > t$ and $DU_t = 0$ otherwise, θ is the slope parameter for the one-time break dummy, $D(T_B)_t = 1$ if $T_B = t$ and $D(T_B)_t = 0$ otherwise, T_B is the breakpoint when a structural break occurs, and its percentage position within all observations is called the break-position $\lambda = (T_B/n) \times 100$. Under the null hypothesis of a unit root process, the empirical distribution of the ADF-SB test would be estimated using 1000

Table 3.16 Empirical distribution of the ADF-SB test statistics

	ADF - SB test ($\omega = 0.125$)						
	0.01	*0.05*	*0.10*	*0.50*	*0.90*	*0.95*	*0.99*
$n = 50$	−4.347	−3.611	−3.301	−2.227	−1.223	−0.852	−0.192
$n = 100$	−4.289	−3.637	−3.360	−2.328	−1.336	−1.007	−0.407
$n = 500$	−4.339	−3.672	−3.380	−2.377	−1.357	−1.046	−0.364
$n = 1000$	−4.199	−3.643	−3.371	−2.378	−1.399	−1.077	−0.462
	ADF - SB test ($\omega = 0.375$)						
	0.01	*0.05*	*0.10*	*0.50*	*0.90*	*0.95*	*0.99*
$n = 50$	−4.581	−3.906	−3.566	−2.396	−1.163	−0.827	−0.069
$n = 100$	−4.427	−3.779	−3.458	−2.388	−1.232	−0.847	−0.215
$n = 500$	−4.405	−3.758	−3.450	−2.381	−1.252	−0.915	−0.175
$n = 1000$	−4.275	−3.713	−3.456	−2.407	−1.314	−0.992	−0.353
	ADF - SB test ($\omega = 0.625$)						
	0.01	*0.05*	*0.10*	*0.50*	*0.90*	*0.95*	*0.99*
$n = 50$	−4.664	−3.852	−3.487	−2.357	−1.103	−0.730	0.119
$n = 100$	−4.487	−3.837	−3.508	−2.413	−1.199	−0.869	−0.091
$n = 500$	−4.349	−3.745	−3.431	−2.429	−1.279	−0.948	−0.224
$n = 1000$	−4.261	−3.720	−3.446	−2.396	−1.273	−0.951	−0.306
	ADF - SB test ($\omega = 0.875$)						
	0.01	*0.05*	*0.10*	*0.50*	*0.90*	*0.95*	*0.99*
$n = 50$	−4.442	−3.802	−3.444	−2.337	−1.336	−0.983	−0.325
$n = 100$	−4.296	−3.665	−3.387	−2.352	−1.365	−1.028	−0.498
$n = 500$	−4.305	−3.708	−3.423	−2.417	−1.418	−1.109	−0.491
$n = 1000$	−4.294	−3.686	−3.410	−2.393	−1.410	−1.124	−0.509

replications of four different sample sizes, namely $T = 50$, $T = 100$, $T = 500$, $T = 1000$ and four break points, namely $\omega = 0.125$, $\omega = 0.375$, $\omega = 0.625$, $\omega = 0.875$ (Cheung et al., 1994; Furuoka, 2017; Yaya et al., 2021). Table 3.16 reports the empirical distribution of the ADF-SB test statistics. As the table indicates, in the case of $\omega = 0.125$, the 0.01 point of distribution was −4.347 when the number of observations was 50, and it increased to −4.199 when the number of observations increased to 1000. Similarly, in the case of $\omega = 0.375$, the 0.05 point 7 of the distribution was −3.906 when the number of observations was 50, and it became −3.713 when the number of observations increased to 1000. For the comparison, the critical values for the ADF-SB test statistics are reported in Table 3.17. The estimated critical values for the ADF-SB test in the current study are generally in line with those values estimated by Perron and Vogelsang (1993), who suggested this unit root test of the ADF-SB test.

Moreover, Furuoka (2017) suggested creating a synthesis between the FADF test and the ADF-SB test by incorporating the Fourier approximation functions and structural break. This synthesised unit root test is known as the FADF-SB test (Furuoka, 2017):

Table 3.17 Critical values for ADF-SB test statistics

	Perron and Vogelsang (1993)		
$[\omega = 0.1]$	*1%*	*5%*	*10%*
$n = 50$	−4.30	−3.58	−3.23
$n = 100$	−4.15	−3.58	−3.24
$n = 1000$	−4.13	−3.52	−3.21
$[\omega = 0.3]$	*1%*	*5%*	*10%*
$n = 50$	−4.67	−3.95	−3.62
$n = 100$	−4.54	−3.92	−3.62
$n = 1000$	−4.41	−4.09	−3.84
$[\omega = 0.6]$	*1%*	*5%*	*10%*
$n = 50$	−4.76	−4.10	−3.79
$n = 100$	−4.59	−3.97	−3.69
$n = 1000$	−4.48	−4.16	−3.64
$[\omega = 0.8]$	*1%*	*5%*	*10%*
$n = 50$	−4.71	−3.99	−3.68
$n = 100$	−4.53	−3.89	−3.57
$n = 1000$	−4.39	−3.84	−3.84
	Current study		
$[\omega = 0.125]$	*1%*	*5%*	*10%*
$n = 50$	−4.34	−3.61	−3.30
$n = 100$	−4.28	−3.63	−3.36
$n = 1000$	−4.19	−3.64	−3.37
$[\omega = 0.375]$	*1%*	*5%*	*10%*
$n = 50$	−4.58	−3.90	−3.56
$n = 100$	−4.42	−3.77	−3.45
$n = 1000$	−4.27	−3.71	−3.45
$[\omega = 0.628]$	*1%*	*5%*	*10%*
$n = 50$	−4.66	−3.85	−3.48
$n = 100$	−4.48	−3.83	−3.50
$n = 1000$	−4.26	−3.72	−3.44
$[\omega = 0.875]$	*1%*	*5%*	*10%*
$n = 50$	−4.44	−3.80	−3.44
$n = 100$	−4.29	−3.66	−3.38
$n = 1000$	−4.29	−3.68	−3.41

$$\Delta y_t = \mu + \beta t + \rho y_{t-1} + \gamma_1 \sin\frac{2\pi kt}{n} + \gamma_2 \cos\frac{2\pi kt}{n} + \delta DU_t + \theta D(T_B)_t + \sum_{i=1}^{p} \Delta y_{t-i} + \varepsilon_t \tag{3.17}$$

Under the null hypothesis of unit root process, the empirical distribution of the FADF-SB test would be estimated using 1000 replications of four different sample sizes, namely $T = 50$, $T = 100$, $T = 500$, $T = 1000$ and two frequencies, namely $k = 1$, $k = 2$,and four break points, namely $\omega = 0.125$, $\omega = 0.375$, $\omega = 0.625$, $\omega = 0.875$ (Cheung et al., 1994; Furuoka, 2017; Yaya et al., 2021). Table 3.18

Table 3.18 Empirical distribution of the FADF-SB test statistics

	FADF - SB test $(k = 1, \omega = 0.125)$						
	0.01	*0.05*	*0.10*	*0.50*	*0.90*	*0.95*	*0.99*
$n = 50$	−5.277	−4.587	−4.229	−3.164	−2.222	−1.942	−1.340
$n = 100$	−5.345	−4.625	−4.305	−3.279	−2.322	−2.048	−1.545
$n = 500$	−5.054	−4.508	−4.218	−3.242	−2.359	−2.096	−1.629
$n = 1000$	−5.088	−4.475	−4.199	−3.266	−2.377	−2.104	−1.538
	FADF - SB test $(k = 1, \omega = 0.375)$						
	0.01	*0.05*	*0.10*	*0.50*	*0.90*	*0.95*	*0.99*
$n = 50$	−5.483	−4.780	−4.39	−3.247	−2.153	−1.810	−1.197
$n = 100$	−5.252	−4.585	−4.286	−3.256	−2.248	−1.944	−1.281
$n = 500$	−5.087	−4.537	−4.253	−3.268	−2.313	−2.003	−1.472
$n = 1000$	−5.110	−4.547	−4.262	−3.267	−2.309	−2.018	−1.398
	FADF - SB test $(k = 1, \omega = 0.625)$						
	0.01	*0.05*	*0.10*	*0.50*	*0.90*	*0.95*	*0.99*
$n = 50$	−5.474	−4.752	−4.366	−3.227	−2.123	−1.773	−1.068
$n = 100$	−5.240	−4.586	−4.290	−3.256	−2.225	−1.900	−1.313
$n = 500$	−5.151	−4.570	−4.267	−3.287	−2.294	−1.981	−1.440
$n = 1000$	−5.002	−4.480	−4.214	−3.247	−2.298	−2.012	−1.419
	FADF - SB test $(k = 1, \omega = 0.875)$						
	0.01	*0.05*	*0.10*	*0.50*	*0.90*	*0.95*	*0.99*
$n = 50$	−5.471	−4.670	−4.302	−3.191	−2.158	−1.884	−1.340
$n = 100$	−5.145	−4.530	−4.228	−3.235	−2.280	−2.023	−1.567
$n = 500$	−5.047	−4.474	−4.198	−3.257	−2.337	−2.099	−1.579
$n = 1000$	−4.975	−4.492	−4.214	−3.248	−2.405	−2.153	−1.573
	FADF - SB test $(k = 2, \omega = 0.125)$						
	0.01	*0.05*	*0.10*	*0.50*	*0.90*	*0.95*	*0.99*
$n = 50$	−5.065	−4.329	−4.006	−2.719	−1.251	−0.768	0.085
$n = 100$	−5.028	−4.377	−4.038	−2.866	−1.462	−1.001	−0.229
$n = 500$	−4.879	−4.315	−4.021	−2.890	−1.574	−1.178	−0.335
$n = 1000$	−4.949	−4.344	−4.011	−2.872	−1.615	−1.212	−0.504
	FADF - SB test $(k = 2, \omega = 0.375)$						
	0.01	*0.05*	*0.10*	*0.50*	*0.90*	*0.95*	*0.99*
$n = 50$	−5.272	−4.433	−4.107	−2.832	−1.391	−0.985	−0.211
$n = 100$	−5.047	−4.356	−4.031	−2.826	−1.516	−1.112	−0.414
$n = 500$	−4.951	−4.324	−4.010	−2.886	−1.684	−1.327	−0.630
$n = 1000$	−4.870	−4.277	−3.984	−2.888	−1.670	−1.304	−0.630
	FADF - SB test $(k = 2, \omega = 0.625)$						
	0.01	*0.05*	*0.10*	*0.50*	*0.90*	*0.95*	*0.99*
$n = 50$	−5.228	−4.414	−4.025	−2.669	−1.243	−0.850	0.044
$n = 100$	−4.922	−4.320	−4.018	−2.790	−1.517	−1.148	−0.320
$n = 500$	−4.815	−4.263	−3.968	−2.848	−1.630	−1.292	−0.568
$n = 1000$	−4.930	−4.298	−3.984	−2.892	−1.714	−1.328	−0.658
	FADF - SB test $(k = 2, \omega = 0.875)$						
	0.01	*0.05*	*0.10*	*0.50*	*0.90*	*0.95*	*0.99*
$n = 50$	−5.336	−4.539	−4.174	−2.866	−1.420	−0.990	−0.243

(continued)

Table 3.18 (continued)

	FADF - SB test ($k = 1, \omega = 0.125$)						
	0.01	*0.05*	*0.10*	*0.50*	*0.90*	*0.95*	*0.99*
$n = 100$	−5.024	−4.399	−4.088	−2.922	−1.547	−1.131	−0.364
$n = 500$	−4.891	−4.330	−4.024	−2.902	−1.597	−1.191	−0.503
$n = 1000$	−4.901	−4.305	−3.996	−2.917	−1.637	−1.212	−0.428

Table 3.19 Empirical distribution of the YOFA test statistics

	0.01	*0.05*	*0.10*	*0.50*	*0.90*	*0.95*	*0.99*
$n = 50$	−3.540	−2.777	−2.373	−1.039	0.265	0.651	1.393
$n = 100$	−3.623	−2.801	−2.381	−1.070	0.244	0.631	1.349
$n = 500$	−3.657	−2.860	−2.452	−1.113	0.294	0.659	1.367
$n = 1000$	−3.500	−2.799	−2.424	−1.102	0.282	0.719	1.468

reports the empirical distribution of the FADF-SB test. As the table indicates, in the case of $k = 1$, $\omega = 0.125$, the 0.01 point of distribution was −5.272 when the number of observations was 50, and it increased to −5.088 when the number of observations increased to 1000. Similarly, in the case of $k = 2$, $\omega = 0.375$,the 0.05 point of distribution was −4.443 when the number of observations was 50, and it increased to −4.277 when the number of observations increased to 1000.

Since the 2010s, the neural network (NN) method has become a popular analytical tool among experts in econometrics. Yaya et al. (2021) suggested that the autoregressive neural network (ARNN) be incorporated into the ADF framework. This ARNN test is known as the Yaya–Ogbonna–Furuoka–Alana (YOFA) test (Yaya et al., 2021)

$$\Delta y_t = \mu + \beta t + k_1[y_{t-1}] + k_2[y_{t-1}]^2 + k_2[y_{t-1}]^3 + \sum_{i=1}^{p} \Delta y_{t-i} + \varepsilon_t \tag{3.18}$$

where k_1 is the slope parameter for linear components, k_2 is the slope parameter for quadratic components and k_3 is the slope parameter for cubic components. Under the null hypothesis of the unit root process, the empirical distribution of the YOFA test would be estimated using 1000 replications of four different sample sizes, namely $T = 50$, $T = 100$, $T = 500$, $T = 1000$ (Cheung et al., 1994; Furuoka, 2017; Yaya et al., 2021). Table 3.19 reports the empirical distribution of the YOFA test.

As the table indicates, in the case of $n = 50$, the 0.01 point of distribution was −3.540, and it increased to −3.500 when the number of observations increased to 1000. However, in the case of $n = 50$, the 0.05 point of distribution was −2.777, and it decreased to −2.877 when the number of observations increased to 1000. Similarly, in the case of $n = 50$,the 0.10 point of distribution was −2.373, and it decreased to −2.424 when the number of observations increased to 1000.

References

Altuzarra, A. (2015). Measuring unemployment persistence by age and gender. *Romanian Journal of Economic Forecasting, 18*(4), 110–133.

Becker, R., Enders, W., & Lee, J. (2006). A stationarity test in the presence of an unknown number of smooth breaks. *Journal of Time Series Analysis, 27*(3), 381–409.

Blanchard, O. J., & Summers, L. H. (1986a). *Hysteresis in unemployment*. NBER Working Paper No.2035.

Blanchard, O. J., & Summers, L. H. (1986b). *Hysteresis and the European unemployment problem*. NBER Working Paper No. 1950.

Blanchard, O., & Summers, L. (1987). Hysteresis in unemployment. *European Economic Review, 31*, 288–295.

Balci, A. I. (2025). Analysis of youth unemployment in Turkey under the impact of COVID-19 within the framework of unemployment hysteresis and the natural rate of unemployment. *Academic Review of Economics and Administrative Sciences, 18*(1), 411–430.

Block, F., & Somers, M. R. (2014). *Power of market fundamentalism: Karl Polanyi's critique*. Harvard University Press.

Caporale, G. M., & Gil-Alana, L. (2014). Youth unemployment in Europe: Persistence and macroeconomic determinants. *Comparative Economic Studies, 56*, 581–591.

Cat, T., & Kirca, M. (2024). Testing the unemployment hysteresis hypothesis for Turkey by age, gender and frequency differences: Evidence from wavelet-based unit root tests. *Journal of Academic Approaches, 15*(3), 1599–1623.

Cheratian, I., Goltabar, S., & Gil-Alaña, L. A. (2023). The unemployment hysteresis by territory, gender, and age groups in Iran. *SN Business & Economics, 3*(2), 44.

Cheung, Y. W., Lai, K. S. and Tran, T. (1994). *Finite-sample critical values of the KPSS test: A response surface approach*. Discussion Papers, University of California, Santa Cruz. https://people.ucsc.edu/~cheung/working.html.

Cook, S. (2008). Joint maximum likelihood estimation of unit root testing equations and GARCH processes: Some finite-sample issues. *Mathematics and Computers in Simulation, 77*(1), 109–116.

Dickey, D. A., & Fuller, W. A. (1979). Distribution of the estimators for autoregressive time series with a unit root. *Journal of the American Statistical Association, 74*, 427–431.

Dickey, D. A., & Fuller, W. A. (1981). Likelihood ratio statistics for autoregressive time series with a unit root. *Econometrica, 49*, 1057–1072.

Enders, W., & Lee, J. (2012). The flexible Fourier form and Dickey-Fuller type unit root tests. *Economic Letters, 117*, 196–199.

Friedman, M. (1968). The role of monetary policy. *American Economic Review, 58*(1), 1–17.

Fuller, W. A. (1976). *Introduction to statistical time series*. John Wiley & Sons.

Furuoka, F. (2017). A new approach to testing unemployment hysteresis. *Empirical Economics, 53*(3), 1253–1280.

Furuoka, F. (2024a). Introduction. In *Disability and employment: Towards a humanistic economy* (pp. 1–10). Springer.

Furuoka, F. (2024b). Patterns and convergence of unemployment rate among people with disabilities: Testing the "Law of one unemployment rate". In *Disability and employment: Towards a humanistic economy* (pp. 69–109). Springer.

Furuoka, F., Gil-Alana, L., Yaya, O. S., & Vo, X. V. (2025). Convergence of gender unemployment gaps in Africa: New evidence from Fourier ADF and KPSS unit root tests with break. *Applied Economics, 1-19*. https://doi.org/10.1080/00036846.2024.2448610

Geweke, J., & Porter-Hudak, S. (1983). The estimation and application of long memory time series models. *Journal of Time Series Analysis, 4*(4), 221–238.

Gil-Alana, L. A., Ozdemir, Z. A., & Tansel, A. (2019). Long memory in Turkish unemployment rates. *Emerging Markets Finance and Trade, 55*(1), 201–217.

Hayashi, F. (2000). *Econometrics*. Princeton University Press.

Kurozumi, E. (2002). Testing for stationarity with a break. *Journal of Econometrics, 108*(1), 63–99.
Kwiatkowski, D., Phillips, P. C. B., Schmidt, P., & Shin, Y. (1992). Testing the null hypothesis of stationarity against the alternative of a unit root. *Journal of Econometrics, 54*, 159–178.
Koustas, Z., & Veloce, W. (1996). Unemployment hysteresis in Canada: an approach based on long-memory time series models. *Applied Economics, 28*(7), 823–831.
Li, Z. Z., Su, C. W., & Tao, R. (2021). Does gender matter for the unemployment hysteresis effect among Asian countries? *International Journal of Manpower, 42*(8), 1527–1544.
MacKinnon, J. G. (1996). Numerical distribution functions for unit root and cointegration tests. *Journal of Applied Econometrics, 11*(6), 601–618.
Narayan, P. K., & Popp, S. (2010). A new unit root test with two structural breaks in level and slope at an unknown time. *Journal of Applied Statistics, 37*(9), 1425–1438.
Narayan, P. K., & Liu, R. (2015). A unit root model for trending time-series energy variables. *Energy Economics, 50*, 391–402.
Narayan, P. K., Liu, R., & Westerlund, J. (2016). A GARCH model for testing market efficiency. *Journal of International Financial Markets, Institutions and Money, 41*, 121–138.
Nnyanzi, J. B., Kilimani, N., & Oryema, J. B. (2024). Hysteresis in youth unemployment in sub-Saharan Africa: Focus on gender, income, and region. *Journal of Developing Areas, 58*(2), 91–126.
O'Higgins, N. (1997). The challenge of youth unemployment. *International Social Security Review, 50*(4), 63–93.
O'Higgins, N. (2001). *Youth unemployment and employment policy: A global perspective*. International Labour Office.
O'Higgins, N. (2016). Youth unemployment. In A. Furlong (Ed.), *Routledge handbook of youth and young adulthood* (pp. 157–171). Routledge.
O'Higgins, N. (2017). *Rising to the youth employment challenge. New evidence on key policy issues*. International Labour Office.
Olubusoye, O. E., Salisu, A. A., & Olofin, S. O. (2023). Youth unemployment in Nigeria: Nature, causes and solutions. *Quality & Quantity, 57*(2), 1125–1157.
Perron, P. (1989). The great crash, the oil price shock, and the unit root hypothesis. *Econometrica, 57*, 1361–1401.
Perron, P., & Vogelsang, T. J. (1992). Testing for a unit root in a time series with a changing mean: corrections and extensions. *Journal of Business & Economic Statistics, 10*(4), 467–470.
Perron, P., & Vogelsang, T. J. (1993). A note on the asymptotic distributions of unit root tests in the additive outlier model with breaks. *Brazilian Review of Econometrics, 13*(2), 18–20.
Polanyi, K. (1944). *The great transformation*. Beacon Press.
Stiglitz, J. E. (2009). Moving beyond market fundamentalism to a more balanced economy. *Annals of Public and Cooperative Economics, 80*(3), 345–360.
Tolvi, J. (2003). Unemployment persistence of different labour force groups in Finland. *Applied Economics Letters, 10*(8), 455–458.
Torun, M., Arica, F., & Azazi, H. (2023). Testing the validity of unemployment hysteresis in Turkic Republics by panel unit root test analysis. *Economic Insights, 12*(2), 61–72.
US Bureau of Labour Statistics. (2025). *BLS data finder*. Accessed on Feb 16 February 2025. https://beta.bls.gov/dataQuery/search
White, J. S. (1958). The limiting distribution of the serial correlation coefficient in the explosive case. *Annals of Mathematical Statistics, 29*, 1188–1197.
Wu, Z. (2009). Youth unemployment in urban China. In *China in the world economy* (pp. 181–194). Routledge.
Yaya, O. S., Ogbonna, A. E., Furuoka, F., & Gil-Alana, L. A. (2021). A new unit root test for unemployment hysteresis based on the autoregressive neural network. *Oxford Bulletin of Economics and Statistics, 83*(4), 960–981.
Yilanci, V., Kırca, M., Canbay, Ş., & Sağlam, M. S. (2024). Unravelling unemployment hysteresis in Nordic countries: A multifaceted analysis of age, gender and frequency differentials. *International Journal of Manpower, 45*(6), 1093–1111.

Yavuz, R. A., Kılıc, C., & Akcan, A. T. (2024). Unemployment hysteresis by gender and youth in the EU: Evidence from new factor PANIC unit root tests with breaks. *International Journal of Manpower, 45*. https://doi.org/10.1108/IJM-05-2024-0314

Zimmermann, K. F. (1991). Ageing and the labour market: Age structure, cohort size and unemployment. *Journal of Population Economics, 4*(3), 177–200.

Chapter 4
Convergence of Age Unemployment Gap: Empirical Analysis of the Second Assumption of the Law of One Unemployment Rate (LOUR)

This chapter is the second analytical chapter of the book. It focuses on the convergence of the age unemployment gap, which is defined as the difference in unemployment between young and older workers, in order to examine LOUR's second assumption of "non-persistence" of the age unemployment gap. The chapter begins with the rationale for studying convergence and reviews major research studies on youth unemployment. Following this, the chapter explains the data and methods used to test LOUR's second assumption. The findings reveal the strength and direction of convergence and highlight how cyclical conditions and institutions shape adjustments. The chapter concludes by summarising the main empirical findings and implications regarding the convergence of the age unemployment gap.

4.1 Introduction

From a historical perspective, youth unemployment has emerged as a major social problem in the second half of the twentieth century. For the first time, youth unemployment became a pressing economic issue in developed countries in the 1980s (Bell & Blanchflower, 2010). At the end of the nineteenth century, the main issue in the labour market was the excessive demand for juvenile workers and their dismal working conditions. There was excessive demand for juvenile workers in certain low-paid jobs. The typical pattern of youth career path in that period was that (1) youth would leave their schools without entering higher learning institutions, (2) they would obtain and work some casual and simple jobs for a few years, and (3) they would join the "reserve arm" of labour. In this sense, youth unemployment was not an issue at that period. However, the problem of the "juvenile work" was that these young workers were employed as casual labourers without proper training for skill development or knowledge accumulation, which would be needed for more stable and permanent employment (Casson, 1979).

Y. Uchiyama, F. Furuoka, *Youth and Employment*,
https://doi.org/10.1007/978-981-95-3257-5_4

In the first half of the twentieth century, the lack of appropriate career paths for young people, rather than youth unemployment, became a major issue in the labour market. The main cause and reason for the absence of the appropriate career path for youth is the decay of apprenticeships. Since the Medieval Age, the apprenticeship ensured that young people aged 14–21 would get appropriate "on-the-job-training" (OJT) opportunities for the period of 5–9 years. However, there was a serious decay in apprenticeship at the beginning of the twentieth century because many employers abandoned apprenticeship, which would provide training and employment opportunities for young people. There was a kind of win-win situation in the apprenticeship. From the perspective of employers, the training program under the apprenticeship is a very practical one, which focuses on business logic rather than theoretical logic and pedagogical reasoning. From the perspective of youth, they would receive money during the apprenticeship, and they would prepare for a better future career at the same time (Tawney, 1909; Beveridge, 1909).

More importantly, Tawney (1909) claimed the decay of apprenticeship caused youth three main problems. Firstly, for a prolonged period, school leavers tended to engage in temporary occupations without the possibility of obtaining more permanent positions. Secondly, they were unable to obtain useful skills and to accumulate appropriate knowledge to become skilled workers. Thirdly, employers failed to exercise appropriate control over these juvenile workers. These young workers often leave their jobs within a short period of time (Tawney, 1909). Similarly, Beveridge (1909) pointed out two main consequences on youth career paths, which derived from the decay of apprenticeship. Firstly, school leavers would have no other choice but they obtain employment in certain "blind alley" occupations. Secondly, within a short period of time, they would leave these "death-end" jobs without receiving any appropriate training.

There are two main types of these "blind alley" occupations for youth at that period. Firstly, the school leavers and young people were often employed in factories as unskilled workers. Secondly, they were also employed as simple manual workers, such as office messengers, delivery workers or shop assistants. There were striking similarities between these two "blind alley" jobs. In this employment, young people entered these occupations not as "learners" but as wage earners. Furthermore, they were doing tasks which were too "simple" or too "light" for the grown people (Beveridge, 1909). In 1910, Rowntree and Lasker conducted intensive social research on youth unemployment in the United Kingdom. They claimed four main reasons why young people ended up working in the "blind alley" jobs. Firstly, school leavers tend to have lower levels of educational achievement. Secondly, some of them were physically weak, and others came from problematic families. Thirdly, they were unable to obtain more appropriate employment under the apprenticeship. Finally, some of them had a preference to work in casual and simple occupations (Rowntree & Lasker, 1911).

In the second half of the twentieth century, there was a widening gap between the young workers and the unemployment of all workers, regardless of age. For instance, most European countries suffered from persistently high youth unemployment in the 1970s. For example, in the case of Italy, the age unemployment gap between the unemployment rate of teenage male workers aged 14–18 and the total male unemployment rate was 15.5 per cent in 1973. Similarly, the age unemployment gap between the unemployment rate of teenage female workers aged 14–18 and the total female unemployment rate was 12.1 per cent in the same year (Casson, 1979). Furthermore, the situation of youth unemployment further deteriorated in the 1980s. For example, the United States faced a serious youth employment crisis in the 1980s. The unemployment rate among high school dropouts was 19.9 per cent in 1979. However, the high school dropouts' unemployment jumped up to 29.7 per cent in 1983 (Bell & Blanchflower, 2010).

More recently, there has been no improvement in the situation of youth employment in the twenty-first century. In 2020, the International Labour Organisation (ILO) published a report on youth employment entitled "Global Employment Trends for Youth 2020". In this report, this international organisation made a conclusion on the dismal situation of global youth employment and claimed that young workers suffer from poverty, and they tend to have informal and less secure employment. According to the ILO report, out of 429 million young workers worldwide, 55 million young workers suffer from extreme poverty. Furthermore, many of them engaged in "precarious" work, which lacked legal and social protection. These young workers would have limited opportunities for training and career progression (International Labour Organisation, 2020). Similarly, Fergusson and Yeates (2021) pointed out that the United Nations proposed the "Sustainable Development Goals (SDGs)" as a global agenda for sustainable and inclusive development and Goal 8.5 of the SDGs clearly stipulated that full employment for all, including young people, would be achieved by 2030. However, the progress is rather slow, and there is a high possibility that full employment for youth will not be achieved in the near future (Fergusson and Yeates, 2021). The United Nations (2018) also admitted to the slow progress toward full employment for youth. It reported that the global unemployment rate decreased from 6.4 per cent in 2000 to 5.6 per cent in 2017. Despite this progress, the youth unemployment rate remained at a high level, which is still 13.0 per cent in the same year. In other words, young people would have a three times higher likelihood of being unemployed than older people (United Nations, 2018).

Furthermore, Fergusson and Yeates (2021) used the new construct of "endemic youth unemployment" (EYU) to describe the dismal state of youth unemployment in recent years. There are three main characteristics of this EYU. Firstly, there is a persistently high level of youth unemployment in the whole decade of the 2010s. Secondly, there is no decline in unemployment or mean-reversion propensity in youth unemployment. In other words, youth unemployment does not seem to decrease drastically after the end of the global financial crisis of the 2000s. Thirdly, there is a rapid increase in the expected level of youth unemployment around the world. More precisely, the expectations of youth unemployment in recent years tend to be higher than in most of the period after the end of the Second World War in 1945 (Fergusson and Yeates, 2021).

Against such a backdrop, the main objective of this chapter is to examine the convergence of the age unemployment gap. From a methodological perspective,

Furuoka (2024a) conducted pioneering research to examine the convergence of the demographic unemployment gaps among different demographic groups. The demographic unemployment gap could be defined as the unemployment gap according to demographic characteristics, such as gender, age and disability. He used several advanced statistical tests and examined whether there would be convergence in the demographic unemployment gaps. This study used his methodological procedure for its empirical analysis.

The theoretical foundation for the analysis of convergence in the age unemployment gap is the second assumption of the Law of One Unemployment Rate (LOUR). This second assumption makes an assumption that there would be no persistence in differences in the unemployment rates between different demographic groups, such as the *disability unemployment gap* or the difference in the unemployment rate between workers with disabilities and workers without disabilities, the *gender unemployment gap* or the difference in the unemployment rate between female workers and male workers, the *age unemployment gap* or difference in the unemployment rate between young workers and older workers. Under this assumption, these unemployment gaps would not be persistent in the absence of labour market frictions, mobility costs, information costs, and labour market discrimination under a competitive labour market with a perfectly flexible wage rate. The validity of this assumption could be tested by whether the age unemployment gap would be persistent or not (Furuoka, 2024a, 2024b; Furuoka et al., 2025).

In other words, the presence of persistence in the age unemployment gap could be considered as evidence to deny the second assumption of the LOUR. For the analysis of the convergence in the age unemployment gap, the current study employs four different types of statistical tests, namely the ADF test (Dickey & Fuller, 1979, 1981), the KPSS test (Kwiatkowski et al., 1992), the Yaya–Ogbonna–Furuoka–Alana (YOFA) test (Yaya et al., 2021) and the KPSS-YOFA test. In other words, this study used two advanced statistical tests, namely the YOFA test and the KPSS-YOFA test, which are based on the autoregressive neural network (ARNN). This is because the ARNN-based approach could be a better method which uses the hidden layers to capture the latent characteristics of time-series data (Yaya et al., 2021).

This chapter consists of five sections. Following this introductory chapter, the second section reviews prominent research on age unemployment gaps. The third section explains the data and methods used to examine the convergence of the age unemployment gap. The fourth section reports the empirical findings on the pattern and convergence of youth unemployment rates. The fifth section is the conclusion.

4.2 Literature Review

Since the 1970s, the persistently high level of youth unemployment has become a major social issue (Casson, 1979; Hess et al., 1994; O'Higgins, 1997). There are numerous studies which have examined the problem of youth unemployment and the age unemployment gap since then (Adams & Mangum, 1978; Casson, 1979). For example, Adams and Mangum (1978) pointed out that the persistently high level of youth unemployment became a national issue in the United States at the end of the 1970s. The unemployment rate among teenagers aged 16–19 was 16.7 per cent in 1977. Furthermore, the unemployment rate among non-white teenagers aged 16–19 was 38.3 per cent. In other words, youth unemployment rates were more than two times higher than the total unemployment rate in the country. Casson (1979) also pointed out that there was a notable trend of an increase in the age unemployment gap, which was the difference in unemployment between young people and older people. Especially, this increase in the age unemployment gap was manifested in the United States. The basic reason for this huge age unemployment gap could be the job-hopping behaviour among young people (Casson, 1979).

There was an increase in the number of studies on youth unemployment in the 1980s. These studies expressed grave concerns about the increase in youth unemployment at that time (Ginzberg, 1980; Sorrentino, 1981; Braverman, 1981). For example, Ginzberg (1980) claimed that there was a rapid increase in youth unemployment in the United States since the 1950s. The youth unemployment rate of teenagers aged 16–19 was 11 per cent in 1955, and it increased to 16 per cent in 1978. The unemployment rate of young people is three times higher than the unemployment rate of older people. In particular, unemployment of non-white Americans was alarmingly high. The unemployment rate of non-white Americans aged 18–19 was around 30 per cent, and that of non-white Americans aged 16–17 was around 40 per cent. Sorrentino (1981) claimed that youth unemployment rates could be used to classify developed countries into countries with high youth unemployment and countries with low youth unemployment rates. There was a common trend of an increase in youth unemployment in both countries with high youth unemployment and countries with low youth unemployment. The first group of countries with high youth unemployment included the United States and Canada. In the case of the United States, the youth unemployment rate increased from 14.7 per cent in 1960 to 16.1 per cent in 1979. Similarly, the youth unemployment rate increased from 13.5 per cent in 1960 to 16.1 per cent in 1979 in Canada. On the other hand, the second group of countries with low young unemployment included Japan and Germany. In the case of Japan, the youth unemployment rate increased from 2.2 per cent in 1960 to 4.9 per cent in 1979. Similarly, the youth unemployment rate increased from 0.3 per cent in 1960 to 3.1 per cent in 1979 in Germany (Sorrentino, 1981). Furthermore, Braverman (1981) pointed out that there was increasing awareness of the seriousness of youth unemployment in the 1970s. Thus, youth unemployment was described as a "ticking bomb" in 1979 when the unemployment rates of Black and African Americans jumped up from 16.5 per cent in 1954 to 36.6 per cent in 1978 in the United States. The unemployment rates of Black and African Americans are extremely high in two states, namely Florida and Illinois. In Florida, the Black and African American unemployment rate was 44.6 per cent in 1978, while that of Illinois was 44.2 per cent in the same year (Braverman, 1981).

In the case of the United Kingdom, there was a rapid rise in youth unemployment due to an economic crisis in the United Kingdom in the 1970s, which effectively ended the economic boom in the post-Second World War period. To reduce youth unemployment, the British government introduced the "Youth Training Scheme" (YTS) in 1980. Participants of this TYS course would receive payment, rather than unemployment insurance, from the government (Gleeson, 1986; Atkinson et al., 1986). With the rise of youth unemployment, some people criticised young people who lacked an appropriate attitude and useful skills. Other people criticised schools which failed to provide young people with vocational training. The YTS training program was especially welcome in the craft industry, where the traditional apprenticeship scheme could not provide training opportunities for young people (Gleeson, 1986; Atkinson et al., 1986; Walker & Burton, 1986).

Furthermore, in the case of Australia, youth unemployment was not a social issue in the 1960s when youth unemployment rates were less than 3 per cent. However, it became a problem in its labour market in the 1970s. More precisely, the unemployment rate of teenagers aged 15–19 was 2.8 per cent in 1965 and increased to 10.1 per cent in 1975, further to 17.1 per cent in 1979. Similarly, the unemployment rate of young people aged 20–24 was 1.5 per cent in 1965 and increased to 5.6 per cent in 1975, further to 9.3 per cent in 1979. The basic cause of youth unemployment in Australia is the mismatch between the skills required for employment and the skills acquired by young people. In August 1980, Australian Prime Minister Malcolm Fraser referred to the "paradox" of youth unemployment. In this paradox in the Australian labour market, there is a co-existence of the "excessive" supply of young workers with the "growing" shortage of skilled workers (Levin, 1983).

A persistently high level of youth unemployment rates remained a social concern, and researchers continued conducting research on this topic in the 1990s (Hammer, 1993, 1997; O'Higgins, 1997). For example, Hammer (1993) explained the cause of youth unemployment by using the theory of labour market segmentation. According to this theory, the primary labour market was dominated by the larger firms with high capital intensity, which could provide workers with stable jobs with higher salaries. By contrast, the secondary labour market was dominated by smaller firms with high labour intensity, which could provide workers with unstable jobs with lower salaries. Young workers tend to obtain employment in the secondary labour market rather than the primary labour market. Hammer (1997) also used the theory of long-term unemployment to explain a cause of persistently high youth unemployment rates. According to this theory, a longer unemployment period would decrease the likelihood of being employed. Young workers tend to fail to obtain employment for a long period of time, which could cause them difficulties in obtaining appropriate employment. Furthermore, O'Higgins (1997) claimed that disability and race are additional factors that increase youth unemployment. The researcher claimed the disability unemployment gap, or the difference in unemployment between people with disabilities and people without disabilities, tends to increase with age. For example, the unemployment rate of people with disabilities aged 16–19 was 25 per cent, while the unemployment rate of people with disabilities aged 20–24 was 32 per cent in the United Kingdom in 1994. Similarly, race is another factor which could contribute to worsening youth unemployment. For instance, the youth unemployment rate among white Americans was 14.5 per cent, while the youth unemployment rate among Black and African Americans was 35.5 per cent in the United States in 1995.

In the case of France and Germany, there was a significant difference in the situation of youth unemployment and their labour market policy in the 1980s. In the case of Germany, the youth unemployment rate marginally increased from 6.5 per cent in 1981 to 8.1 per cent in 1987. By contrast, there was a rapid increase in youth unemployment in France. In the country, the youth unemployment rate increased drastically from 17.5 per cent in 1981 to 23.0 per cent in 1987. The low level of youth unemployment in Germany could be derived from the successful apprenticeship program in the country. Approximately two-thirds of young people in Germany received the apprenticeship program, and the total number of apprentices amounted to 740 thousand youth. By contrast, the apprenticeship has played a minor role in youth employment in France. However, the problem of apprenticeship in Germany is that the cost to employers for providing the apprenticeship programs tends to be higher than the benefit to employers of the programs. In other words, this apprenticeship program could not be sustainable unless employers were willing to support this loss-making program (Hess et al., 1994).

Furthermore, in the case of Norway, youth unemployment was not a major issue in the labour market in the 1970s. However, there was a rapid increase in the youth unemployment rate in the 1980s. For example, the unemployment rate of teenagers aged 16–19 increased from 9.8 per cent in 1978 to 13.2 per cent in 1982. Similarly, the unemployment rate of young people aged 20–24 increased from 3.6 per cent in 1978 to 5.3 per cent in 1982. Particularly, there was a serious problem in youth unemployment among lower secondary school leavers. For example, the unemployment rate among the tenth-year school leavers (i.e. lower secondary school education plus a supplementary one year's education) was 25 per cent. On the other hand, the unemployment rate among the twelfth-year school leavers (i.e. lower secondary education plus upper secondary education) was much lower, and it is only 10 per cent. In other words, a longer period of education in secondary school could enhance employability among school leavers (Lindbekk, 1989).

In the 2000s, researchers continued to make efforts to understand the causes and effects of youth unemployment in various countries (O'Higgins, 2001; Breen, 2005; Mroz & Savage, 2006). For example, O'Higgins (2001) pointed out that youth unemployment emerged as a global concern since the 1990s. Many countries suffer from high youth unemployment. In the case of the Philippines, the female youth unemployment rate was 18.5 per cent, and the male youth unemployment rate was 14.6 per cent in 1997. Furthermore, in Zimbabwe, the unemployment rate of teenagers aged 15–19 was 18.9 per cent in the same year. Similarly, some Eastern European countries also faced serious problems with youth unemployment rates. In the case of Poland, the youth unemployment rate was 24.7 per cent in 1997, and the youth unemployment rate in Hungary was 16.0 per cent in the same year (O'Higgins, 2001). Breen (2005) pointed out that there was a discrepancy between countries with high youth unemployment rates and countries with low youth unemployment. Among the first groups of countries with high youth unemployment, the youth unemployment rate was 34 per cent in Italy and 30 per cent in Greece in 1998. By contrast, among the second group of countries with low youth unemployment, the youth unemployment rate was 7 per cent in Austria and 4 per cent in Switzerland in the same year. Mroz and Savage (2006) pointed out the presence of the "scaring" effect of long-term unemployment on youth unemployment. In other words, long-term unemployment among young people would have a persistently high negative impact on their wages and prospects of obtaining employment. They claimed that if young workers aged 22 experience a six-month spell of unemployment, this negative experience would contribute to a decrease in the expected level of their wage rate by 8 per cent when the worker reaches the age of 23. This worker's wage would be 5 per cent lower than the wages of workers without unemployed experience when the workers reach the age of 26 (Mroz & Savage, 2006).

In the case of the United Kingdom, the Labour government launched a labour market intervention policy for youth known as the "New Deal for Young People" (NDYP) in 1998. This ambitious "workfare" consists of two stages of intervention, namely the "gateway" program and the supported placement program. The NDYP began with the "gateway" program, in which unemployed youth would be required to attend compulsory "consultation" sessions for job search activities for six months. If the job search were not successful, these unemployed youth would be placed into subsidised jobs for the next six months. This intervention program was very effective for young people to obtain employment. A survey study indicated that 60 per cent of participants in this supported replacement program obtained employment after the end of "subsided" employment (Gregg, 2001; Olle, 2022).

Furthermore, in the case of South Africa, Lam et al. (2009) mentioned that there are two main issues of youth unemployment in the country. Firstly, many youths were involved in the resistance against apartheid, and they also suffered from political instability after the end of the apartheid regime. Secondly, many youths could not attain a good education due to social turbulence in the power transition. Thus, this cohort of youth in South Africa could be called the "lost generation" who would not enjoy the stability of politics and would be deprived of job opportunities. As a consequence, the unemployment rate of youth aged 15–24 was 59 per cent in 2005. Particularly, the unemployment rate among African South Africans is higher than that of white South Africans. In Cape Town, the unemployment rate of African South African youth aged 15–22 (i.e., the share of unemployed youth in all youth who were not pursuing formal education) was 58 per cent, and that of the white South African youth aged 15–22 was only 11 per cent in 2001 (Lam et al., 2009).

More recently, empirical analysis of youth unemployment has remained a popular topic in the field of labour economics and youth studies. Researchers examined youth unemployment in the context of the post-global financial crisis in the 2010s. Particularly, they focused on the emergence of the "precariat", in which young people tend to work in part-time and temporary jobs (Caporale & Gil-Alana, 2014; Furlong, 2016; Roberts, 2016). For example, Caporale and Gil-Alana (2014) identified three main reasons for high youth employment, namely low level of human capital endowment among youth, lack of experience among youth, which is known as the "youth experience gap" and mismatch between skills acquired by youth through education and those required by employers, which is known as "skill mismatch". Furlong (2016) claimed that in the youth transition from school to the workplace, employment provides a means to sustain independent living. Without appropriate employment, it is difficult for youth to make a living without getting support from parents or the government. In the 1950s and 1960s, the main problem of youth employment was job-hopping, which was practised by many young people due to low pay and long working hours in the manufacturing sectors, such as textile factories. However, at the end of the 1970s, the manufacturing sectors ceased to play a role in providing sufficient employment opportunities for youth in many developed countries. Additionally, the global financial crisis in the second half of the 2000s contributed to the destruction of stable and long-term employment contracts with young workers. As a consequence, young people in this decade are known as the "lost generation" who cannot obtain stable and full-time employment. Instead, they could manage to obtain some unstable and temporary "precarious" employment since the 2010s. The emergence of the "precariat" in the aftermath of the global financial crisis is an interesting new phenomenon in the labour market. These "precarious workers" are not a homogeneous group of people. Some precarious workers would have high wages, such as digital nomads, and others would have simple manual work with low pay, such as food delivery workers (Furlong, 2016; MacDonald, 2016). Roberts (2016) introduced the mechanism of reproduction to explain youth unemployment. This mechanism is a social structure, such as an education system, which would maintain and reproduce inequalities between the lower class and upper class across generations. For example, a group of working-class students in high schools tended to have unique values and culture, which were not conducive to school knowledge. They considered school knowledge as useless and intended to become "real men" by doing "real jobs" in the coal mines, steel mills and shipyards. However, rapid social changes since the 1970s, such as deindustrialisation, economic structural change, technological progress and globalisation, have contributed to destroying job opportunities for young people in these "local" industries. Most young people can manage to obtain employment and work experience in some part-time jobs with temporary contracts in a post-industrial society. However, young people tend to have an "epistemological fallacy" in which they cannot comprehend the power of reproduction to enhance class inequalities in this new form of social structure (Roberts, 2016). Until the 2000s, Roulstone (2016) claimed that mainstream youth studies tended to ignore the presence of youth with disabilities who suffered double risks of the age-related risk (i.e. high unemployment rate of young people) and disability-related risk (i.e. high unemployment rate of people with disabilities). Until that point, the main unit of analysis in the youth studies is the youth without disabilities. However, there are two crises which affect the youth transition among young people with disabilities. Firstly, the rise of the deindustrialisation process in developed countries contributes to prolonging the transition of young people with disabilities to adulthood. Secondly, the widespread idea of "neo-liberal" work tends to promote self-reliance without relying on the welfare system and to stress flexibility without ensuring stable and full-time employment. Due to the effects of these two crises, youth studies started paying attention to the similarities and differences between young people with disabilities and young people without disabilities (Roulstone, 2016).

In the case of the European Union (EU), besides high youth unemployment, the rise of the young NEET (i.e. Not in Employment, Education or Training) rate became a social issue in the 2010s. The young NEET could be defined as young people who have joined neither employment nor education. The young NEET rate could be calculated as the share of the NEET in the total number of young people. There was a rapid increase in the young NEET rate in Europe in the 2010s. The NEET rate among young people aged 15–24 in Europe was around 16 per cent in 2006 and increased to 21 per cent in 2011, further to 23 per cent in 2013. There is a close connection between the long-term young unemployment rate and the young NEET rate because many unemployed young people become discouraged workers if they cannot obtain employment for a long period of time. These discouraged workers among young people would become NEET in the long run (O'Higgins, 2016). European policymakers preferred to use the young NEET rate, rather than youth unemployment, to measure the problem and issue in youth employment because there are two major measurement problems in the unemployment rate. Firstly, the youth unemployment rate is measured as the share of unemployed youth in the total number of youths in the labour market. However, the majority of youth participated in education, not in the labour market. Secondly, youth unemployment is based on the number of job seekers. It could not take into account the discouraged workers. Thus, the European Council adopted the Europe 2020 strategy to promote smart growth, sustainable growth and inclusive growth in 2010. In the bold strategy, a standardised definition to measure the NEET is used to deal with the youth employment problem in the European Union (Mascherini, 2016). However, the policy focus of the NEET problem could contribute to playing down the importance of eliminating the barriers to work for young people with disabilities by stressing the removal of disengagement among young people (Roulstone, 2016).

Despite the wealth of literature on youth unemployment, there are no empirical studies to examine whether the gap in unemployment rates between young people and older people would converge or not. A notable exception is a study conducted by Furuoka (2024a). He defined the age unemployment gap, or the "youth-total" unemployment gap, which is the difference between youth unemployment and total unemployment. He claimed the age unemployment gap was around 15 per cent in early 2010 and decreased to around 7 per cent at the end of the decade. The COVID-19 pandemic made a negative impact on widening the age unemployment gap. The age unemployment gap was 8.2 per cent in January 2020 and slightly decreased to 8.5 per cent in the following month. Furthermore, the age unemployment gap jumped up from 9.5 per cent in March 2020 to 18.2 per cent in the following month. However, the unemployment gap decreased from 17.5 per cent in April 2020 to 11.7 per cent in May 2020, further to 8.8 per cent in June 2020.

4.3 Data and Methods

The main objective of this empirical analysis is to examine the convergence of the unemployment gap between young workers and prime-age workers. For this purpose, this study used two standard statistical tests, the ADF test (Dickey & Fuller, 1979, 1981) and the KPSS test (Kwiatkowski et al., 1992) and two advanced statistical tests, which are based on the autoregressive neural network (ARNN), namely the Yaya–Ogbonna–Furuoka–Alana (YOFA) test (Yaya et al., 2021) and the KPSS-YOFA test. In other words, this study would suggest a new KPSS-type test or the KPSS-YOFA test to examine the convergence of the age unemployment gap. This new test could synthesise the methodological advantage of the KPSS stationarity test and the YOFA test's autoregressive neural network (ARNN) framework. If these tests point to the presence of convergence in the age unemployment gap, these findings are contradictory to the second assumption of the LOUR.

In this study, there will be two different age unemployment gaps in the empirical analysis. The first age unemployment gap is the difference in the unemployment rate between teenage workers with or without disabilities aged 16–19 and four types of older demographic groups, namely the lower prime-aged workers aged 25–34, the middle prime-aged workers aged 35–44, the upper prime-aged workers aged 45–54 and older workers aged 55–64. The second age unemployment gap is the difference in the unemployment rate between young workers with or without disabilities aged 20–24 and four types of other demographic groups, namely the lower prime-aged workers aged 25–34, the middle prime-aged workers aged 35–44, the upper prime-aged workers aged 45–54 and older workers aged 55–64.

4.4 Empirical Evidence

For the purpose of data analysis, four different statistical tests are used to examine the age unemployment gaps, namely the ADF test, the KPSS test, the YOFA test and the KPSS-YOFA test. In other words, these tests are employed to examine whether the age unemployment gap would diverge (i.e. unit root process) or converge (i.e. stationary process). Firstly, the empirical findings from the ADF test are reported in Table 4.1. As the findings in the table indicated, the ADF test failed to reject the null hypothesis of no convergence in all eight kinds of age unemployment gaps among people with disabilities. In other words, both the unemployment rates of teenage workers with disabilities aged 16–19 and the unemployment rates of young workers with disabilities aged 20–24 would not converge with the unemployment rate of prime-aged and older workers with disabilities aged 25–64. Furthermore, the ADF test could reject the null hypothesis of no convergence in all four kinds of age unemployment gaps between teenage workers without disabilities aged 16–19 and prime-aged and older workers without disabilities aged 25–64. This means that the unemployment rates of teenage workers without disabilities could converge with the

Table 4.1 Empirical findings from the ADF test

Age unemployment gaps (people with disabilities)	ADF statistics	Age unemployment gaps (people without disabilities)	ADF statistics
PWD16–19 vs PWD25–34	−1.462	*PND16–19 vs PND25–34*	−3.601*
PWD16–19 vs PWD35–44	−1.713	*PND16–19 vs PND35–44*	−3.903*
PWD16–19 vs PWD45–54	−1.356	*PND16–19 vs PND45–54*	−3.901*
PWD16–19 vs PWD55–64	−1.107	*PND16–19 vs PND55–64*	−3.601*
PWD20–24 vs PWD25–34	−2.657	*PND20–24 vs PND25–34*	−2.747
PWD20–24 vs PWD35–44	−2.703	*PND20–24 vs PND35–44*	−3.309
PWD20–24 vs PWD45–54	−2.512	*PND20–24 vs PND45–54*	−3.178
PWD20–24 vs PWD55–64	−2.235	*PND20–24 vs PND55–64*	−2.520

Notes: * denotes the significance of 5%; 1%, and 5% critical values for the ADF test are −4.191 and − 3.547 (see Table 3.12)

Table 4.2 Empirical findings from the YOFA test

Age unemployment gaps (people with disabilities)	YOFA statistics	Age unemployment gaps (people without disabilities)	YOFA statistics
PWD16–19 vs PWD25–34	−1.460	*PND16–19 vs PND25–34*	−2.778*
PWD16–19 vs PWD35–44	−1.771	*PND16–19 vs PND35–44*	−2.175
PWD16–19 vs PWD45–54	−1.420	*PND16–19 vs PND45–54*	−3.466*
PWD16–19 vs PWD55–64	−1.256	*PND16–19 vs PND55–64*	−3.202*
PWD20–24 vs PWD25–34	−1.631	*PND20–24 vs PND25–34*	−1.492
PWD20–24 vs PWD35–44	−1.735	*PND20–24 vs PND35–44*	−3.600**
PWD20–24 vs PWD45–54	−1.529	*PND20–24 vs PND45–54*	−3.197*
PWD20–24 vs PWD55–64	−1.305	*PND20–24 vs PND55–64*	−2.038

Notes: ** denotes the significance of 1%; * enotes the significance of 5%; 1% and 5% critical values for the YOFA test are −3.540 and −2.777 (see Table 3.19)

unemployment rates of prime-aged and older workers without disabilities aged 25–64. By contrast, the ADF failed to reject the null hypothesis of no convergence in all four kinds of age unemployment gaps between young workers without disabilities aged 20–24 and prime-aged and older workers without disabilities aged 25–64.

Secondly, the empirical findings from the YOFA test are reported in Table 4.2. As the findings in the table indicated, the YOFA test confirmed the empirical findings from the ADF test that there would be no convergence in all eight kinds of age unemployment gaps among people with disabilities. It means that both the ADF test and the YOFA test indicated the non-convergence of unemployment rates of teenage and young workers with disabilities aged 16–24 and unemployment rates of prime-aged and older workers with disabilities aged 25–64. Furthermore, the YOFA test also confirmed the empirical findings from the ADF test that there would be convergence in all four kinds of age unemployment gaps between teenage workers without disabilities aged 16–19 and the prime-aged and older workers without disabilities aged 25–64, except the age unemployment gap between teenage workers without disabilities aged 16–19 and the middle prime-aged workers without

Table 4.3 Empirical findings from the KPSS test

Age unemployment gaps (people with disabilities)	KPSS statistics	Age unemployment gaps (people without disabilities)	KPSS statistics
PWD16–19 vs PWD25–34	0.154	*PND16–19 vs PND25–34*	0.147
PWD16–19 vs PWD35–44	0.155	*PND16–19 vs PND35–44*	0.144
PWD16–19 vs PWD45–54	0.151	*PND16–19 vs PND45–54*	0.147
PWD16–19 vs PWD55–64	0.150	*PND16–19 vs PND55–64*	0.146
PWD20–24 vs PWD25–34	0.187*	*PND20–24 vs PND25–34*	0.172*
PWD20–24 vs PWD35–44	0.177*	*PND20–24 vs PND35–44*	0.173*
PWD20–24 vs PWD45–54	0.161*	*PND20–24 vs PND45–54*	0.185*
PWD20–24 vs PWD55–64	0.156	*PND20–24 vs PND55–64*	0.175*

Notes: * denotes the significance of 5%; 1% and 5% critical values for the KPSS test are 0.158 and 0.216 (see Table 4.6)

disabilities aged 35–44. On the other hand, the ADF test failed to reject the null hypothesis of no convergence in the age unemployment gap between unemployment rates of young workers without disabilities aged 20–24 and the unemployment rates of prime-aged workers without disabilities aged 35–55. However, the YOFA test could reject the null hypothesis for this age unemployment gap. On the other hand, both the ADF test and the YOFA indicated there would be no convergence in the age unemployment gap for young workers without disabilities aged 20–24 and lower prime-aged workers without disabilities 25–34, as well as another age unemployment gap between young workers without disabilities aged 20–24 and older workers without disabilities 55–64.

Thirdly, the empirical findings from the KPSS test are reported in Table 4.3. Regarding age unemployment gaps of teenage workers with disabilities aged 16–19 with prime-aged and older workers with disabilities aged 25–64, the empirical findings from the KPSS test are contrary to the empirical findings from the ADF test and the YOFA test. More precisely, the KPSS test indicates the convergence of age unemployment gaps between teenage workers with disabilities aged 16–19 and the prime-aged and older workers with disabilities aged 25–64. However, both the ADF test and the YOFA test indicated the non-convergence in this age unemployment gap. On the other hand, regarding age unemployment gaps between young workers with disabilities aged 20–24 and prime-aged and older workers with disabilities aged 25–64, the KPSS test confirmed the empirical findings from the ADF test and the YOFA test, except for the age unemployment gap between young workers with disabilities aged 20–24 and older workers with disabilities aged 55–64. Furthermore, regarding age unemployment gaps of teenage workers without disabilities aged 16–19 with prime-aged and older workers without disabilities aged 25–64, the KPSS test confirmed the empirical findings from the ADF test that there is convergence in this age unemployment gap. Similarly, regarding age unemployment gaps of young workers without disabilities aged 20–24 with prime-aged and older workers without disabilities aged 25–64, the KPSS test also confirmed the empirical findings from the ADF test that there is no convergence in this age unemployment gap.

Table 4.4 Empirical findings from the KPSS-YOFA test

Age unemployment gaps (people with disabilities)	KPSS-YOFA statistics	Age unemployment gaps (people without disabilities)	KPSS-YOFA statistics
PWD16–19 vs PWD25–34	0.255**	*PND16–19 vs PND25–34*	0.196**
PWD16–19 vs PWD35–44	0.321**	*PND16–19 vs PND35–44*	0.173**
PWD16–19 vs PWD45–54	0.290**	*PND16–19 vs PND45–54*	0.235**
PWD16–19 vs PWD55–64	0.267**	*PND16–19 vs PND55–64*	0.212**
PWD20–24 vs PWD25–34	0.163**	*PND20–24 vs PND25–34*	0.242**
PWD20–24 vs PWD35–44	0.171**	*PND20–24 vs PND35–44*	0.213**
PWD20–24 vs PWD45–54	0.243**	*PND20–24 vs PND45–54*	0.199**
PWD20–24 vs PWD55–64	0.259**	*PND20–24 vs PND55–64*	0.163**

Notes: ** denotes the significance of1%; 1%and 5%critical values for the KPSS-YOFA test are 0.091 and 0.068 (see Table 4.13)

Fourthly, the empirical findings from the KPSS-YOFA test are reported in Table 4.4. Regarding age unemployment gaps between teenage workers with disabilities aged 16–19 and older workers with disabilities aged 25–64, the empirical findings from the KPSS-YOFA test conformed with the findings from the ADF test and the YOFA test that there is no convergence in these age unemployment gaps. Similarly, regarding age unemployment gaps between young workers with disabilities aged 20–24 and older workers with disabilities aged 25–64, the KPSS-YOFA test also confirmed the empirical findings from the ADF test, the YOFA test and the KPSS test that there is no convergence in these age unemployment gaps. However, regarding age unemployment gaps between teenage workers without disabilities aged 16–19 and older workers without disabilities aged 25–64, the KPSS-YOFA test failed to confirm the empirical findings from the ADF test and the KPSS test. Both the ADF test and the KPSS test indicated that there is convergence in these age unemployment gaps, while the KPSS-YOFA test indicated the non-convergence. Regarding age unemployment gaps of young workers without disabilities aged 20–24 with prime-aged and older workers without disabilities aged 25–64, the KPSS-YOFA test also confirmed the empirical findings from the ADF test and the KPSS test that there is no convergence in this age unemployment gap.

The findings of the empirical analysis on the convergence of the age unemployment gap are summarised in Table 4.5. As the table indicates, these findings could be summarised into three insights. Firstly, there is no convergence in the over-majority of sixteen different age unemployment gaps. In other words, no convergence in the twelve age unemployment gaps, namely all four age unemployment gaps between teenage workers with disabilities aged 16–19 and older workers with disabilities aged 25–64, all four age unemployment gaps between young workers with disabilities aged 20–24 and older workers with disabilities aged 25–64 as well as all four age unemployment gaps between young workers without disabilities aged 20–24 and older workers without disabilities aged 25–64. Secondly, there is convergence in less than one-quarter of the sixteen different age unemployment gaps. In other words, convergence was found in only three age unemployment gaps, namely

Table 4.5 Summary of findings on the convergence of the age unemployment gap

Age unemployment gaps (people with disabilities)	ADF test	YOFA test	KPSS test	KPSS-YOFA test	Number of Statistical tests which indicated convergence	Overall
PWD16–19 vs PWD25–34	No convergence	No convergence	Convergence	No convergence	1/4	No convergence
PWD16–19 vs PWD35–44	No convergence	No convergence	Convergence	No convergence	1/4	No convergence
PWD16–19 vs PWD45–54	No convergence	No convergence	Convergence	No convergence	1/4	No convergence
PWD16–19 vs PWD55–64	No convergence	No convergence	Convergence	No convergence	1/4	No convergence
PWD20–24 vs PWD25–34	No convergence	No convergence	No convergence	No convergence	0/4	No convergence
PWD20–24 vs PWD35–44	No convergence	No convergence	No convergence	No convergence	0/4	No convergence
PWD20–24 vs PWD45–54	No convergence	No convergence	No convergence	No convergence	0/4	No convergence
PWD20–24 vs PWD55–64	No convergence	No convergence	Convergence	No convergence	1/4	No convergence
PND16–19 vs PND25–34	Convergence	Convergence	Convergence	No convergence	3/4	Convergence
PND16–19 vs PND35–44	Convergence	No convergence	Convergence	No convergence	2/4	Indecisive
PND16–19 vs PND45–54	Convergence	Convergence	Convergence	No convergence	3/4	Convergence
PND16–19 vs PND55–64	Convergence	Convergence	Convergence	No convergence	3/4	Convergence
PND20–24 vs PND25–34	No convergence	No convergence	No convergence	No convergence	0/4	No convergence
PND20–24 vs PND35–44	No convergence	Convergence	No convergence	No convergence	1/4	No convergence
PND20–24 vs PND45–54	No convergence	Convergence	No convergence	No convergence	1/4	No convergence
PND20–24 vs PND55–64	No convergence	No convergence	No convergence	No convergence	0/4	No convergence

all four age unemployment gaps between teenage workers without disabilities aged 16–19 and older workers without disabilities aged 24–64, except the age unemployment gap between teenage workers without disabilities aged 16–19 and the middle prime-aged workers without disabilities aged 35–44. Thirdly, empirical findings are indecisive regarding the age unemployment gap between teenage workers without disabilities aged 16–19 and the middle prime-aged workers without disabilities aged 35–44. In other words, the empirical analysis indicated that two statistical tests, namely the ADF test and the KPSS test, showed convergence, and the other two tests, namely the ADF-YOFA test and the KPSS-YOFA test, implied no convergence.

In a nutshell, these four statistical tests seem to indicate that there is no convergence in the age unemployment gaps. These tests especially produce consistent findings for unemployment rates of people with disabilities. For example, empirical findings indicated that there is no convergence in the age unemployment gap between teenage workers with disabilities aged 16–19 and the other four older workers with disabilities aged 25–64. Similarly, there is no convergence in the age unemployment gap between young workers with disabilities aged 20–24 and older workers with disabilities aged 25–64. On the other hand, there are minor differences in the empirical findings on the unemployment rates of workers without disabilities. For example, the empirical findings indicated that there is a convergence of the age unemployment gap between teenage workers without disabilities aged 16–19 and three demographic groups, namely, the lower prime-aged workers without disabilities aged 25–34, the upper prime-aged workers without disabilities aged 45–54 and older workers without disabilities aged 55–64. By contrast, the findings indicated that there is no convergence in the age unemployment gap between young workers without disabilities aged 20–24 and older workers without disabilities aged 25–64.

4.5 Conclusion

This chapter used several sophisticated statistical methods to examine the convergence of age unemployment gaps. The empirical findings on this convergence offer some empirical evidence that young unemployment rates would not converge with the unemployment rates of older workers. Firstly, statistical tests indicated that there is no convergence in age unemployment gaps between unemployment rates of teenage workers with disabilities aged 16–19 and unemployment rates of older workers with disabilities. Secondly, empirical findings indicated that there is no convergence in age unemployment gaps between the unemployment rate of young workers with disabilities aged 20–24 and the unemployment rates of older workers with disabilities. Thirdly, findings also showed that there is no convergence in the age unemployment gap between the unemployment rate of young workers without disabilities aged 20–24 and the unemployment rates of older workers without disabilities. On the other hand, statistical tests also indicated that there could be a convergence in the age unemployment gap between the unemployment rate of workers without disabilities aged 16–19 and the unemployment rates of older workers without disabilities.

Despite these minor discrepancies in the findings, empirical analysis on the convergence of the age unemployment gap does not seem to offer some evidence to support the second assumption of the Law of One Unemployment Rate (LOUR). In other words, the empirical findings indicated that the unemployment rates of young workers do not seem to converge with the unemployment rates of elderly workers. It means that there would be persistence in the age unemployment gap between young workers and elderly workers.

Appendix: KPSS-Type Tests for the Empirical Analysis of the Law of One Unemployment Rate (LOUR)

This study uses the five different KPSS-type stationarity tests to test the Law of One Unemployment Rate (LOUR). The theoretical origin of the stationarity test is the consistency of the regression coefficient. The null hypothesis is the consistency, while the alternative hypothesis is the random walk. This hypothesis is the reverse case of the hypothesis for the unit root test, whose null hypothesis is a unit root or random walk. Therefore, the stationarity test could be called the "reversed" unit root test (Choi & Kurozumi, 2014). The consistency of the regression coefficient could be examined by using the following equations (Tanaka, 1983; Nabeya & Tanaka, 1988; Kwiatkowski et al., 1992):

$$y_t = x_t\beta_t + z_t\gamma + u_t \tag{4.1}$$

where y_t is the sequence of scalar observations, which is the variable of interest, x_t is the nonstochastic fixed sequence, β_t is a coefficient parameter, z_t is the sequence of deterministic components, γ is a coefficient parameter for the deterministic components, u_t is the sequence of independent Gaussian random variables with mean zero and variance $\delta^2 > 0$, $\varepsilon_t \sim NID(0, \delta^2)$. The coefficient parameter is the random walk process (Tanaka, 1983; Nabeya & Tanaka, 1988; Kwiatkowski et al., 1992):

$$\beta_t = \beta_{t-1} + \varepsilon_t \tag{4.2}$$

where ε_t is the sequence of independent Gaussian random variables with mean zero and variance $\{\delta^2 \times \theta\} \geq 0$, $\varepsilon_t \sim NID(0, \{\delta^2 \times \theta\})$. The null hypothesis of consistency of the coefficient parameter could be expressed (Tanaka, 1983; Nabeya & Tanaka, 1988; Kwiatkowski et al., 1992):

$$H_0 : \theta = 0 \tag{4.3}$$

On the other hand, the alternative hypothesis of the random walk coefficient parameter could be expressed (Tanaka, 1983; Nabeya & Tanaka, 1988; Kwiatkowski et al., 1992):

$$H_1 : \theta > 0 \tag{4.4}$$

Furthermore, Eq. (4.1) could be simplified by setting. $x_t = 1$ and $z_t = t$ (Tanaka, 1983; Nabeya & Tanaka, 1988; Kwiatkowski et al., 1992):

$$y_t = \beta_t + \gamma t + u_t \tag{4.5}$$

where t is the deterministic trend, and γ is the coefficient parameter for the trend. The partial sum of regression residuals could be calculated as (Tanaka, 1983; Nabeya & Tanaka, 1988; Kwiatkowski et al., 1992):

$$S_t = \sum\nolimits_{i=1}^{t} e_i \tag{4.6}$$

where n is the number of observations, S_t is the partial sum of the regression residual and e_t is the regression residual. Using a partial sum of regression residuals, the Lagrange Multiplier (LM) statistic could be estimated as (Tanaka, 1983; Nabeya & Tanaka, 1988; Kwiatkowski et al., 1992):

$$LM = \sum_{t=1}^{n} S_t^2 / \widehat{\delta_u^2} \tag{4.7}$$

where LM is the Lagrange Multiplier statistic and $\widehat{\delta_u^2}$ is the estimate of error variance which could be calculated as (Tanaka, 1983; Nabeya & Tanaka, 1988; Kwiatkowski et al., 1992):

$$\widehat{\delta_u^2} = \frac{1}{n} \sum\nolimits_{t=1}^{n} e_t^2 \tag{4.8}$$

Based on Corollary 3 in MacNeill (1978), the partial sum of regression residuals would converge in probability to the Brownian bridge (MacNeill, 1978):

$$S_t \xrightarrow{p} \int_0^1 \psi(r) V(r)\, dr \tag{4.9}$$

where $\psi(r)$ is nonnegative weight function and $V(r)$ is the Brownian bridge which could be expressed as $V(r) = W(r) - rW(1)$ and $W(r)$ is a Wiener process. Based on Eq. (2.5) in Nabeya and Tanaka (1988), the LM statistic could be expressed as (Tanaka, 1983; Nabeya & Tanaka, 1988; Kwiatkowski et al., 1992):

$$LM = \frac{y'MD_xA_TD_xMy}{y'My} \tag{4.10}$$

where My is the residual from Eq. (4.1), in the denominator, $y'\ My$ could be considered as the sum of squared residuals (SSR). In other words, SSR could be expressed as (Tanaka, 1983; Nabeya & Tanaka, 1988; Kwiatkowski et al., 1992):

$$SSR = n \times \widehat{\delta}_u^2 \tag{4.11}$$

where $\widehat{\delta}_u^2$ is the estimate of residual variances from Eq. (4.1). In Eq. (4.10), My is replaced by e_t and $y'\ My$ is replaced by $n \times \delta_u^2$ (Tanaka, 1983; Nabeya & Tanaka, 1988; Kwiatkowski et al., 1992):

$$LM = \frac{e_t'D_xA_TD_xe_t}{n \times \delta_u^2} \tag{4.12}$$

where e_t is the residual from Eq. (4.1). The matrix D_x is the identity matrix, which could be ignored. Therefore, Eq. (4.12) could be simplified as (Tanaka, 1983; Nabeya & Tanaka, 1988; Kwiatkowski et al., 1992):

$$LM = \frac{e_t'A_Te_t}{n \times \delta_u^2} \tag{4.13}$$

where A_t is a matrix which is used to create the R_t which is the "reverse" partial sum of residuals (Tanaka, 1983; Nabeya & Tanaka, 1988; Kwiatkowski et al., 1992):

$$e'A_Te = \sum\nolimits_{t=1}^{n} R_t \tag{4.14}$$

where R_t is the reverse partial sum, which could be expressed as (Tanaka, 1983; Nabeya & Tanaka, 1988; Kwiatkowski et al., 1992):

$$R_t = \sum\nolimits_{i=t}^{n} e_t \tag{4.15}$$

where e_t is the residual from Eq. (4.1). It means that the numerator of the LM statistic in Eq. (4.7) seems to be different from the numerator of the LM statistic in Eq. (4.12). This is because the former relies on the "forward" partial sum of residuals, and the latter relies on the "reverse" partial sum of residuals. However, $S_t = R_t$ because the sum of the residuals would be zero (Tanaka, 1983; Nabeya & Tanaka, 1988; Kwiatkowski et al., 1992).

This study employs the four types of KPSS-type stationarity tests, namely the KPSS test (Kwiatkowski et al., 1992); the Fourier KPSS (FKPSS) test (Becker et al., 2006); the KPSS with structural break (KPSS-SB) test (Kurozumi, 2002) and the Fourier KPSS with structural break (FKPSS-SB) test (Furuoka, 2017). Each of these

Table 4.6 Empirical distribution of the KPSS test statistics

	0.01	*0.05*	*0.10*	*0.50*	*0.90*	*0.95*	*0.99*
$n = 50$	0.021	0.028	0.032	0.062	0.129	0.158	0.216
$n = 100$	0.019	0.025	0.030	0.059	0.121	0.147	0.212
$n = 500$	0.017	0.024	0.028	0.058	0.122	0.150	0.215
$n = 1000$	0.017	0.024	0.029	0.056	0.116	0.147	0.219

Table 4.7 Critical values for the KPSS test

	0.10	*0.05*	*0.01*
MacNeill (1978)	0.119	0.147	0.217
Nabeya and Tanaka (1988)	0.119	0.147	0.217
Kwiatkowski et al. (1992)	0.119	0.146	0.216
Cheung et al. (1994)	0.119	0.148	0.218
Current study	0.116	0.147	0.219

four KPSS-type tests would obtain its residual from the different equations. For the first KPSS-type test or the KPSS test (Kwiatkowski et al., 1992), the residuals would be obtained from the following equation (Kwiatkowski et al., 1992):

$$y_t = \mu + \beta t + e_t \tag{4.16}$$

where μ is the intercept, t is a deterministic trend, and β is the slope parameter for the trend. Under the null hypothesis of a stationary process, the empirical distribution of the KPSS test would be estimated using 1000 replications of four different sample sizes, namely $T = 50$, $T = 100$, $T = 500$, $T = 1000$ (Cheung et al., 1994; Furuoka, 2017; Yaya et al., 2021). Table 4.6 reports the empirical distribution of the KPSS test. As the table indicates, in the case of $n = 50$, the 0.90 point of distribution was 0.129, and it decreased to 0.116 when the number of observations increased to 1000. Similarly, in the case of $n = 50$, the 0.95 point of distribution was 0.158, and it decreased to 0.147 when the number of observations increased to 1000. For the comparison, the critical values for the KPSS test statistics are reported in Table 4.7. The estimated critical values for the KPSS test in the current study are generally in line with those values estimated by MacNeill (1978) and Nabeya and Tanaka (1988), who suggested the precursor of the KPSS test, as well as Kwiatkowski et al. (1992), who suggested this stationarity test.

For the second KPSS-type test or the Fourier KPSS (FKPSS) test (Becker et al., 2006), the residuals would be obtained from the following equation (Becker et al., 2006):

$$y_t = \mu + \beta t + \gamma_1 \, sin \frac{2\pi kt}{n} + \gamma_2 \, cos \frac{2\pi kt}{n} + e_t \tag{4.17}$$

where sin is the sine function, cos is the cosine function, $\pi = 3.1416$, k is the frequency for the Fourier approximation function, γ_1 is the slope coefficient for the sine function and γ_2 is the slope coefficient for the cosine function. Under the null

Table 4.8 Empirical distribution of the FKPSS test statistics

	FKPSS test ($k = 1$)						
	0.01	*0.05*	*0.10*	*0.50*	*0.90*	*0.95*	*0.99*
$n = 50$	0.015	0.018	0.020	0.031	0.049	0.057	0.073
$n = 100$	0.013	0.016	0.018	0.029	0.048	0.055	0.072
$n = 500$	0.012	0.015	0.017	0.027	0.046	0.054	0.071
$n = 1000$	0.011	0.014	0.016	0.027	0.046	0.053	0.072
	FKPSS test ($k = 2$)						
	0.01	*0.05*	*0.10*	*0.50*	*0.90*	*0.95*	*0.99*
$n = 50$	0.016	0.021	0.024	0.048	0.114	0.144	0.223
$n = 100$	0.015	0.019	0.022	0.045	0.107	0.136	0.204
$n = 500$	0.013	0.017	0.020	0.041	0.098	0.129	0.199
$n = 1000$	0.013	0.017	0.020	0.040	0.098	0.125	0.201

hypothesis of a stationary process, the empirical distribution of the FKPSS test would be estimated using 1000 replications of four different sample sizes, namely $T = 50$, $T = 100$, $T = 500$, $T = 1000$ and two frequencies, namely $k = 1$, $k = 2$ (Cheung et al., 1994; Furuoka, 2017; Yaya et al., 2021). Table 4.8 reports the empirical distribution of the FKPSS test. As the table indicates, in the case of $k = 1$, the 0.95 point of distribution was 0.057 when the number of observations was 50, and it decreased to 0.053 when the number of observations increased to 1000. Similarly, in the case of $k = 2$, the 0.99 point of distribution was 0.223 when the number of observations was 50, and it decreased to 0.200 when the number of observations increased to 1000. Interestingly, the range of the empirical distribution of FKPSS in the case of $k = 1$ is narrower than that of the empirical distribution in the case of $k = 2$. For the comparison, the critical values for the FKPSS test statistics are reported in Table 4.9. The estimated critical values for the FKPSS test in the current study are generally in line with those values estimated by Becker et al. (2006), who suggested this stationarity test of the FKPSS test.

For the third KPSS-type test or the KPSS with structural break (KPSS-SB) test (Kurozumi, 2002), the residuals would be obtained from the following equation (Kurozumi, 2002):

$$y_t = \mu + \beta t + \delta DU_t + \theta D(T_B)_t + e_t \tag{4.18}$$

where δ is the slope parameter for the structural break dummy, $DU_t = 1$ if $T_B > t$ and $DU_t = 0$ otherwise, θ is the slope parameter for the one-time break dummy, $D(T_B)_t = 1$ if $T_B = t$ and $D(T_B)_t = 0$ otherwise, T_B is the breakpoint when a structural break occurs. Under the null hypothesis of a stationary process, the empirical distribution of the KPSS-SB test would be estimated using 1000 replications of four different sample sizes, namely $T = 50$, $T = 100$, $T = 500$, $T = 1000$ and four break points, namely $\omega = 0.125$, $\omega = 0.375$, $\omega = 0.625$, $\omega = 0.875$ (Cheung et al., 1994; Furuoka, 2017; Yaya et al., 2021). Table 4.10 reports the empirical distribution of the KPSS-SB test. As the table indicates, in the case of $\omega = 0.375$, the 0.99

Table 4.9 Critical values for the FKPSS test

Becker et al., (2006)		$k = 1$		
		0.10	*0.05*	*0.01*
	$n = 100$	0.047	0.054	0.071
	$n = 500$	0.046	0.053	0.072
	$n = 1000$	0.046	0.053	0.071
		$k = 2$		
		0.10	*0.05*	*0.01*
	$n = 100$	0.103	0.132	0.202
	$n = 500$	0.099	0.127	0.196
	$n = 1000$	0.099	0.127	0.195
Current study		$k = 1$		
		0.10	*0.05*	*0.01*
	$n = 100$	0.048	0.055	0.072
	$n = 500$	0.046	0.054	0.071
	$n = 1000$	0.046	0.053	0.072
		$k = 2$		
		0.10	*0.05*	*0.01*
	$n = 100$	0.107	0.126	0.204
	$n = 500$	0.098	0.129	0.199
	$n = 1000$	0.098	0.125	0.201

point of distribution was 0.171 when the number of observations was 50, and it decreased to 0.162 when the number of observations increased to 1000. Similarly, in the case of $\omega = 0.625$, the 0.95 point of distribution was 0.119 when the number of observations was 50, and it decreased to 0.116 when the number of observations increased to 1000. For the comparison, the critical values for the KPSS-SB test statistics are reported in Table 4.11. The estimated critical values for the KPSS-SB test in the current study are generally in line with those values estimated by Kurozumi (2002), who suggested this stationarity test of the KPSS-SB test.

For the fourth KPSS-type test or the Fourier KPSS with structural break (FKPSS-SB) test (Furuoka, 2017), the residuals would be obtained from the following equation (Furuoka, 2017):

$$y_t = \mu + \beta t + \gamma_1 \sin\frac{2\pi kt}{n} + \gamma_2 \cos\frac{2\pi kt}{n} + \delta DU_t + \theta D(T_B)_t + e_t \tag{4.19}$$

Under the null hypothesis of stationary process, the empirical distribution of the FKPSS-SB test would be estimated using 1000 replications of four different sample sizes, namely $T = 50$, $T = 100$, $T = 500$, $T = 1000$ and two frequencies, namely $k = 1$, $k = 2$,and four break points, namely $\omega = 0.125$, $\omega = 0.375$, $\omega = 0.625$, $\omega = 0.875$ (Cheung et al., 1994; Furuoka, 2017; Yaya et al., 2021). Table 4.12 reports the empirical distribution of the FKPSS-SB test. As the table indicates, in the

Table 4.10 Empirical distribution of the KPSS-SB test statistics

	KPSS - SB test ($\omega = 0.125$)						
	0.01	*0.05*	*0.10*	*0.50*	*0.90*	*0.95*	*0.99*
$n = 50$	0.018	0.024	0.027	0.049	0.095	0.116	0.167
$n = 100$	0.017	0.022	0.025	0.047	0.096	0.117	0.166
$n = 500$	0.016	0.021	0.024	0.045	0.095	0.118	0.166
$n = 1000$	0.016	0.021	0.024	0.046	0.093	0.117	0.174
	KPSS - SB test ($\omega = 0.375$)						
	0.01	*0.05*	*0.10*	*0.50*	*0.90*	*0.95*	*0.99*
$n = 50$	0.019	0.025	0.029	0.053	0.104	0.126	0.178
$n = 100$	0.017	0.023	0.026	0.049	0.098	0.123	0.171
$n = 500$	0.016	0.021	0.025	0.046	0.096	0.117	0.167
$n = 1000$	0.016	0.021	0.025	0.046	0.095	0.117	0.162
	KPSS - SB test ($\omega = 0.625$)						
	0.01	*0.05*	*0.10*	*0.50*	*0.90*	*0.95*	*0.99*
$n = 50$	0.019	0.025	0.028	0.051	0.100	0.119	0.164
$n = 100$	0.017	0.022	0.026	0.049	0.097	0.118	0.160
$n = 500$	0.016	0.021	0.024	0.046	0.095	0.118	0.165
$n = 1000$	0.015	0.021	0.025	0.046	0.095	0.116	0.165
	KPSS - SB test ($\omega = 0.875$)						
	0.01	*0.05*	*0.10*	*0.50*	*0.90*	*0.95*	*0.99*
$n = 50$	0.019	0.024	0.028	0.051	0.102	0.125	0.174
$n = 100$	0.017	0.023	0.026	0.048	0.099	0.121	0.169
$n = 500$	0.016	0.021	0.025	0.047	0.096	0.118	0.166
$n = 1000$	0.015	0.020	0.024	0.045	0.094	0.117	0.172

Table 4.11 Critical values for the KPSS-SB test

Kurozumi (2002)		*0.10*	*0.05*	*0.01*
	$\omega = 0.10$	0.097	0.120	0.177
Current study		*0.10*	*0.05*	*0.01*
	$\omega = 0.125$	0.093	0.117	0.174

case of $k = 1$, $\omega = 0.125$, the 0.95 point of distribution was 0.047 when the number of observations was 50, and it decreased slightly to 0.046 when the number of observations increased to 1000. Similarly, in the case of $k = 2$, $\omega = 0.375$, the 0.99 point of distribution was 0.045 when the number of observations was 50, and it increased to 0.041 when the number of observations increased to 1000.

Finally, this paper suggests using a new KPSS-type test, which is based on the neural network (NN) method, which has become a useful analytical tool among experts in econometrics since the 2010s. Yaya et al. (2021) suggested a new autoregressive neural network (ARNN) in the ADF framework. This ARNN test is known as the Yaya–Ogbonna–Furuoka–Alana (YOFA) test (Yaya et al., 2021). In other words, the new KPSS type test could be called the KPSS-YOFA test, which obtained residual from the following equation (Yaya et al., 2021):

Table 4.12 Empirical distribution of the FKPSS-SB test statistics

	FKPSS - SB test $(k = 1, \omega = 0.125)$						
	0.01	*0.05*	*0.10*	*0.50*	*0.90*	*0.95*	*0.99*
$n = 50$	0.014	0.017	0.018	0.027	0.042	0.047	0.059
$n = 100$	0.012	0.015	0.017	0.026	0.041	0.048	0.061
$n = 500$	0.011	0.014	0.016	0.024	0.040	0.046	0.061
$n = 1000$	0.011	0.013	0.015	0.024	0.040	0.046	0.062
	FKPSS - SB test $(k = 1, \omega = 0.375)$						
	0.01	*0.05*	*0.10*	*0.50*	*0.90*	*0.95*	*0.99*
$n = 50$	0.014	0.016	0.018	0.027	0.043	0.049	0.063
$n = 100$	0.012	0.015	0.017	0.026	0.042	0.048	0.061
$n = 500$	0.011	0.013	0.015	0.025	0.041	0.047	0.061
$n = 1000$	0.011	0.013	0.015	0.024	0.041	0.047	0.063
	FKPSS - SB test $(k = 1, \omega = 0.625)$						
	0.01	*0.05*	*0.10*	*0.50*	*0.90*	*0.95*	*0.99*
$n = 50$	0.014	0.017	0.018	0.028	0.043	0.049	0.061
$n = 100$	0.012	0.015	0.017	0.026	0.042	0.048	0.062
$n = 500$	0.011	0.013	0.015	0.024	0.040	0.047	0.060
$n = 1000$	0.011	0.013	0.015	0.024	0.040	0.046	0.061
	FKPSS - SB test $(k = 1, \omega = 0.875)$						
	0.01	*0.05*	*0.10*	*0.50*	*0.90*	*0.95*	*0.99*
$n = 50$	0.014	0.016	0.018	0.027	0.042	0.048	0.060
$n = 100$	0.012	0.015	0.016	0.026	0.041	0.047	0.061
$n = 500$	0.011	0.013	0.015	0.024	0.040	0.047	0.062
$n = 1000$	0.011	0.013	0.015	0.024	0.040	0.046	0.060
	FKPSS - SB test $(k = 2, \omega = 0.125)$						
	0.01	*0.05*	*0.10*	*0.50*	*0.90*	*0.95*	*0.99*
$n = 50$	0.015	0.018	0.020	0.034	0.074	0.092	0.143
$n = 100$	0.013	0.016	0.019	0.033	0.070	0.089	0.139
$n = 500$	0.012	0.015	0.017	0.031	0.069	0.088	0.127
$n = 1000$	0.011	0.015	0.017	0.031	0.067	0.088	0.130
	FKPSS - SB test $(k = 2, \omega = 0.375)$						
	0.01	*0.05*	*0.10*	*0.50*	*0.90*	*0.95*	*0.99*
$n = 50$	0.015	0.018	0.021	0.037	0.080	0.097	0.145
$n = 100$	0.013	0.017	0.019	0.035	0.077	0.098	0.145
$n = 500$	0.012	0.015	0.018	0.032	0.071	0.089	0.127
$n = 1000$	0.012	0.015	0.017	0.032	0.067	0.087	0.143
	FKPSS - SB test $(k = 2, \omega = 0.625)$						
	0.01	*0.05*	*0.10*	*0.50*	*0.90*	*0.95*	*0.99*
$n = 50$	0.015	0.018	0.021	0.035	0.074	0.093	0.133
$n = 100$	0.013	0.017	0.019	0.034	0.071	0.088	0.137
$n = 500$	0.012	0.015	0.017	0.031	0.070	0.088	0.130
$n = 1000$	0.012	0.015	0.017	0.031	0.066	0.082	0.126

(continued)

Table 4.12 (continued)

	FKPSS - SB test ($k = 2, \omega = 0.875$)						
	0.01	*0.05*	*0.10*	*0.50*	*0.90*	*0.95*	*0.99*
$n = 50$	0.015	0.018	0.021	0.038	0.083	0.105	0.155
$n = 100$	0.013	0.017	0.019	0.034	0.077	0.099	0.145
$n = 500$	0.012	0.015	0.017	0.032	0.072	0.091	0.135
$n = 1000$	0.012	0.015	0.017	0.031	0.069	0.090	0.139

Table 4.13 Empirical distribution of the KPSS-YOFA test statistics

	0.01	*0.05*	*0.10*	*0.50*	*0.90*	*0.95*	*0.99*
$n = 50$	0.019	0.023	0.025	0.037	0.059	0.068	0.091
$n = 100$	0.015	0.018	0.020	0.031	0.053	0.063	0.082
$n = 500$	0.012	0.015	0.017	0.029	0.051	0.060	0.081
$n = 1000$	0.011	0.015	0.017	0.028	0.050	0.058	0.082

$$\Delta y_t = \mu + \beta t + k_1[y_{t-1}] + k_2[y_{t-1}]^2 + k_2[y_{t-1}]^3 + \sum_{i=1}^{p} \Delta y_{t-i} + \varepsilon_t \tag{4.20}$$

where k_1 is the slope parameter for linear components, k_2 is the slope parameter for quadratic components and k_3 is the slope parameter for cubic components, and p is number of lagged differences. Under the null hypothesis of a stationary process, the empirical distribution of the KPSS-YOFA test would be estimated using 1000 replications of four different sample sizes, namely $T = 50$, $T = 100$, $T = 500$, $T = 1000$ (Cheung et al., 1994; Furuoka, 2017; Yaya et al., 2021). Table 4.13 reports the empirical distribution of the KPSS-YOFA test. As the table indicates, in the case of $n = 50$, the 0.95 point of distribution was 0.068, and it decreased to 0.058 when the number of observations increased to 1000. Similarly, in the case of $n = 50$, the 0.99 point of distribution was 0.091, and it decreased to 0.082 when the number of observations increased to 1000. It should be noted that the range of the empirical distribution of KPSS-YOFA in the case of $n = 1000$ is narrower than that of the empirical distribution in the case of $n = 50$.

References

Adams, A. V., & Mangum, G. I. (1978). *Lingering crisis of youth unemployment*. W.E. Upjohn Institute for Employment Research.

Atkinson, P., Dickinson, H., & Erben, M. (1986). The classification and control of vocational training for young people. In S. Walker & L. Burton (Eds.), *Youth, unemployment and schooling* (pp. 151–166). Open University Press.

Becker, R., Enders, W., & Lee, J. (2006). A stationarity test in the presence of an unknown number of smooth breaks. *Journal of Time Series Analysis, 27*(3), 381–409.

Bell, D. N., & Blanchflower, D. G. (2010). *Youth unemployment: Déjà Vu?* Institute for the Study of Labour (IZA) Discussion Paper No. 4705.
Beveridge, W. H. (1909). *Unemployment: A problem of industry*. Longmans.
Braverman, M. (1981). Youth, unemployment, and work with young adults. *Journal of Library History, 16*(2), 353–364.
Breen, R. (2005). Explaining cross-national variation in youth unemployment: Market and institutional factors. *European Sociological Review, 21*(2), 125–134.
Caporale, G. M., & Gil-Alana, L. (2014). Youth unemployment in Europe: Persistence and macroeconomicdeterminants. Comparative Economic Studies, 56, 581-591.
Casson, M. (1979). *Youth unemployment*. Springer.
Cheung, Y. W., Lai, K. S., & Tran, T. (1994). *Finite-sample critical values of the KPSS test: A response surface approach*. Discussion Papers, University of California, Santa Cruz. https://people.ucsc.edu/~cheung/working.html
Choi, I., & Kurozumi, E. (2014). The ET Interview: Professor Katsuto Tanaka. *Econometric Theory, 30*(2), 474–490.
Dickey, D. A., & Fuller, W. A. (1979). Distribution of the estimators for autoregressive time series with a unit root. *Journal of the American Statistical Association, 74*, 427–431.
Dickey, D. A., & Fuller, W. A. (1981). Likelihood ratio statistics for autoregressive time series with a unit root. *Econometrica, 49*, 1057–1072.
Fergusson, R., & Yeates, N. (2021). *Global youth unemployment: History, governance and policy*. Edward Elgar.
Furlong, A. (2016). The changing landscape of youth and young adulthood. In A. Furlong (Ed.), *Routledge handbook of youth and young adulthood* (pp. 19–27). Routledge.
Furuoka, F. (2017). A new approach to testing unemployment hysteresis. *Empirical Economics, 53*, 1253–1280.
Furuoka, F. (2024a). Patterns and convergence of unemployment rate among people with disabilities: Testing the "law of one unemployment rate". In *Disability and employment: Towards a humanistic economy* (pp. 69–109). Springer.
Furuoka, F. (2024b). Introduction. In *Disability and employment: Towards a humanistic economy* (pp. 1–10). Springer.
Furuoka, F., Gil-Alana, L., Yaya, O. S., & Vo, X. V. (2025). Convergence of gender unemployment gaps in Africa: New evidence from Fourier ADF and KPSS unit root tests with break. *Applied Economics, 2025*, 1–19. https://doi.org/10.1080/00036846.2024.2448610
Ginzberg, E. (1980). Youth unemployment. *Scientific American, 242*(5), 43–49.
Gleeson, D. (1986). Further education, free enterprise and the curriculum. In S. Walker & L. Burton (Eds.), *Youth, unemployment and schooling* (pp. 46–67). Open University Press.
Gregg, P. (2001). The impact of youth unemployment on adult unemployment in the NCDS. *Economic Journal, 111*(475), 626–653.
Hammer, T. (1993). Explanations of youth unemployment. *Young, 1*(3), 11–22.
Hammer, T. (1997). History dependence in youth unemployment. *European Sociological Review, 13*(1), 17–33.
Hess, L. E., Petersen, A. C., & Mortimer, J. T. (1994). Youth, unemployment and marginality: The problem and the solution. In A. C. Petersen & J. T. Mortimer (Eds.), *Youth unemployment and society* (pp. 3–33). Cambridge University Press.
International Labour Organisation. (2020). *Global employment trends for youth 2020*. International Labour Organisation.
Kurozumi, E. (2002). Testing for stationarity with a break. *Journal of Econometrics, 108*(1), 63–99.
Kwiatkowski, D., Phillips, P. C. B., Schmidt, P., & Shin, Y. (1992). Testing the null hypothesis of stationarity against the alternative of a unit root. *Journal of Econometrics, 54*, 159–178.
Lam, D., Leibbrandt, M., & Mlatsheni, C. (2009). Education and youth unemployment in South Africa. In S. R. Kanbur & J. Svejnar (Eds.), *Labour markets and economic development* (pp. 90–109). Routledge.

Levin, H. M. (1983). Youth unemployment and its educational consequences. *Educational Evaluation and Policy Analysis, 5*(2), 231–247.

Lindbekk, T. (1989). Education for life, vocational education and social integration in Norway. *Comparative Education, 25*(1), 19–28.

MacDonald, R. (2016). Precarious work. In A. Furlong (Ed.), *Routledge handbook of youth and young adulthood* (pp. 156–1163). Routledge.

MacNeill, I. B. (1978). Properties of sequences of partial sums of polynomial regression residuals with applications to tests for change of regression at unknown times. *Annals of Statistics, 6*, 422–433.

Mascherini, M. (2016). NEETs in the European agenda: Characteristics and policy debate. In A. Furlong (Ed.), *Routledge handbook of youth and young adulthood* (pp. 180–187). Routledge.

Mroz, T. A., & Savage, T. H. (2006). The long-term effects of youth unemployment. *Journal of Human Resources, 41*(2), 259–293.

Nabeya, S., & Tanaka, K. (1988). Asymptotic theory of a test for the constancy of regression coefficients against the random walk alternative. *Annals of Statistics, 16*, 218–235.

O'Higgins, N. (1997). The challenge of youth unemployment. *International Social Security Review, 50*(4), 63–93.

O'Higgins, N. (2001). *Youth unemployment and employment policy: A global perspective*. International Labour Organisation.

O'Higgins, N. (2016). Youth unemployment. In A. Furlong (Ed.), *Routledge handbook of youth and young adulthood* (pp. 141–155). Routledge.

Olle, H. (2022). *The new deal for young people (NDYP)*. Edge Foundation Paper No. 13.

Roberts, K. (2016). Socio-economic reproduction. In A. Furlong (Ed.), *Routledge handbook of youth and young adulthood* (pp. 28–35). Routledge.

Roulstone, A. (2016). Youth and disability: Growing up, getting out, getting on? In A. Furlong (Ed.), *Routledge handbook of youth and young adulthood* (pp. 83–97). Routledge.

Rowntree, B. S., & Lasker, B. (1911). *Unemployment: A social study*. Macmillan.

Sorrentino, C. (1981). Youth unemployment: An international perspective. *Monthly Labour Review, 104*(7), 3–15.

Tanaka, K. (1983). Non-normality of the Lagrange multiplier statistic for testing the constancy of regression coefficients. *Econometrica, 51*, 1577–1582.

Tawney, R. H. (1909). The economics of boy labour. *Economic Journal, 19*(76), 517–537.

United Nations. (2018). *Academic impact: SDG hub for Goal 8 dated 17 December 2018*. Retrieved June 6, 2025, from https://www.un.org/en/academic-impact/sdgsinacademia-sdg-hub-goal-8

Walker, S., & Burton, L. (1986). Introduction. In S. Walker & L. Burton (Eds.), *Youth, unemployment and schooling* (pp. 1–8). Open University Press.

Yaya, O. S., Ogbonna, A. E., Furuoka, F., & Gil-Alana, L. A. (2021). A new unit root test for unemployment hysteresis based on the autoregressive neural network. *Oxford Bulletin of Economics and Statistics, 83*(4), 960–981.

Chapter 5
High-End Gig Work: Case in Thailand

This chapter is the third analytical chapter. It examines the reception of high-end gig work in Thailand and its broader labour and socio-economic implications. It begins by outlining how the expansion of internet access and platform-based economic structures has reshaped youth employment and facilitated the rise of high-end gig work. The chapter then reviews relevant literature on cloud work and online freelancing and focuses on institutional frameworks, employment modalities, and gendered labour dynamics in Southeast Asia, particularly in Thailand. It then details the methodological framework that draws on semi-structured interviews with nine high-end gig workers based in Bangkok, and explains the sampling criteria, interview protocols, and the thematic analysis approach. Findings from the interviews are organised around four themes: self-reliance under structural constraints; the intersection of discretion and regulation; the revaluation of marginalised labour; and non-linear career paths beyond institutional norms. The chapter concludes by relating these themes to broader theoretical debates. In addition, it synthesises its contributions to understanding the complex realities and evolving challenges of high-end gig work in the Global South.

5.1 Introduction

Changes in connectivity, as well as the specification of new labour market entrants due to the rapid spread of the internet, have brought about the rise of digital labour that transcends geographical boundaries (Donovan et al., 2016; Graham et al., 2017; Vallas & Schor, 2020; Woodcock & Graham, 2019). According to a report by the International Telecommunication Union (ITU), the United Nations' specialised information and communications technology (ICT) agency, 68 per cent of the world's population (about 4.5 billion people) had internet access in 2024 (ITU, 2024). Personal internet usage rates by region in 2024 were Europe (91 per cent), the Americas (87 per cent), the Commonwealth of Independent States (CIS) (92 per

Y. Uchiyama, F. Furuoka, *Youth and Employment*,
https://doi.org/10.1007/978-981-95-3257-5_5

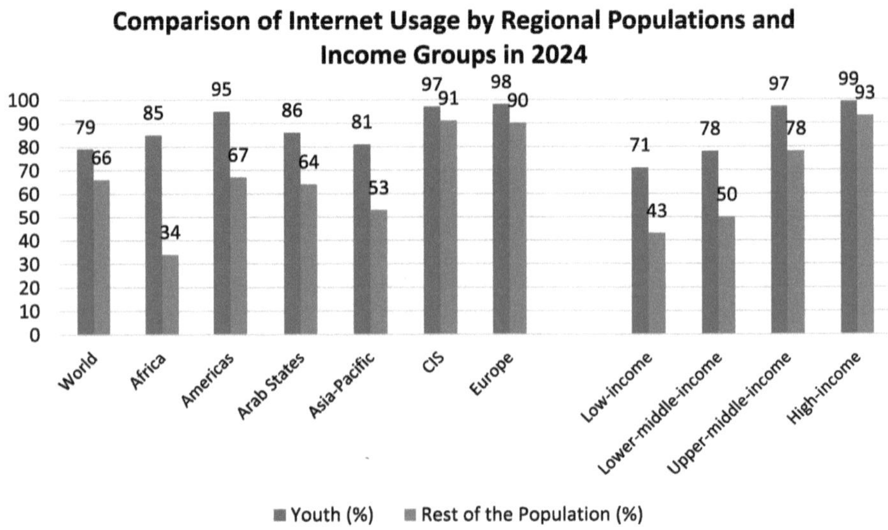

Fig. 5.1 Comparison of internet usage by regional populations and income groups in 2024. Source: ITU (2024)

cent), Asia-Pacific (66 per cent) and Africa (38 per cent). This prevalence varies widely depending on the inclusion of high-income and low-income country groups, whether they are urban or rural, or by gender (see ITU, 2024). Figure 5.1 illustrates the percentage of individuals using the internet in 2024, comparing youth (ages 15–24) with the rest of the population across various regions and income groups. Globally, internet usage is significantly higher among youth (79%) compared to other age groups (66%). The disparity is most pronounced in low-income regions (71% for youth vs. 43% for others) and least significant in high-income areas (99% vs. 93%). Regionally, Africa demonstrates the largest gap between youth (85%) and the rest of the population (34%), highlighting ongoing digital divides. Conversely, Europe and the CIS exhibit the highest overall internet penetration rates, with minimal differences between youth and other populations. These trends underscore the influence of regional and economic factors on digital accessibility, particularly for younger demographics.

Additionally, the on-demand commerce structure, where online platforms mediate workers and end-users, continues to give rise to various forms of "gig work" or "platform work" (Gandini, 2021; Stewart & Stanford, 2017; Uchiyama et al., 2022). The International Labour Organisation (ILO) states that gig work can be broadly divided into two main employment categories: "crowd work", which is featured online-based and globally organised (e.g., Upwork, CrowdSource, Amazon Mechanical Turk) and "on-demand gig work", which is managed online, and the actual work is done offline (e.g., Uber, Grab, TaskRabbit, Foodpanda). This section focuses on crowdwork (including high-skill freelancers), whilst on-demand gig work involving offline work is dealt with in the next chapter.

Table 5.1 Key demographic and digital indicators in Southeast Asian Countries in 2023

Country/ column	Population	Population ages 65 and above (%)	Unemployment rate (%)	Youth unemployment rate (15–24)	Internet penetration rate (%)
Brunei	458,949	7	5.91	18.6	99***
Cambodia	17,423,880	6	0.4**	0.8	57***
Indonesia	281,190,067	7	5.32	13.9	69
Laos	7,664,993	5	1.2***	2.2	66***
Malaysia	35,126,298	7	3.62	12.5	98
Myanmar	51,133,798	7	1.5*	9.7	44**
Philippines	114,891,119	5	4.35	6.9	75***
Singapore	5,917,648	13	2.1***	8.3	94
Thailand	71,702,435	15	1.3***	5.3	90
Vietnam	100,352,192	9	2.32***	6.2	78

Notes: Latest data: *2020, **2021, ***2022
Source: World Bank

Crowd work serves as an intermediary marketplace that connects crowdsourcers—comprising companies, institutions, and individuals—with crowd workers via an online platform, where all tasks are conducted and completed entirely online (De Stefano, 2016; Prassl & Risak, 2017). Crowdsourcing is broadly divided into two main categories: "microwork" and "online freelancing" (Margaryan, 2019; Wood et al., 2018). Microwork primarily involves simple tasks, such as image tagging and data entry, which can be completed quickly and are typically managed through algorithms. Conversely, online freelancing is distinguished by more complex tasks that require specialised skills, such as graphic design or data analysis, with remuneration and contract terms negotiated directly between the freelancer and the client.

Previous research has extensively examined typologies (Estellés-Arolas et al., 2015; Howcroft & Bergvall-Kåreborn, 2018; Kazai et al., 2011), business models (Durward et al., 2016; Gol et al., 2019; Kittur et al., 2013) and employment characteristics (Berg, 2015; Deng & Joshi, 2016; Durward et al., 2020) of crowd work. However, the social and economic implications of this form of work, particularly its impact on youth employment, remain underexplored. Crowd work is gaining popularity not only in the Global North, where internet infrastructure is well developed, but also in the Global South, where digital access remains uneven (Donini et al., 2017; Newlands & Lutz, 2021). Despite this, discussions of the gig economy in the Global South often disproportionately focus on on-demand app-based gig work involving offline service delivery. Consequently, there is a notable scarcity of research on the effects of crowd work, which occurs entirely online, on young people.

This chapter focuses on the Southeast Asian (SEA) region and examines high-end crowd and freelance gig workers, especially the younger generation in Thailand. Table 5.1 summarises key demographic and digital indicators in SEA. Whilst each country exhibits different characteristics, these two countries were chosen based on factors such as their respective demographics, employment conditions, and Internet penetration levels. Thailand has the highest proportion of the population aged 65 and over (15%) among ASEAN countries, coupled with a relatively low youth unemployment rate (5.3%). However, the rapid decline in birth rates and the ageing population in Thailand have raised concerns regarding a shrinking workforce. In this context, crowd work is increasingly attracting attention as a flexible form of employment that may address labour shortages and provide new opportunities in an ageing society.

Therefore, this chapter explores the reception of emerging forms of work, such as crowd work and online freelancing, among young people and examines their contribution to employment within the socio-economic contexts of Thailand. By conducting semi-structured interviews and media analysis with crowd workers in Bangkok, Thailand. This study seeks to elucidate both the significance and the challenges of high-skilled gig work for youths in the Global South, with a particular focus on SEA.

5.2 Crowd Work

The crowdsourcing market plays an intermediary role between physical and digital services by matching crowdsourcers, such as firms, institutions, and individuals, with an unspecified number of crowd workers who can take on their own tasks (Blohm et al., 2018; Durward et al., 2020; Howcroft & Bergvall-Kåreborn, 2018). In other words, this marketplace enables the simultaneous mobilisation of a huge workforce for complex and large-scale tasks by an intermediary connecting geographically dispersed workers (crowdsourcers) with crowdsourcers on an online platform (Kittur et al., 2013). Crowd work can function as an open-ended online business. Specifically, clients seek workers with a range of skills in a marketplace, and workers who match their requirements accept online work orders and carry out tasks. After workers finish the task, they can receive financial remuneration from the client. De Stefano (2016) mentioned that crowd work is mainly characterised as monotonous and voluminous micro-tasks, and unit costs are lower than without the use of a platform. This generally requires judgments and assessments of emotions and nuances that are not possible with artificial intelligence, but the low-cost work attracts consumers and consequently allows them to take advantage of geographical differences in skills and labour costs (De Stefano, 2016). In the case of crowd work, tasks are judged and paid for in different ways, with payment only proceeding for tasks that exceed a certain quality, or on a first-come, first-served basis (De Stefano, 2016; Tubaro, 2021). In addition, some platforms set a minimum amount of remuneration for certain tasks, whilst others allow workers to set their own remuneration (Stewart & Stanford, 2017). Furthermore, digital microwork involves very little physical human contact (Howcroft & Bergvall-Kåreborn, 2018). From the discussion of prior literature, the author classifies the types of crowd work according to the

Table 5.2 Classification of crowd work

Classification	Description	Key features	Method	Examples
Individual freelance marketplace	Freelance-based work where workers complete tasks individually and remotely.	Professional and creative work; speculative payment; initiated by workers.	First Offer	iStockphoto, Apple App Store
Crowd work	Tasks assigned to an unspecified number of gig workers with no individual focus.	Paid microtasks initiated by requesters; modular and fragmented work.	Cheapest Offer	Amazon Mechanical Turk, UpWork
Microtask crowd work	Segmented tasks completed for small fees.	Utilises workers' assets; managed digitally but often conducted offline.	Quality Requirement	TaskRabbit
Contest crowd work	Tasks performed simultaneously by a large group, rewarding the highest quality.	Unpaid/speculative work; creativity-focused; initiated by requesters.	Best Quality	TopCoder, Threadless, InnoCentive

Source: Schmidt (2017), Howcroft and Bergvall-Kåreborn (2018), Jäger et al. (2019), Duggan et al. (2020), Author's modification

nature of the crowd work operation: individual freelance marketplace, crowd work, microtask crowd work, and contest crowd work (Table 5.2).

The individual freelance marketplace refers to a form of freelance work where tasks are assigned to and completed by individuals working remotely, typically focusing on creative or professional projects with speculative payment structures. In contrast, crowd work distributes tasks to an unspecified number of gig workers, emphasising modularity and scalability rather than individual assignments. Microtask crowd work comprises small, segmented tasks managed digitally, for which workers receive minimal fees. Finally, contest crowd work represents a crowdsourcing model where large groups of workers simultaneously perform tasks without subdivision, with payment awarded to the submission judged to be of the highest quality (Duggan et al., 2020; Schmidt, 2017).

Each of these categories aligns with distinct methods of crowd work. For instance, platforms such as Amazon Mechanical Turk utilise a "First Offer" system, where the first worker to accept a task secures the contract, whereas freelancer.com employs a "Cheapest Offer" model, prioritising the lowest bid. Conversely, "Best Quality" models, exemplified by platforms like TopCoder, focus on selecting the most qualified worker, whilst "Quality Requirement" methods ensure participants meet minimum standards, often verified through platform-based assessments (Jäger et al., 2019). These differences reflect the variety of mechanisms employed by crowd work platforms, including variations in task allocation, remuneration structures and worker selection processes.

One advantage of the crowd work business model is that crowdsourcers can alleviate professional shortages and local economic stagnation by utilising a flexible workforce and providing individuals with new income and social mobility opportunities. Crowdsourcers can also maintain a work-life balance by controlling the acceptance of their contracts due to their flexibility and self-employed nature (Jäger et al., 2019). In addition, many young people are finding opportunities due to their digital adaptability (Brewer et al., 2016). However, it also involves risks such as low wages and lack of benefits, poor quality due to piece-rate payment, as well as the risk of unskilled labour and reduced quality of life for workers due to task fragmentation (Kittur et al., 2013). In addition, various problems in the algorithmic management of workers specific to platform businesses arise (Uchiyama et al., 2024). Furthermore, crowd work may cause employment contractual problems of non-payment of the minimum wage (i.e. wage damping) due to the low unit cost of the work (Wood et al., 2019). In order to deal with it, crowd work platforms benefit from minimum wage payment relief, tax benefits and regulatory avoidance by positioning employers as self-employed (Prassl & Risak, 2016). In the performance assessment, the platforms digitise the management and performance of workers from legal and fair perspectives to prevent bias (Howcroft & Bergvall-Kåreborn, 2018). Such on-demand tasks, with limited communication channels and their lack of monitoring compared to traditional office tasks, can lead to workers being treated as interchangeable and unreliable, reducing their motivation and sense of responsibility (Kittur et al., 2013). The expansion of crowdwork has shattered the illusion of innovation neutrality and highlights the reality that digital technologies are designed to serve platform capitalist interests (Howcroft & Bergvall-Kåreborn, 2018).

Despite being exposed to tenuous relationships with companies and precarious employment and remuneration structures, crowd workers, particularly freelancers, establish identities independent of the organisations they work for. They build their careers not only through individual strategies but also by leveraging collective approaches. Within their professional communities, freelancers engage in situational learning and facilitate remuneration processes, which enable many to eventually transition back into full-time employment (Schwartz, 2018).

5.3 Crowd Work in Southeast Asia

In SEA, online gig work has emerged as a promising means of economic development, offering workers the opportunity to participate in the global marketplace without being tied to long-term employment contracts. This form of work is believed to increase workers' labour participation rates and productivity, thereby increasing their chances of escaping poverty (Graham et al., 2018). In particular, the high proportion of young workers in the region and the prevailing climate for flexibility in terms of work-life balance have contributed significantly to the spread of online gig work (Serafica & Oren, 2022; Uchiyama et al., 2022). Furthermore, crowd work can be a useful option for workers, especially in regions with underdeveloped labour markets (Pfeiffer & Kawalec, 2020). The Online Labour Index (OLI) is the first economic indicator to measure trends in the online gig economy, produced jointly by

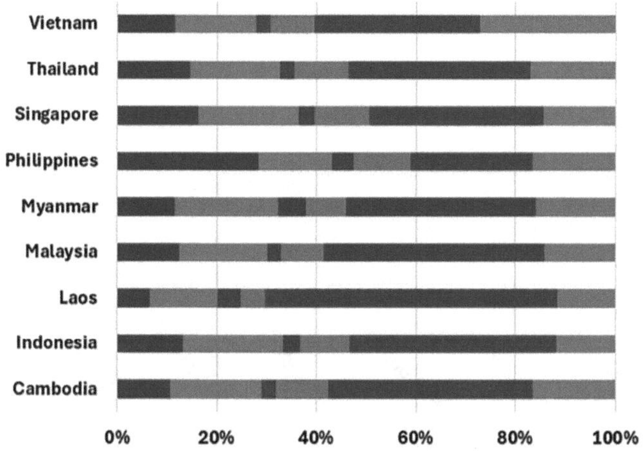

Fig. 5.2 Online labour demand in Southeast Asia. Notes: Brunei is not in the data. Source: OLI (2020), Stephany et al. (2021)

the International Labour Organisation (ILO) and the Oxford Internet Institute at the University of Oxford (Stephany et al., 2021). Figure 5.2 and Appendix show the crowd gig work in SEA occupational distribution and identify overall regional trends and country-specific characteristics.

There were marked differences in the distribution of occupations in crowd work between countries. A common trend is the importance of software development and technical occupations in many countries. In Laos, for example, 58.7% of crowd workers work in this sector, while in Indonesia, the proportion is also high at 41.4%. On the other hand, document writing and translation occupy a high share in Vietnam (27.1%) and the Philippines (16.5%), reflecting the excellent language skills and ability of workers in these countries to respond to international markets. The creative sector is also prominent in Singapore (20.2%) and Malaysia (17.9%), indicating that these countries function as centres of the creative economy. On the other hand, 28.2% of workers in the Philippines and 16.3% in Singapore are employed in the clerical and data entry sectors. This trend indicates that differences in the economic structure and skill sets of different countries have a strong influence on occupational distribution. In the region as a whole, crowd work in SEA exhibits diverse characteristics depending on country-specific skill levels, economic conditions and ICT infrastructure. In some countries, high-value-added sectors such as software development and creative fields play a major role, whilst in other countries, low-value-added sectors such as office work and data entry dominate. Figure 5.3 illustrates the percentages of online female crowd workers in Southeast Asia.

The distribution of female crowd workers and freelancers in SEA shows clear country-specific characteristics. In data entry and clerical work, the Philippines (71.3%) and Indonesia (61.3%) have high proportions of women in these key occupations. In creative fields, Myanmar has by far the highest proportion

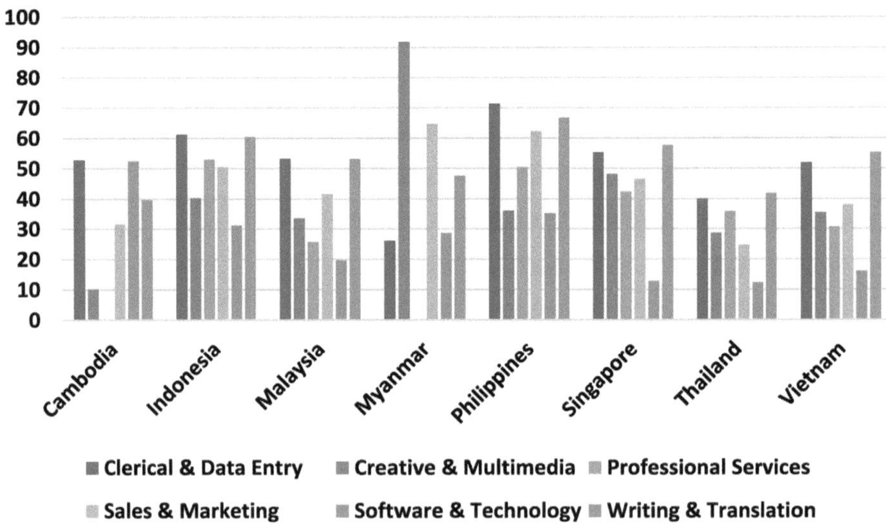

Fig. 5.3 Online female workers in Southeast Asia. Source: OLI (2020)

(91.8%), with distinct regional characteristics. In Professional Services and Sales & Marketing, Indonesia (53% and 50.6% respectively) and the Philippines (50.5% and 62.3% respectively) lead the way, with women also playing an important role in these sectors. In Software & Technology, on the other hand, Cambodia (52.5%) has the highest proportion of women, but the proportion of women is lower than in other sectors. In Writing & Translation, the Philippines (66.8%) and Indonesia (60.5%) have the highest percentages, indicating the importance of women's language skills as a revenue opportunity.

The income potential that transcends the constraints of local markets, coupled with rising unemployment, has attracted a significant number of young people to online gig work. In the SEA region, many workers rely on crowd work as their primary source of income. In contrast, in the US and Western Europe, it is more commonly utilised as a supplementary job or a means to gain specific work experience (Gerber & Krzywdzinski, 2019). Despite extensive research on gig work in SEA, relatively little attention has been paid to crowd work and online freelancing compared to on-demand app-based gig work (e.g., ridesharing and food delivery). Notably, the Philippines, which hosts the third-largest number of online freelancers globally, is frequently highlighted in research on SEA. Its prominence is attributed to the scale of its digital workforce and its numerous policy initiatives in this domain (Bayudan-Dacuycuy & Kryz Baje, 2021; Soriano, 2021).

Graham et al. (2017) examine microtask and freelance skills work in the Philippines, Malaysia, and Vietnam, where digital labour platforms offer flexible working arrangements and new income opportunities independent of local labour market constraints. Online freelance workers in SEA tend to migrate in search of better employment opportunities, contrasting with workers in high-income countries, who often relocate for scenic landscapes or recreational purposes (Zander & Garnett, 2021). Whilst some workers benefit from economic opportunities and freedoms unavailable in traditional labour markets, they also face vulnerabilities, including contract terminations and declining hourly wages. For instance, microtask workers in Vietnam and the Philippines may accept rates below what is considered fair, given their qualifications and experience, to secure work amidst growing competition. Meanwhile, highly skilled workers, such as accountants, may initially earn substantial incomes through digital platforms but later face challenges in negotiating new contracts, placing them at a disadvantage (Graham et al., 2017).

In Vietnam, younger workers from Generation Z exhibit a greater willingness to participate in the gig economy compared to Generations X and Y. This trend is influenced by their risk perceptions, skills, preference for flexible working hours, affinity for platform economies, and current income levels (Cao & Pham, 2024). Crowd work is expanding rapidly in the Philippines, leveraging the population's high English proficiency and familiarity with Western culture. The country ranks third globally in the number of online freelancers, following the United States and India, with workers engaged in diverse tasks ranging from data entry and customer service to content creation and web development (Bayudan-Dacuycuy et al., 2020; Serafica & Oren, 2022). Crowd work has also emerged as a flexible alternative within the Business Process Outsourcing (BPO) sector in the Philippines. In 2013, the Philippines' government partnered with platforms such as Elance, Odesk (now Upwork), and Freelancer.com to promote digital labour. This initiative offered new opportunities for workers dissatisfied with BPO practices, as well as for unemployed youth and returning migrants (Soriano, 2021).

Nevertheless, the oversupply of workers on some platforms has led to a decline in wages. In the Philippines, women are more engaged in platform labour than men, yet they face challenges such as low wages, inadequate social protection, and slow skill development (Bayudan-Dacuycuy et al., 2020). Digital labour influencers play a key role in the expansion of crowd work by mentoring new entrants and fostering solidarity through community building with workers and clients (Soriano et al., 2021). However, these influencers' activities may inadvertently increase workers' dependence on platforms and obscure structural issues in their working environments.

In Malaysia, the COVID-19 pandemic and the state-led "Digital Malaysia" initiative have spurred the rapid adoption of crowd work and online freelancing. The programme has particularly encouraged low-income groups (B40) to participate in gig work. However, it has also highlighted persistent issues, including the absence of social security, the prevalence of short-term contracts, and low wages (Ali et al., 2023; Uchiyama et al., 2024). According to Uchiyama et al. (2025)'s study among university students in Malaysia, students tended to prefer entrepreneurial, skill-based freelancers rather than ride-hailing and food delivery services (Uchiyama et al., 2025). In Myanmar, digital labour has emerged as a new source of income following political and economic reforms in 2011. However, the sector remains primarily reliant on local clients, and institutional barriers such as the unavailability of PayPal and restrictions on foreign currency accounts hinder participation in international platforms (Galpaya & Senanayake, 2018).

Whilst the growth of crowd work and online freelance gig work in SEA has been significant, research specific to this regional context remains underdeveloped. Institutional challenges, including inadequate protections for workers' rights and practical barriers to their implementation, persist, requiring more comprehensive academic and policy-focused engagement.

5.4 Crowd Work in Thailand

In Thailand, the public and private sectors have recognised the importance of developing the skills of the workforce for the transition to a digital economy, but there is still a shortage of workers with intermediate and advanced skills and digital skills in the freelance market, which is expected to grow in global markets including the EU and the USA (Layraman & Sirarujanon, 2024). The government's "Thailand 4.0" policy aims to move from an efficiency-driven to an innovation-driven economy, and youth skills development is seen as key to its success. Puriwat and Tripopsakul (2020) found that Thai youth have significant deficiencies in digital and information skills. This skills shortage is attributed to the fact that the education curriculum does not meet the demands of the digital employment market, widening the gap between young people and the labour market. Another challenge is the lack of support for young people, particularly low-skilled young people, to participate in the digital economy (Intaratat, 2021).

The distinct hierarchical structure of Thai society affects the development of the digital economy and the gig economy. Whilst the elite and wealthy gain easy access to the digital economy through education and networks, lower-income and rural residents tend to lack these opportunities. This disparity further widens the differences in skills and employment opportunities that exist between urban and rural areas (Leung & Cossu, 2019). In particular, start-up ecosystems and co-working spaces have developed in major cities such as Bangkok and Chiang Mai, and it is the wealthy and young elites who mainly benefit from this infrastructure. On the other hand, rural workers and low- and middle-income groups tend to be left out of these ecosystems.

Internet use in Thailand is becoming increasingly diverse, particularly among the younger generation, against a backdrop of mobile internet penetration. Unmarried, well-educated urban women show more diverse usage trends and a wider range of online activities than men (Lopez-Sintas et al., 2020). However, gender disparities in working conditions remain, with around 9 million women and 11.2 million men working in the informal work sector in 2022 (Sutassanamarlee et al., 2024).

Bangkok-based freelancers use online courses and workshops to improve their skills and increase their adaptability to the global market. They also participate in global online communities through social networking sites and forums to promote information exchange and collaboration (Sattayathamrongthian & Vanpetch, 2023).

In addition, they are strengthening their human and social capital by using platforms such as Behance and Dribbble to publicise their portfolios and establish a digital footprint. Conversely, freelancers in rural areas have limited access to these educational resources and networks, putting them at a disadvantage compared to urban workers. This imbalance is a stark illustration of the impact of social stratification on the development of the digital economy in Thailand.

Chiang Mai is highly popular, especially among westerners, as the "digital nomad capital", with its low cost of living, robust infrastructure and mild climate (Thompson, 2019). Digital nomads contribute significantly to the local economy, creating demand for co-working and co-living spaces, but challenges such as the rising cost of living and economic disparity with local residents have also emerged (Jiwasiddi et al., 2024). Local freelancers in Chiang Mai also face issues such as competition from digital nomads and difficulties in accessing fair remuneration, and policy interventions are needed to address these challenges.

A fair remuneration system, strengthened social protection, and promotion of skills development through collaboration between educational institutions and industry are essential for the sustainable development of Thailand's gig economy. Whilst there is an urgent need to promote digital skills education in rural areas and low-income groups, policies are required to address the advancement of AI and automation technologies. Increased support for occupations that require creativity and advanced human skills is expected to increase the sustainability of gig workers (Brynjolfsson & McAfee, 2014; Tanoamchard & Ceienwattanasook, 2024).

5.5 Methodology

This study examines the acceptance of high-skilled gig work, particularly crowd work and online freelancing, in Thailand, and seeks to empirically elucidate how these work forms contribute to employment within a socio-economic context. Adopting a multi-method qualitative research approach, it specifically investigates the implications for youth employment in the Global South (Tashakkori & Teddlie, 2010).

In order to comprehensively understand the experiences of these workers, this study conducted semi-structured interviews with nine individuals aged 23 to 34 who reside in Bangkok, Thailand, and engage in crowdwork or online freelancing through digital labour platforms and websites. This study includes both Thai and foreign nationals who can speak English for the interview. The workers included not only those engaged in microtasks but also those involved in tasks requiring specialised skills. Although the sample size is relatively small, this aligns with the conventional approach of detailed qualitative research aimed at identifying subtle differences and common patterns in individual experiences (Braun & Clarke, 2006).

The semi-structured interviews are designed around demographic questions and four key sections: reasons for choosing motivation and career choice, work organisation and autonomy, economic and social impacts, and career prospects. Questions were comprehensively calibrated on participants' reasons for choosing crowd work, their experience of platform competition, wage structure and access to social protection. In addition, the study explored skills development, career trajectories and the sustainability of crowd working as a long-term employment option in an evolving digital labour market. These interviews were conducted in co-working spaces and cafes in Bangkok or via Zoom, each lasting approximately 30–45 minutes. With the participants' permissions, all interviews are recorded and transcribed verbatim for analysis. Given the tendency for crowd workers' networks to form through online channels, the study employed snowball sampling, recruiting participants through initial contacts and social media outreach.

For data analysis, this study employs thematic analysis, integrating insights from the semi-structured interviews. Thematic analysis is a qualitative method that systematically identifies patterns within data, enabling a deeper exploration of the research phenomenon (Braun & Clarke, 2006). The analysis was conducted in four stages to identify key aspects of crowd workers' experiences and to derive policy implications related to their working conditions (Uchiyama et al., 2022).

The first stage involved transcribing the recorded interviews and compiling verbatim transcripts. Supplementary notes were taken during interviews to highlight key points, refine data organisation, and guide the analytical focus. The second stage comprised open coding, where key terms and phrases related to working conditions were identified and categorised while preserving the original intent of participants' statements. In the third stage, axial coding was employed to refine and integrate the codes from the previous step, establishing relationships between key elements and identifying structural patterns in crowd workers' experiences. The final stage, selective coding, involved the identification of core themes and their corresponding subthemes, which were then organised into a structured framework. Extracted themes were visually mapped and cross-referenced with demographic and employment-related data, such as working hours, years of experience, and income levels, to provide a holistic interpretation of crowd workers' socio-economic conditions.

By examining the cases of Bangkok, this study provides empirical insights into the socio-economic implications of high-skilled crowdwork in SEA, a key region within the Global South. The findings contribute to an understanding of how platform-mediated gig work shapes young workers' career trajectories and broader labour market transformations in the digital economy.

5.6 Findings

This study conducted semi-structured interviews with nine young freelance workers (R-1 to R-9) active in Thailand. Their demographic characteristics clearly reflect the diversifying career structures in today's high-skilled labour and digital economy, as shown in Table 5.3. The participants' ages ranged from 24 to 34, with six women and three men. The data from this study also revealed some gender-based

Table 5.3 Demographics of respondents

Respondents: R-(k)	Age	Gender	Occupation	Education	Work arrangement	Experiences	Average monthly income (THB[a])
R-1	32	Female	Language Tutor (English)	Bachelor	Part-time	3 years	20,000 THB
R-2	24	Male	Research Assistant	Master	Full-time	2 years 6 months	20,000 THB
R-3	27	Female	Interior Designer	Bachelor	Part-time		20,000 THB
R-4	29	Female	Math Tutor, Exam Proctor, Graphic Designer	Bachelor	Part-time	4 years	10,000 THB
R-5	26	Female	Web Designer	Bachelor	Part-time	2 years	8000 THB
R-6	31	Male	Policy Advisor and Political Consultant	Master (pursuing a PhD)	Part-time	4 years	30,000 THB
R-7	25	Female	Accountant	Bachelor	Full-time	4 years	70,000 THB
R-8	24	Male	Research Assistant	Bachelor	Full-time	1 year	18,000 THB
R-9	34	Female	Language Tutor (French)	Bachelor	Full-time		30,000 THB

Source: Authors

[a]1 THB=0.31 USD (as of 16 June 2025)

occupational choice tendencies. For example, women were more prevalent in language education (R-1, R-9) and accounting/design-related roles (R-3, R-4, R-5, R-7), while men were more common in policy support and research assistance roles (R-2, R-6, R-8). In terms of educational background, all participants held at least a bachelor's degree, and in the case of R-6, the simultaneous pursuit of doctoral studies and practical professional development indicates a distinctive and strategically hybrid career trajectory. The occupational fields are education, language, design, and accounting, which are representative of freelance work and require a certain level of specialisation and skills. Particularly noteworthy is the growing prevalence of non-regular and freelance employment among young individuals in knowledge-intensive sectors. Regarding employment status, five individuals (R-1, R-3, R-4, R-5, R-6) were classified as part-time workers, choosing this arrangement to balance family responsibilities, full-time employment, or prioritise flexible time management. On the other hand, four individuals (R-2, R-7, R-8, R-9) were full-time workers, with freelance work serving as their primary source of income or professional identity. Thus, the freelance employment form is not necessarily limited to one-off or low-skilled work but is being redefined by young workers in the middle class who seek high specialisation, temporal flexibility, and autonomy.

5.6.1 Exploring Self-Reliance Under Structural Constraints

This study identified that freelancers and crowd workers in Bangkok, Thailand, sought autonomy under existing structural constraints, which led to their main motivation for entering the field and their career choices. In addition to positive narratives such as free will and flexibility, there are various structural factors behind this, including a lack of employment opportunities, institutional exclusion, family responsibilities, and discrepancies with the market value of expertise.

5.6.1.1 Lifestyle-Aligned Flexibility with Supplementary Income

Multiple interviewees highlighted flexibility in employment as their primary motivation. This did not simply refer to discretion over working hours but was emphasised from the perspective of harmonising with overall lifestyle. As examples, they specified balancing childcare (R-1), reducing commuting time (R-2), securing additional income (R-3, R-4), and addressing mismatches between academic qualifications and full-time work (R-5). R-1, who has children and whose husband works overseas, stated that she needed to work in a way that was compatible with her responsibilities as a mother and household chores, and that remote work through a platform played an important role in supporting her household finances. R-3 and R-4, who work full-time during the week, use weekends and weekday evenings to utilise their skills to secure freelance work through platforms or referrals. Additionally, R-4 leverages the advantage of working at a university to apply online for one-time examiner positions, which are only open to staff with a bachelor's degree or higher and frequently conducts these exams at the venue. These two career choices intersect at the structural context of the advancement of platform technology, the absence of institutional support, and the effective utilisation of benefits.

5.6.1.2 Flexible Self-Fulfilment Through Specialisation

Online freelance work is not just a place to utilise traditional skills, but also an opportunity to benefit from building digital labour skills in areas such as technology literacy, digital communication, and multi-tasking project management. R-5 and R-9 chose online freelancing as a field where they could maximise their language and educational skills, demonstrating a strong desire for self-fulfilment through work. After graduating from university, they worked as full-time employees at companies in sectors different from their desired fields but felt constrained by standardised job duties within the framework of regular employment. Following their transition to freelance work, while direct engagement with clients and the development of bespoke materials and skills posed ongoing challenges, such practices nevertheless served as a means of reclaiming a sense of self-efficacy and creativity in relation to their originally envisioned mode of labour. Interestingly, R-9 stated that "the competence of a freelance language teacher is proven by students' reactions and parents' trust", indicating that a new professional identity is emerging based on performance and relationships rather than traditional qualifications.

5.6.1.3 Adaptation to Institutional Barriers and Strategic Circumvention

In some cases, the transition to freelance work was not a clear aspiration but rather a passive response to institutional barriers and occupational stagnation (R-2 and R-7). In Thailand, interior design is classified as an unskilled occupation under the institutional classification system, resulting in relatively low wages. To meet the wage standards required for local employment, significant experience and corporate capital are necessary, limiting opportunities to a few foreign companies. Therefore, due to legal restrictions on foreign workers, R-7 had to give up his original aspiration to become an interior designer and continue working for his family's accounting firm, where he was able to work as an online freelancer. Although working as an accountant appears to be a high-income profession, in reality, it is a "choice without options" formed by institutional exclusion. Another participant with a degree in fine arts also mentioned that they started graphic design as a side job because the field was difficult to connect with practical work, and there were few opportunities for regular employment (R-4). Such cases demonstrate that the disconnect between the education system and the labour market acts as a structural factor pushing youths into informal freelance work outside the system.

5.6.1.4 Divergence in Perceptions of Long-Term Careers

Interestingly, even among those who engage in the same high-skilled freelance work, there was a clear divergence between those who view it positively as a long-term career and those who view it as a temporary transitional phase. Some of them explicitly stated their intention to transition to institutional occupations such as universities or international organisations in the future, positioning their current work as a place to accumulate skills and gain experience (R-2, R-6, and R-8). On the other hand, R-1 and R-5 expressed a desire to become independent in marketing their services without relying on platforms, as they believed that stable trust relationships with clients would enable them to operate their own classrooms. They envisioned an entrepreneurial, independent career path that was not tied to institutional frameworks. While the entry of youths into freelancing may appear voluntary, it is in fact shaped by a constellation of structural conditions, including professional norms, differential access to urban resources, and institutional constraints. This demonstrates that the freelancing work arrangement carries multifaceted meanings in career development.

5.6.2 Intersection of Discretion and Regulation in Labour Schemes

Regarding the organisation and autonomy of work, this section reveals the process by which youths engaged in freelance work manage their daily labour. Although autonomy and flexibility are often seen as advantages, in practice, they are constantly negotiated in response to labour market insecurity, platform design, everyday life demands, and power imbalances between workers and clients.

5.6.2.1 Redefining Autonomy

Many participants highlighted the ability to manage their own working hours as a key advantage of freelancing (R-3, R-5, R-6, R-9). However, it is important to carefully assess whether this truly represents genuine autonomy. For example, since R-5 and R-6 each have full-time jobs during the day, their design work is limited to weekends and late nights. R-1 also needs to work between childcare duties, and this is not a choice made to balance their main job and childcare, but rather a product of an unavoidable structural necessity. This interpretation varies depending on whether one chooses not to access formal employment or is unable to access it, but flexibility in time can also be interpreted to compensate for gaps or free time. While it may appear on the surface that flexible time management is possible, the reality is that this free time is carved out within the strong constraints of living conditions such as gender, generation, class, and family responsibilities.

5.6.2.2 Discretion in Work and Potential Asymmetry

Freelancers with a certain level of expertise enjoy a high degree of discretion in their work and autonomous work design. For example, those with experience in education and consulting select projects that match their areas of expertise and design their own course content and delivery styles (R-6, R-9). One freelancer, whose students are mostly overseas, took advantage of the time difference to spend their days off and teach at night (R-9). Another, R-6, combined offline research activities with online policy advocacy, achieving a flexible schedule that balanced their lifestyle and work. In contrast, those engaged in outsourcing-type work have very limited room for negotiation regarding work content, remuneration, and deadlines, and their freedom in selecting work tends to be nominal (R-2, R-8). When serving as assistants in university research projects, their schedules and workloads are largely dependent on the discretion of the project leader, and they are constantly busy with daily work preparations. In fact, concerns have been raised that if they do not follow the work assignments within the project, there will be no next project, suggesting a structural vulnerability in which the power asymmetry with clients and the possibility of rejection leading to immediate exclusion lie behind the superficial freedom (R-2). This resonates with the fact that the "freedom of choice" seen in platform work is only formally functional, especially in low-skill areas.

5.6.2.3 Spatial Autonomy and Social Isolation

While the ability to work online is an advantage for many participants, it also carries the risk of weakening social connections. Whereas R-9 stated that due to the nature of their job, there are days when they do not speak to anyone all day when there are no classes, R-8 also mentioned that there are days when their motivation declines due to feelings of loneliness. Furthermore, unlike office work, such jobs primarily involve social interaction, which is a major challenge. This is particularly amplifying feelings of loneliness among foreigners in other countries (R-7). The spatial autonomy of being able to work anywhere simultaneously creates psychological stress in the form of social isolation. This isolation can also become a barrier to professional growth and career development through a lack of evaluation and feedback. This differs from the competitive, constantly evaluated labour forms like microtasks or contest-based gig work that the author also does. With microtasks, workers can always see their ranking and position in the crowd job pool through task assignments and accuracy displays, allowing them to develop skills specific to those tasks. On the other hand, even in high-end gigs, the ease of the tasks means they have little impact on career development, and the complete absence of face-to-face communication with clients inevitably leads to feelings of loneliness. In other words, the freedom to work anywhere is shown to be intertwined with the absence of a support network.

5.6.2.4 Formation of Autonomy Through Recursive Specialisation and Learning

Some participants were independently rebuilding their careers while acquiring and improving the skills necessary for their work in their own way. This was particularly evident among online tutors who had frequent interactions with students and received irregular requests. Accounts of beginning work with limited confidence in teaching materials, yet gradually developing a personalised curriculum through trial and error (R-9), alongside practices that emphasise the need for flexible lesson planning due to last-minute student queries (R-4), indicate a steady process of skill development and the internalisation of professional competence beyond formal work tasks Such self-directed learning implies the formation of expertise based on experience, independent of institutional certification or qualifications. The recursive development of professional skills, in which understanding client needs arises not through formal instruction but through experience, involves more than the simple accumulation of techniques. It requires continuous reflection and refinement of one's own practice, indicating a form of recursive expertise (R-3). Autonomy in freelance work through platforms is neither monolithic nor absolute but is conditionally constituted within multiple contexts such as living structures, market pressures, institutional backgrounds, and human relationships. Considering that relentless learning efforts underpin the freedom they experience, their autonomy is conditional, requiring constant negotiation with institutions and structures.

5.6.3 Compensation and Re-evaluation of Marginalised Labour

The perspectives of youths regarding the economic and social impacts of platform-based freelance and crowd work are extremely important. While gig work is often highlighted for its flexibility and freedom, regardless of skill level, the reality is that it does not necessarily guarantee economic stability or social recognition. The analysis results of this study reveal that beneath the façade of independence lie various forms of marginalisation, which pose challenges that negatively impact participants' lives and work.

5.6.3.1 Income Instability and Pressure on Living Costs

Many participants (R-2, R-5, R-7) pointed to income instability as the biggest challenge of working as freelancers. Even if they have a certain level of income, it fluctuates greatly from month to month, making it difficult to manage rent and food expenses (R-5). Furthermore, this situation is also affected by delays in payments from clients and customers (R-2, R-9). Especially in central Bangkok, where living costs are significantly higher than in other Thai cities, they face daily challenges in managing their household finances due to the aforementioned issues. This explains their pursuit of supplementary work or additional opportunities beyond full-time employment, as they actively seek and engage in alternative sources of income (R-8).

5.6.3.2 Social Recognition and Professional Identity

As online freelancers and crowd workers are basically treated as independent contractors in Thailand, they lack formal employment contracts and organisational affiliation. This often results in a lack of social recognition, such as social security and pension benefits, and a minimum wage, making it difficult to establish a professional identity. Therefore, those who work full-time must purchase private insurance at their own expense. Furthermore, the pension system is insufficient to guarantee a secure retirement without formal employment-based contributions. Part-time workers continue this work, dependent on the benefits of full-time employment, and this gap in perception highlights the societal perception that the legitimacy of a profession is supported by institutional frameworks. Additionally, their social presence is primarily constructed through word-of-mouth from clients and customers. For instance, R-1 and R-9 mention that positive feedback from students and parents, as well as reviews on platforms and social media, form personal networks that lead to student acquisition. Furthermore, they mention that providing customised lesson plans tailored to individual learning needs and maintaining open communication with parents to track students' progress contribute to the continuous acquisition of new students through word-of-mouth (R-1, R-4). This phenomenon is distinctive in that non-institutional forms of recognition are actively shaping an emergent professional reality.

5.6.3.3 Work–Life Boundary Erosion and Psychological Strain

While most participants acknowledged the convenience of online-based gig work, they also expressed concerns about the blurring of the boundary between work and private life. In cases where business with overseas clients had become routine, participants particularly reported feeling compelled to respond to requests during nights and weekends, resulting in a sustained state of hyper-responsiveness and inability to disconnect (R-7, R-9). For example, respondents who frequently communicate with overseas clients mentioned that due to time zone differences, meetings and responses often extend into the late hours of the night (R-9). While such flexible time management may appear to be self-directed, it shifts the responsibility for self-management excessively onto the individual, increasing the risk of psychological stress and burnout. While the advent of platforms and crowd-based environments has markedly reduced spatial constraints on work, full-time freelancers tend to unconsciously normalise a state of perpetual availability.

5.6.3.4 Struggle Between Economic Independence and Marginal Employment

Many participants viewed freelance work positively and took pride in being able to support their households with their own skills. For example, some expressed joy at being able to cover their children's education expenses with their own income (R-1), while others noted that they could now earn enough to make ends meet even as part-time workers (R-1, R-6). R-1 is pursuing a formal teacher certification programme with the goal of achieving full-time independence in the future. On the other hand, concerns about the inadequacy of the social security system and uncertainty about the future remain strong. Specifically, some participants expressed concerns about their future prospects in the absence of stable income or employment conditions equivalent to those of regular employees, leading them to maintain freelance work as a supplementary or part-time engagement (R-4, R-5).

5.6.4 Non-linear Career Paths Outside the System

This section provides a multifaceted analysis of the future career plans of young high-end gig workers. While freelance work may appear attractive at first glance, its prospects are complexly intertwined with factors such as their outlook, anxieties, institutional constraints, and self-strategies.

5.6.4.1 Career Perception as a Temporary Stepping Stone

Many young freelancers view their current work style as a means of accumulating skills and building experience, with the goal of eventually transitioning to a more stable institutional occupation or becoming independent. As a result, they are proactive in pursuing self-directed learning and enrolling in specialised courses to acquire new skills. For example, R-6, who is enrolled in a doctoral programme, represents the elite tier of high-skilled freelancers who are institutionally integrated as advisors to government organisations and thus enjoy a more stable income. He views freelance work as part of his career development but aims to transition to a research position in the future, indicating a desire to keep freelance work secondary. On the other hand, there are also voices calling for a return to institutionalised employment due to concerns that non-institutionalised work experience is not sufficiently recognised in resumes (R-3). Particularly among part-time freelancers, there is a strong tendency to prioritise securing full-time employment in the long term. This tendency to return to formal employment is driven by structural constraints such as the scarcity of freelance projects and low pay in Thailand. As a result, some freelancers seek higher-paying, more stable projects and prefer to work with overseas clients (R-5). While overseas markets offer relatively competitive pay, language and payment system barriers also exist, highlighting the complexity of career choices.

5.6.4.2 Desire for Transition to Institutional Employment and Barriers

Some participants stated that while their current work arrangements were self-selected, their ideal future career would be institutional employment at a government agency or educational institution. R-1 stated their intention to leverage their current experience to obtain a formal teaching licence, with the aim of transitioning into full-time online teaching or establishing their own language school, using platform-based work as a stepping stone for long-term career development. R-2 and R-8 are working as research assistants to accumulate knowledge and learn project management skills, with the goal of securing full-time research positions. However, such institutional transitions require access to structural resources, making their feasibility highly dependent on an individual's social and economic background. Notably, all respondents held at least a bachelor's degree, qualifying them as high-skilled gig workers. This suggests that they possess both the motivation and capacity to move within formal labour market structures, provided the necessary institutional pathways are accessible.

5.6.4.3 Specialisation and Independent Careers for Freelancers

Some freelancers regard their current employment status as a viable long-term career path and express aspirations to become specialists by broadening their client base and further developing their skill sets. The career prospects of young freelancers are not uniform, and a variety of ideas emerge that freely move between the inside and outside of the system. Among those engaged in the education services sector, there is a strong belief in the long-term sustainability of their current roles. This confidence is grounded in the perception that parents continue to prioritise their children's education even during periods of economic downturn (R-1). On the other hand, there is also a strategic approach of starting with platform-based work while aiming for greater independence by developing one's own website or brand in the future (R-4, R-9). Some individuals find fulfilment in multiple side jobs while maintaining a part-time position at a university within the institutional framework, creating a hybrid career path that combines institutional stability with autonomous professional identity (R-4). Additionally, efforts to support family-run accounting businesses while pursuing creative professions such as interior design symbolise the construction of an independent professional identity not reliant on institutional frameworks (R-7). In this way, a recurring pattern emerges in which individuals pursue diverse career paths while maintaining a balance between autonomy and flexibility on the periphery of existing institutional structures, without becoming fully integrated into them.

5.7 Discussion

This chapter examines the employment experiences of young high-skilled gig workers based in Bangkok, Thailand, offering a multifaceted analysis of emerging forms of gig work in the Global South, particularly within the Southeast Asian context. Drawing on institutional, lifestyle, and occupational perspectives, the findings yield critical insights into the region's structural conditions and contribute to addressing notable gaps in the existing literature on youth and gig employment.

Most interviewees emphasised flexibility and autonomy as their motives for choosing crowd work or online freelancing. While this reflects the superficial essence of gig work, it was often a result of structural conditions such as family responsibilities, incompatibility with regular employment, and barriers to accessing certain occupations. These factors indicate that crowd work and online freelancing function as countermeasures to institutional exclusion and the rigidity of the regular employment market. At the same time, this reinforces the empirical evidence of the ambivalence of platform work, where freedom and constraints coexist in the workplace (Rosenbohm & Hoose, 2022; Wu et al., 2022).

What was notable among gig workers in Bangkok, Thailand, was their experience-driven career development, in which they rebuilt their expertise through practice without relying on institutional qualifications or employment frameworks. For example, freelance lecturers refined their skills through trial and error in response to the reactions of their students and parents, regardless of whether they had certificates, and eventually developed their own curricula. In addition, one respondent combined their experience in education with part-time graphic design work to form a career that utilised multiple skills across different fields (R-4). As Schwartz (2018) points out, this means that the formation of unique identities through the autonomous development of skills by crowd workers can also be seen in the context of Southeast Asia. Meanwhile, this point is logically connected to the current situation in which educational institutions in Southeast Asia are unable to systematically provide digital skills and practical skills (Puriwat & Tripopsakul, 2020), highlighting the importance of career development outside of institutional frameworks.

Furthermore, this study found that the apparent benefits of spatial autonomy were offset by a trade-off with social isolation. These factors appear to influence feelings of loneliness and the maintenance of motivation, indicating that platform work may be experiencing an erosion of its organisational cohesion as a result of the geographical dispersal of the workforce (Uchiyama et al., 2024). This can also be described as the thinning of social capital accompanying the ongoing remote work and freelancing trends across Southeast Asia, and it is a concrete manifestation of the lack of social embeddedness in platform work (Tubaro, 2021). Within platform capitalism, youths face the risk of serious problems directly linked to a lack of professional evaluation and growth opportunities. Thus, it will be an important challenge for them to accumulate social capital while maintaining connections within digital platforms (Tóth et al., 2022). There was a certain degree of divergence and fluidity in terms of long-term career awareness. The analysis shows that there was a clear division between those who use gig work as a temporary stepping stone to institutional employment and those who strategically pursue freelance gigs as a long-term career. As Zander and Garnett (2021) point out, this strategy of building a better career in a multi-track, non-linear manner across institutional boundaries aligns with the career fluidity unique to youths in Southeast Asian urban areas.

In terms of institutional design, Southeast Asian countries, including Thailand, lack mature institutional responses to the expansion of online labour, including crowd work. This is due to the use of a dichotomy between "employee" and "independent contractor" in the classification of gig work employment in Southeast Asia, which lacks flexibility in defining the boundaries between the two. This has often been highlighted as an issue in the ride-hailing and food delivery sectors, but high-end gig workers with university degrees or higher are also facing the same situation. They have limited access to social security systems and are required to pay for insurance out of their own pockets. This system is particularly burdensome for those in the early stages of their careers. In addition, concerns about unstable remuneration, late payments, and opaque evaluation systems on platforms were also commonly expressed. This situation is not unique to Thailand but represents a structural challenge across Southeast Asia. To ensure the sustainability of platform work and the participation of youths, a fundamental redesign of the institutional framework surrounding high-skilled gig work is essential. Based on the conditions, the study strategically provides four suggestions for youths' gig employment.

First, it is necessary to introduce minimum wage standards for high-skilled gig workers and establish a payment guarantee system from service providers. While low-skilled gig work is overly dependent on wage levels on the platform, high-skilled gig work has wage levels that vary to some extent depending on skills. However, its continuity is unstable, and clarifying minimum standards is extremely important from the perspective of fair evaluation of professional skills and livelihood security for those engaged in professional work. This could be complemented by establishing a backup system to help youth gig workers with little experience stabilise their businesses.

Second, the inclusion of high-skilled gig workers in social security systems such as employment insurance and pensions should be institutionally guaranteed. The reality that freelancers with a certain level of income, similar to full-time workers, are outside the system and therefore face future uncertainty has come to light. Singapore's Platform Workers Bill, which came into effect in January 2025, will serve as a benchmark for the region in terms of expanding access to social insurance systems. The health insurance and pension systems covered by this bill will be key to supporting the sustainability of their careers and trust in the system.

Third, it is essential to expand practical skills education tailored to rural areas and low-income groups to address the digital skills divide caused by regional and income disparities. However, empirical research shows that employment opportunities for freelancers and crowd workers are concentrated in urban areas, and that opportunities to acquire marketable skills are unevenly distributed across regions and social classes. Therefore, the regional redistribution of skills education is key to the democratisation of freelance and crowd work.

Fourth, in freelance and crowd work, which tends to rely on individual contracts, it is essential to foster collective bargaining power through professional associations and collaboration between platforms. As Uchiyama and Furuoka (2025) point out, while some parts of Europe and the United States are making progress in improving the status of workers through strikes and demonstrations, in Southeast Asia, the lack of institutional support and the weakness of workers' bargaining power remain prominent. Particularly in the gig sector of this region, regardless of skill level, power imbalances with platforms and institutional deficiencies leave little room for expressing opinions or improving working conditions. There is also a strong tendency to passively rely on government decisions, and even among high-end workers, there is little movement toward organisation, as seen in food delivery services, with information asymmetry and a lack of negotiation tools making working conditions vulnerable.

Therefore, the formation of networks outside of platforms and the building of bargaining power through industry associations are important institutional foundations for restoring workers' self-determination and voice.

5.8 Conclusion

This chapter qualitatively examines the acceptance and experiences of young, highly skilled crowd workers and online freelance gig workers residing in Bangkok, Thailand. It particularly reveals that these workers have chosen to engage in labour forms mediated by digital platforms and social media under structural constraints such as exclusion or incompatibility with institutional employment frameworks, family responsibilities, and disparities in access to urban resources. Many participants had developed their expertise through experiential learning and trial and error, without relying on traditional institutional qualifications or employment systems. This process of reflexive specialisation offers insights into existing discussions on gig work for youths, serving as a significant career development pathway that compensates for the mismatch between institutional education and digital skill demands in Southeast Asia. On the other hand, the characteristics of high-end gig work, such as spatial autonomy and flexibility, also encompass negative aspects such as social isolation and psychological exhaustion, clearly demonstrating how the concept of freedom in gig work is inseparable from structural constraints. Furthermore, this study revealed a divergence in career awareness between those who view gig work as a long-term professional occupation and those who aspire to transition to institutional employment. This non-linear and fluid career development suggests a new phase of labour that cannot be fully captured by the traditional framework centred on employment stability. This chapter contributes to youth and employment studies by empirically clarifying the social significance and challenges of young, highly skilled platform workers through a case example from Bangkok, thereby illuminating new horizons for career development under platform capitalism and presenting the complex interplay of work, learning, and identity formation outside of institutional frameworks.

Appendix: Percentage of Online Labour Demand in SEA

Country	Clerical and data entry	Creative and multimedia	Professional services	Sales and marketing support	Software dev. and tech.	Writing and translation
Cambodia	10.5	18.6	2.9	10.6	40.8	16.6
Indonesia	13.3	20.1	3.1	10.2	41.4	11.8
Laos	6.5	13.6	4.5	5.1	58.7	11.5
Malaysia	12.4	17.9	2.5	8.7	44.4	14.1
Myanmar	11.7	20.7	5.5	8.1	38.3	15.8
Philippines	28.2	15.1	4.2	11.5	24.4	16.5
Singapore	16.3	20.2	3.2	10.9	35	14.4
Thailand	14.7	18	2.8	11	36.6	16.9
Vietnam	11.6	16.3	2.7	8.9	33.4	27.1

Source: OLI (2020), Stephany et al. (2021)

References

Ali, M., Hussain, H. I., Nisar, Q. A., Yenwen, C., Hamid, B. A., & Mahomed, Z. (2023). Developing a social security micro-takaful model for the gig economy workforce. *Cuadernos de Economía, 46*(130), 73–86.

Bayudan-Dacuycuy, C., & Kryz Baje, L. (2021). *Decent work in crowdwork: Gendered takeaways from an online survey in the Philippines*.

Bayudan-Dacuycuy, C., Orbeta, A. C., Serafica, R. B., & Baje, L. K. C. (2020). *Online work in the Philippines: Some lessons in the Asian context*.

Berg, J. (2015). Income security in the on-demand economy: Findings and policy lessons from a survey of crowdworkers. *Comparative Labour Law & Policy Journal, 37*, 543–576.

Blohm, I., Zogaj, S., Bretschneider, U., & Leimeister, J. M. (2018). How to manage crowdsourcing platforms effectively? *California Management Review, 60*, 122–149. https://doi.org/10.1177/0008125617738255

Braun, V., & Clarke, V. (2006). Using thematic analysis in psychology. *Qualitative Research in Psychology, 3*(2), 77–101. https://doi.org/10.1191/1478088706qp063oa

Brewer, R., Morris, M. R., & Piper, A. M. (2016). "Why would anybody do this?" Understanding older adults' motivations and challenges in crowd work. In *Proceedings of the 2016 CHI conference on human factors in computing systems*.

Brynjolfsson, E., & McAfee, A. (2014). *The second machine age: Work, progress, and prosperity in a time of brilliant technologies*. W.W. Norton & Company.

Cao, T. M., & Pham, A. N. (2024). Generation differences in the gig economy in Vietnam. *Ho Chi Minh City Open University Journal of Science - Economics Business Administration, 14*(3), 59–76.

De Stefano, V. (2016). The rise of the "just-in-time workforce": On-demand work, crowdwork, and labour protection in the "gig economy". *Comparative Labour Law Policy Journal, 37*(3), 461–471.

Deng, X. N., & Joshi, K. D. (2016). Why individuals participate in micro-task crowdsourcing work environment: Revealing crowdworkers' perceptions. *Journal of the Association for Information Systems, 17*(10), 3–673.

Donini, A., Forlivesi, M., Rota, A., & Tullini, P. (2017). Towards collective protections for crowdworkers: Italy, Spain and France in the EU context. *Transfer: European Review of Labour and Research, 23*(2), 207–223.

Donovan, S. A., Bradley, D. H., & Shimabukuro, J. O. (2016). *What does the gig economy mean for workers?*

Duggan, J., Sherman, U., Carbery, R., & McDonnell, A. (2020). Algorithmic management and app-work in the gig economy: A research agenda for employment relations and HRM. *Human Resource Management Journal, 30*(1), 114–132. https://doi.org/10.1111/1748-8583.12258

Durward, D., Blohm, I., & Leimeister, J. M. (2016). Crowd work. *Business & Information Systems Engineering, 58*, 281–286.

Durward, D., Blohm, I., & Leimeister, J. M. (2020). The nature of crowd work and its effects on individuals' work perception. *Journal of Management Information Systems, 37*(1), 66–95. https://doi.org/10.1080/07421222.2019.1705506

Estellés-Arolas, E., Navarro-Giner, R., & González-Ladrón-de-Guevara, F. (2015). Crowdsourcing fundamentals: Definition and typology. *Advances in Crowdsourcing*, 33–48.

Galpaya, H., & Senanayake, L. (2018). Online freelancing: Potential for digital gig work in India, Sri Lanka and Myanmar. In *22nd Biennial Conference of the International Telecommunications Society (ITS): "Beyond the boundaries: Challenges for business, policy and society", Seoul, Korea, 24th–27th June, 2018*. International Telecommunications Society (ITS).

Gandini, A. (2021). Digital labour: An empty signifier? *Media, Culture & Society, 43*(2), 369–380.

Gerber, C., & Krzywdzinski, M. (2019). Brave new digital work? New forms of performance control in crowdwork. In *Work and labour in the digital age* (Vol. 33, pp. 121–143). Emerald Publishing.

Gol, E. S., Stein, M.-K., & Avital, M. (2019). Crowdwork platform governance toward organisational value creation. *The Journal of Strategic Information Systems, 28*(2), 175–195.

Graham, M., Hjorth, I., & Lehdonvirta, V. (2017). Digital labour and development: Impacts of global digital labour platforms and the gig economy on worker livelihoods. *Transfer: European Review of Labour and Research, 23*(2), 135–162. https://doi.org/10.1177/1024258916687250

Graham, M., Lehdonvirta, V., Wood, A., Barnard, H., & Hjorth, I. (2018). Could online gig work drive development in lower-income countries? In *Future of work in the global south.*

Howcroft, D., & Bergvall-Kåreborn, B. (2018). A typology of crowdwork platforms. *Work, Employment and Society, 33*(1), 21–38. https://doi.org/10.1177/0950017018760136

Intaratat, K. (2021). Digital skills scenario of the workforce to promote the digital economy in Thailand under & post-COVID-19 pandemic. *International Journal of Research and Innovation in Social Science, 10*, 116–127.

ITU. (2024). *Measuring digital development—Facts and Figures 2024.* https://www.itu.int/hub/publication/d-ind-ict_mdd-2024-4/

Jäger, G., Zilian, L. S., Hofer, C., & Füllsack, M. (2019). Crowdworking: Working with or against the crowd? *Journal of Economic Interaction and Coordination, 14*, 761–788.

Jiwasiddi, A., Schlagwein, D., Cahalane, M., Cecez-Kecmanovic, D., Leong, C., & Ractham, P. (2024). Digital nomadism as a new part of the visitor economy: The case of the "digital nomad capital" Chiang Mai, Thailand. *Information Systems Journal, 34*, 1493–1535.

Kazai, G., Kamps, J., & Milic-Frayling, N. (2011). Worker types and personality traits in crowdsourcing relevance labels. In *Proceedings of the 20th ACM International Conference on Information and Knowledge Management.*

Kittur, A., Nickerson, J. V., Bernstein, M., Gerber, E., Shaw, A., Zimmerman, J., …, Horton, J. (2013). The future of crowd work. In *Proceedings of the 2013 conference on computer-supported cooperative work, San Antonio, Texas, USA*. https://doi.org/10.1145/2441776.2441923

Layraman, T., & Sirarujanon, N. (2024). Job security on freelance employees' perception of online delivery, Chiang Mai, Thailand. *NIDA Development Journal, 60*(1–2), 1–18.

Leung, W.-F., & Cossu, A. (2019). Digital entrepreneurship in Taiwan and Thailand: Embracing precarity as a personal response to political and economic change. *International Journal of Cultural Studies, 22*(2), 264–280.

Lopez-Sintas, J., Lamberti, G., & Sukphan, J. (2020). The social structuring of the digital gap in a developing country. The impact of computer and internet access opportunities on internet use in Thailand. *Technology in Society, 63*, 101433.

Margaryan, A. (2019). Workplace learning in crowdwork: Comparing microworkers' and online freelancers' practices. *Journal of Workplace Learning, 31*(4), 250–273.

Newlands, G., & Lutz, C. (2021). Crowdwork and the mobile underclass: Barriers to participation in India and the United States. *New Media & Society, 23*(6), 1341–1361.

Pfeiffer, S., & Kawalec, S. (2020). Justice expectations in crowd and platform-mediated work. The Economic and Labour Relations Review, 31(4), 483–501. doi:10.1177/1035304620959750

Prassl, J., & Risak, M. E. (2016). Uber, TaskRabbit, & Co: Platforms as employers? Rethinking the legal analysis of crowdwork. *Comparative Labour Law and Policy Journal, 37*, 604–619.

Prassl, J., & Risak, M. (2017). The legal protection of crowdworkers: Four avenues for workers' rights in the virtual realm. In P. Meil & V. Kirov (Eds.), *Policy implications of virtual work* (pp. 273–295). Springer. https://doi.org/10.1007/978-3-319-52057-5_11

Puriwat, W., & Tripopsakul, S. (2020). Preparing for Industry 4.0--Will youths have enough essential skills? Evidence from Thailand. *International Journal of Instruction, 13*(3), 89–104.

Rosenbohm, S., & Hoose, F. (2022). Ambivalences of platform work: The gig economy in Germany. In *The Routledge handbook of the gig economy* (pp. 324–336). Routledge.

Sattayathamrongthian, M., & Vanpetch, Y. (2023). *A qualitative examination of Thai freelancers' business model enhancement through the integration of social and human capital in the global market*. E3S Web of Conferences.

Schmidt, F. (2017). *Digital labour markets in the platform economy: Mapping the political challenges of crowd work and gig work* (9783958617452). http://library.fes.de/pdf-files/wiso/13164.pdf.

Schwartz, D. (2018). Embedded in the crowd: Creative freelancers, crowdsourced work, and occupational community. *Work and Occupations, 45*(3), 247–282.

Serafica, R. B., & Oren, Q. C. A. (2022). *Exploring policies and initiatives for online workers in the Philippines*.

Soriano, C. R. R. (2021). Digital labour in the Philippines: Emerging forms of brokerage. *Media International Australia, 179*(1), 23–37.

Soriano, C. R., Cabalquinto, E. C., & Panaligan, J. H. (2021). Performing "digital labour bayanihan": Strategies of influence and survival in the platform economy. *Sociologias, 23*, 84–111.

Stephany, F., Kässi, O., Rani, U., & Lehdonvirta, V. (2021). Online Labour Index 2020: New ways to measure the world's remote freelancing market. *Big Data & Society, 8*(2). https://doi.org/10.1177/20539517211043240

Stewart, A., & Stanford, J. (2017). Regulating work in the gig economy: What are the options? *Economic and Labour Relations Review, 28*(3), 420–437. https://doi.org/10.1177/1035304617722461

Sutassanamarlee, D., Chandam, C., Suttisome, P., Lek-Uthai, A., & Jamme, H.-T. (2024). *Narrowing the gender divide: Thailand's platform economy and digital work*.

Tanoamchard, W., & Ceienwattanasook, K. (2024). The future of work and the impact of automation on jobs in the gig economy in Thailand: A review of literature. *Scholar: Human Sciences, 16*(1), 77–88.

Tashakkori, A., & Teddlie, C. (2010). *SAGE handbook of mixed methods in social & behavioural research* (2nd ed.). https://doi.org/10.4135/9781506335193

Thompson, B. Y. (2019). The digital nomad lifestyle: (Remote) work/leisure balance, privilege, and constructed community. *International Journal of the Sociology of Leisure, 2*(1), 27–42.

Tóth, Z., Nemkova, E., Hizsák, G., & Naudé, P. (2022). Social capital creation on professional sharing economy platforms: The problems of rating dependency and the non-transferability of social capital. *Journal of Business Research, 144*, 450–460. https://doi.org/10.1016/j.jbusres.2022.01.090

Tubaro, P. (2021). Disembedded or deeply embedded? A multi-level network analysis of online labour platforms. *Sociology, 55*(5), 927–944.

Uchiyama, Y., Furuoka, F., & Akhir, M. N. M. (2022). Gig workers, social protection and labour market inequality: Lessons from Malaysia. *Jurnal Ekonomi Malaysia, 56*(3), 165–184.

Uchiyama, Y., Furuoka, F., & Omar, S. A. (2024). The rise and contestation of platform capitalism: Evidence from two food delivery blackouts in Malaysia. *Journal of Industrial Relations*. https://doi.org/10.1177/00221856241294107

Uchiyama, Y., Omar, S. A., Furuoka, F., Nikitina, L., Pazim, K. H., & Lim, B. (2025). Malaysian university students' understanding and perceptions of the gig economy. *Institutions and Economies, 17*(2), 121–142.

Uchiyama, Y., & Furuoka, F. (2025). Uberisation and Resistance to Online Food Delivery Gig Work in Asia: Lessons from Malaysia. Journal of Contemporary Asia, 1–18. https://doi.org/10.1080/00472336.2024.2449081

Vallas, S., & Schor, J. B. (2020). What do platforms do? Understanding the gig economy. *Annual Review of Sociology, 46*(1), 273–294.

Wood, A. J., Lehdonvirta, V., & Graham, M. (2018). Workers of the Internet unite? Online freelancer organisation among remote gig economy workers in six Asian and African countries. *New Technology, Work and Employment, 33*(2), 95–112.

Wood, A. J., Graham, M., Lehdonvirta, V., & Hjorth, I. (2019). Good gig, bad gig: Autonomy and algorithmic control in the global gig economy. *Work Employment and Society, 33*(1), 56–75. https://doi.org/10.1177/0950017018785616

Woodcock, J., & Graham, M. (2019). *The gig economy. A critical introduction*. Polity.

Wu, P. F., Zheng, R., Zhao, Y., & Li, Y. (2022). Happy riders are all alike? Ambivalent subjective experience and mental well-being of food-delivery platform workers in China. *New Technology, Work and Employment, 37*(3), 425–444.

Zander, K. K., & Garnett, S. T. (2021). Trade-offs in destination choices among the urban populations in three Southeast Asian countries. *Population, Space and Place, 27*(8), e2460.

Chapter 6
On-Demand App Gig Work for Youth: A Case in Malaysia

This chapter is the fourth analytical chapter. It examines the employment realities of young on-demand app-based gig workers in Malaysia. It situates e-hailing and food delivery work within the country's expanding platform economy and shifting youth employment landscape. The chapter proceeds to review relevant literature on youth labour and platform work in Southeast Asia and outlines key features of the platform labour market and regulatory frameworks in the region. It then presents the methodology, which draws on semi-structured interviews with 85 young gig workers across 11 Malaysian states, and explains the sampling criteria, interview design, and thematic analysis. A short profile of respondents is provided. The findings reveal how young app-based workers navigate precarious conditions by flexibly configuring their work between employment and self-employment amid regulatory ambiguity, blurred labour status, and growing collective awareness. The chapter interprets these dynamics within broader institutional constraints and concludes by emphasising the need for inclusive and adaptive youth employment governance.

6.1 Introduction

Rapid digitisation, including the introduction of smartphones and technological developments, has encouraged the rise of "online app-based gig workers" who use online platforms to replace and complement their work on a task basis (Donovan et al., 2016; Kassi & Lehdonvirta, 2018). They are moving away from traditional full-time, permanent employment, and many tend to earn multiple incomes from a variety of freelance and temporary jobs (UNCTAD, 2020). Transport platforms, such as ride-hailing and courier services, play an integral role in society as they are closely connected to people's lives due to their local nature (Kalleberg & Dunn, 2016). It may be inevitable that the taxi and courier industries, which have traditionally functioned as part of the social infrastructure, would gain popularity as major platform actors in the wave of digitalisation.

Y. Uchiyama, F. Furuoka, *Youth and Employment*,
https://doi.org/10.1007/978-981-95-3257-5_6

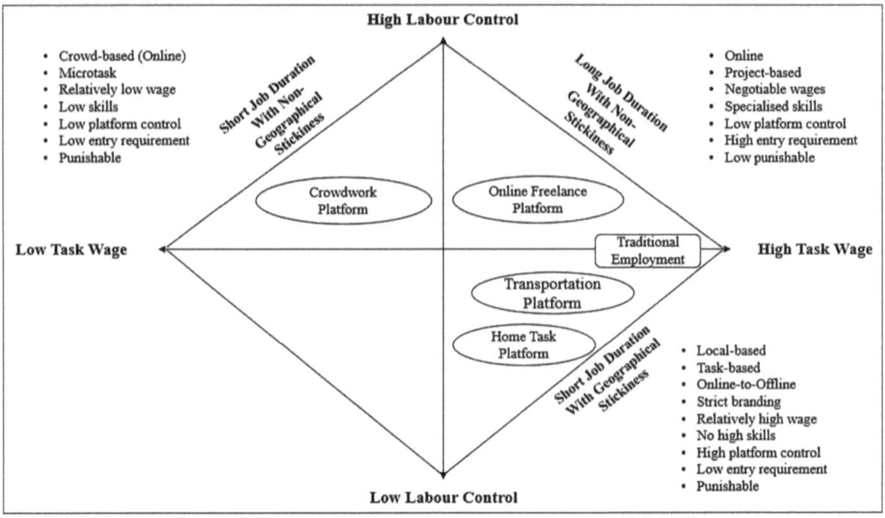

Fig. 6.1 Gig labour job scale types. Source: Authors

As highlighted by Woodcock (2021), the various innovations resulting from the rise of platform technology (e.g. booking systems, pre-fixed fees, safety) have led to a renewal of the resistance that prevailed in traditional markets. As a result, platforms have succeeded in the great invention of effectively mediating between customers, drivers, restaurants and riders (Kost et al., 2020; Stewart & Stanford, 2017). As the essence of the gig economy lies in the employment patterns of workers, this fundamental change in the traditional labour market ecosystem has brought about profound changes in the way people work (Adams et al., 2018; Uchiyama et al., 2023; Vallas, 2019). As seen in Fig. 6.1, the scale of work in gig work is classified in terms of four dimensions: labour domination, task wage, duration and geographical dependence (De Groen et al., 2016; Jarrahi et al., 2020; Kalleberg & Dunn, 2016).

On-demand app-based gig work, represented by transport platforms, differs from crowd work platforms and online freelance platforms in terms of geographical dependence. Entry into task-based services based on online-to-offline (O2O) services does not require high skills, as only background checks and competency tests are required. Transport platforms are highly branded, and drivers and riders are signposted to companies (Kalleberg & Dunn, 2016). For instance, they carry logos and advertisements on their vehicles and wear platform uniforms to work. In other words, they are remotely and highly controlled as billboards on the platform. Whilst it is difficult to calculate an accurate average income estimate for gig workers who work in a variety of ways, they may earn more than the minimum wage due to performance-based income and the tendency to operate services in major cities. As one example, Uber claims that the median hourly wage for Uber drivers in New York is $30.35 per hour, and the median annual income is $90,766 (Tran & Sokas, 2017).

Table 6.1 Number and percentage of people employed by employment status, Q1 2020-Q4 2024 in Malaysia

Year	Quarter	Total (000s)	Employer	Employee	Own account worker	Unpaid family worker
2020	I	15243.5	585.1 (3.8%)	11378.2 (74.6%)	2658.8 (17.4%)	621.4 (4.1%)
	II	14883.7	499.6 (3.4%)	11270.4 (75.7%)	2516.3 (16.9%)	597.4 (4.0%)
	III	15095.6	451.4 (3.0%)	11526.7 (76.4%)	2533.3 (16.8%)	584.3 (3.9%)
	IV	15161.6	485.1 (3.2%)	11703.8 (77.2%)	2439.5 (16.1%)	533.3 (3.5%)
2021	I	15236.5	491.4 (3.2%)	11677.1 (76.6%)	2534.0 (16.6%)	534.1 (3.5%)
	II	15207.3	460.0 (3.0%)	11610.5 (76.3%)	2611.8 (17.2%)	525.0 (3.5%)
	III	15274.8	476.8 (3.1%)	11692.7 (76.5%)	2581.5 (16.9%)	523.8 (3.4%)
	IV	15440.7	486.9 (3.2%)	11772.3 (76.2%)	2651.5 (17.2%)	529.9 (3.4%)
2022	I	15574.9	529.1 (3.4%)	11822.1 (75.9%)	2708.4 (17.4%)	515.3 (3.3%)
	II	15701.2	558.5 (3.6%)	11873.6 (75.6%)	2772.9 (17.7%)	496.3 (3.2%)
	III	15831.1	568.7 (3.6%)	11934.4 (75.4%)	2836.1 (17.9%)	491.8 (3.1%)
	IV	15941.7	571.8 (3.6%)	12001.9 (75.3%)	2878.2 (18.0%)	489.3 (3.1%)
2023	I	16,062	581.7 (3.6%)	12056.5 (75.1%)	2935.9 (18.3%)	487.9 (3.0%)
	II	16146.1	585.2 (3.6%)	12102.0 (75.0%)	2968.6 (18.4%)	490.3 (3.0%)
	III	16250.9	586.1 (3.6%)	12190.1 (75.0%)	2982.8 (18.4%)	491.9 (3.0%)
	IV	16346.7	588.6 (3.6%)	12265.5 (75.0%)	2998.9 (18.3%)	493.7 (3.0%)
2024	I	16401.2	596.8 (3.6%)	12299.7 (75.0%)	3015.8 (18.4%)	488.9 (3.0%)
	II	16591.2	597.0 (3.6%)	12432.3 (74.9%)	3063.8 (18.5%)	498.0 (3.0%)
	III	16249.9	599.9 (3.6%)	12524.1 (74.9%)	3095.8 (18.5%)	497.3 (3.0%)
	IV	16306.2	602.4 (3.6%)	12568.3 (74.8%)	3123.5 (18.6%)	494.5 (3.0%)

Source: Department of Statistics Malaysia (2025a)

In Malaysia, gig workers working in e-hailing and online food delivery platforms are recognised and representative of gig work in the country. Gig work has traditionally opened doors to a wide range of people due to its flexible and meritocratic nature (Malay Mail, 2023). In Malaysia, the gig economy labour market is expanding rapidly, particularly in the areas of e-hailing and p-hailing (motorbike-based delivery services), where young people are entering the sector. According to Dr. Mohammed Azman, CEO of SOCSO, approximately 600,000 people are engaged in e-hailing and p-hailing nationwide (Malay Mail, 2023). This growth is closely linked to labour market trends, particularly among young people, with around 20% of those who passed the Sijil Pelajaran Malaysia (SPM) (Secondary School Completion Examination) expressing interest in gig work after graduation, particularly through on-demand applications such as p-hailing and e-hailing. On-demand app-based jobs such as p-hailing and e-hailing are growing in popularity (The Star, 2023). The number and percentage of people employed by work status in Malaysia from Q1 2020 to Q4 2024 are shown in Table 6.1 (Department of Statistics Malaysia, 2025a).

In addition, approximately 70 per cent of SPM graduates in 2021 aspire to careers as independent contractors or entrepreneurs rather than in traditional corporate employment (Department of Statistics Malaysia, 2022; Yee, 2022). This trend reflects the changing attitudes of young people in the labour market, particularly the attraction of gig work as a flexible income without higher education (Free Malaysia Today, 2023). To support the entry of these young people into the gig work market, the Government has reduced the minimum age for p-hailing from 21 to 18 (The Star, 2023), facilitating greater employment opportunities. The relatively low initial entry costs of e-hailing and p-hailing, and the fact that young people can start as soon as they have a driving licence, smartphone and a Malaysian bank account, are also factors that encourage young people to enter the market (Free Malaysia Today, 2023). A survey conducted by Statistics Malaysia of 6657 people engaged in vehicle dispatch services between March and December 2022 found that 97.71% of p-hailing drivers were aged between 15 and 30, indicating that gig work is supported by the youth (Free Malaysia Today, 2023).

However, previous research has not focused on how young people perceive the working environment and social security in on-demand app gig work employment. Although the entry of young people into on-demand app gig work is increasing rapidly in emerging economies such as Malaysia and in the Global South, there is a lack of research focusing on the young people who support these labour markets. Research on young gig workers has the potential to provide important policy implications for the development of sustainable and decent working environments.

Research by Uchiyama et al. (2025) shows that Malaysian university students have a limited understanding of gig work and consider it a long-term career option. Accordingly, many of them still tend to prioritise traditional formal employment. In particular, many perceive gig work as "high-skilled freelance work", suggesting insufficient knowledge of on-demand gig work such as e-hailing and p-hailing. This knowledge gap reflects a misalignment between normative values about gig work and differences in perceptions between levels of education and actual work experience. Reasons for this include a lack of social security, unclear labour rights and income insecurity. Concerns about working as a gig worker include the uncertainty of minimum wage guarantees and employment contracts, and these factors undermine the attractiveness of gig work (Stewart & Stanford, 2017). Furthermore, increased competition between platforms tends to compress gig workers' remuneration packages, for which they do not have the right to join labour unions or bargain collectively (Uchiyama et al., 2024). Although the government provides a minimal social insurance scheme through the Social Security Organisation (SOCSO), many gig workers are not actually enrolled in this scheme (Malay Mail, 2023).

Whilst on-demand app gig work is an attractive option for young people, it faces the challenge of lagging institutional governance that supports it, as well as surfacing their vulnerability due to ambiguity in labour regulation and lack of social protection. This remains under-researched as to how young people perceive the precariousness of gig-work employment in the first place, and how they themselves perceive the need for labour regulation and protection. Using Malaysia as a case study, this section aims to identify the work attitudes and perceptions of regulation and social security of young ride-hailing and p-hailing gig workers. Semi-structured interviews were conducted with young people working in the ride-hailing and p-hailing sectors across Malaysia to analyse their motivations for entering gig work, perceptions of the need for regulation and their assessment of the working environment.

The employment patterns of this type of gig worker in Malaysia show similar trends to those in neighbouring Southeast Asian countries or in other parts of Asia. By articulating the perspectives of young gig workers, this paper develops new perspectives and reveals the reality of gig work employment for young people in non-Western countries. On 23 October 2024, a new regulatory framework in the classification of platform workers, including on-demand app gig workers, will come into force within the EU prefectures, and they are entitled to almost the same social security and benefits as employees (European Council, 2024). Southeast Asian countries are also gradually reviewing their regulatory frameworks, such as Singapore, which enacted the Platform Workers Act in January 2025, placing gig workers between employees and independent contractors (Ministry of Manpower, 2024). This study aims to contribute to the global debate on the employment conditions of young on-demand gig workers by exploring the Malaysian case. In addition, in terms of policy implications, this section is expected to contribute to policy recommendations in strengthening platform regulation through a review of labour market policies for young people. As many countries in Southeast Asia have inadequate social security for workers, the findings of this study contribute to the formation of comprehensive informal labour policies.

6.2 Overview of the Gig Economy in Malaysia

The continued stagnation of the manufacturing sector and the rapid growth of digital platforms due to the development of ICT have changed the nature of the structure of the Malaysian economy, particularly from traditional full-time employment to mainstream independent work classified as gig work, a new type of work style (Stewart & Stanford, 2017). According to the Labour Force Statistics Report of the Ministry of Economic Affairs, there were an estimated 3.12 million self-employed people, including gig workers, as of December 2024 (Department of Statistics Malaysia, 2025b). Many traditional occupations have taken on aspects of gig work in Malaysia as various professions have partnered with online platforms and apps; according to Harun et al. (2020), about 216 professions in Malaysia have aspects of gig work (Harun et al., 2020).

Ng et al. (2017) and Uchiyama et al. (2022) identified the following factors as contributing to the increase in gig workers in Malaysia: (1) accelerated industry and job change due to rapid technological progress; (2) changes in employment relationships leading to greater worker independence and job instability; and (3) the impact of the pandemic (Ng et al., 2017; Uchiyama et al., 2022). In the context of this emerging trend, the Malaysian Government has identified the gig economy as an important driver of economic growth and has been working to promote it. As the first national initiative on the gig economy, the Government announced the "Digital

Malaysia" strategy in 2012. The strategy aimed to support the livelihoods of the bottom 40% of income earners through microwork and online freelancing, with 340,000 microworkers contributing RM2.23 billion to the Malaysian economy by 2020 (Asohan, 2012; Fu, 2019; Graham et al., 2017). Subsequently, as part of the 12th Malaysia Plan (2021–2025), the Malaysian Government identified the gig economy as a new source of economic growth to drive GDP growth (Lim, 2021). Former Prime Minister Mahathir Mohamad has also highlighted the importance of the gig economy in this plan in terms of sustainable economic growth. Furthermore, in March 2020, the Central Bank of Malaysia (BNM), the Malaysian Digital Economy Corporation (MDEC) and the United Nations Capital Development Fund (UNCDF) launched the Financial Innovation Gig Economy Challenge in collaboration with APEC Malaysia 2020. The programme aims to promote the economic stability of gig workers and build good relationships with platform operators, which is essential to support flexible working. This initiative was also part of measures to mitigate the damage to the domestic economy caused by the COVID-19 pandemic and to achieve a sustainable economic recovery by supporting businesses in digitalising (Bank Negara Malaysia, 2020). On 5 June 2020, former Prime Minister Muhyiddin Yassin allocated RM75 million under the National Economic Recovery Plan to promote the gig economy and protect the social safety net for workers in the informal sector. This national strategy, developed as the 'Malaysian Digital Economy Blueprint', aims to develop flexible regulations for the gig economy sector so that 40% of the workforce leaves full-time employment and enters the gig economy (Economic Planning Unit, 2021).

On-demand app gig work in Malaysia can mainly be described by the ride-hailing and p-hailing sectors. In Malaysia, ride-hailing is referred to as e-hailing. According to the Ministry of Transport Malaysia, e-hailing services are intermediary operations that book public transport through electronic apps and include e-hailing vehicles and taxis. An e-hailing vehicle is a private vehicle that passengers book via an app and has a capacity of 4–11 persons, including the driver (Ministry of Transport Malaysia, 2023). Thirty-two e-hailing applications were officially licensed and operating in Malaysia as of 6 February 2025. These include Grab, which originated in Malaysia and is the largest tech giant in Southeast Asia, Bolt, an Estonian company with global operations, and AirAsia ride, operated by the airline AirAsia. Furthermore, motorbike food, beverage and goods delivery services are broadly defined as p-hailing (parcel delivery) in Malaysia. Market competitors in Malaysia include GrabFood and Foodpanda, which are developing dominant market presence across Malaysia, while Shoppeefood and airasiafood are also major players in and around Kuala Lumpur (Furuoka et al., 2022; Uchiyama & Furuoka, 2024).

6.3 Challenges of Gig Workers in Malaysia

At first glance, Malaysia's growing on-demand, app-based gig economy not only contributes to the country's economic development but also provides flexible, task-based employment opportunities for diverse worker groups and increased convenience for consumers.

Despite these apparent benefits, numerous challenges have emerged, primarily because work practices and organisational systems within the on-demand gig economy differ markedly from conventional employment structures. From a macro perspective, the tripartite relationship among gig workers, digital platforms, and customers (or, in the context of food delivery services, a four-way relationship including restaurants) is a configuration inadequately captured by the traditional, bilateral employer-employee dynamic presumed by neoliberalism and advanced capitalism (Gandhi et al., 2019; Healy & Pekarek, 2024; Uchiyama et al., 2023). At a micro level, gig workers in Malaysia, similar to those in most other countries, lack clear legal recognition and are treated by platforms as independent contractors rather than employees, thus positioning them as freelancers or workers engaged on a task-by-task basis (Radzi et al., 2022). Consequently, Malaysian gig workers remain excluded from labour protections established under the Employment Act 1955 (Act 265), the Labour Ordinance (Chap. 67, Sabah), and the Labour Ordinance (Chap. 76, Sarawak) (Uchiyama et al., 2022). This exclusion facilitates their enclosure within platform capitalism, allowing profit extraction through commodification and simultaneously increasing their vulnerability by detaching them from wage guarantees and social protections (Uchiyama et al., 2024; Wood & Monahan, 2019). Concurrently, the food delivery and ride-hailing markets in Malaysia exemplify on-demand gig work, characterised by oligopolistic dominance of select platforms, notably Grab, AirAsia Ride, Foodpanda, and ShopeeFood, despite competition from numerous other applications (Uchiyama & Furuoka, 2024). This pattern is observable across most Southeast Asian countries.

Zakaria (2020) highlights government initiatives and their limitations in addressing the complexities surrounding gig worker management in Malaysia. Although the Malaysian government introduced legislative policies targeting gig workers and established support schemes, such as the "Penjana Gig" grant and SOCSO/EPF enrolment programmes, actual participation among self-employed individuals in social security systems remained at only 7% in 2020 (Zakaria, 2020). Furthermore, despite implementing a special withdrawal scheme during the COVID-19 pandemic, long-term support for gig workers remains inadequate. Post-pandemic developments, including a 30% reduction in driver availability and surge pricing increases of up to 400%, exacerbated consumer dissatisfaction, prompting governmental consideration of regulatory interventions in the e-hailing sector. However, industry stakeholders criticised governmental responses as insufficient, resulting in increased tensions. Consequently, the excessive commodification of labour by dominant platforms catalysed collective resistance among urban food delivery riders.

Uchiyama et al. (2024) examined two significant blackouts in Malaysia's food delivery sector as part of a sustained process of gig worker resistance to platform capitalism. These strikes, occurring in 2022 and 2024, provide insights into the evolution of worker mobilisation, their specific demands, and structural shifts within platform capitalism. The 2022 blackout united riders from multiple platforms, including Grab, Foodpanda, and ShopeeFood, calling for enhanced wages, improved bonus schemes, and comprehensive social security coverage. Conversely, the 2024 blackout, predominantly involving Grab riders, targeted specific system improvements. A common element in both strikes was the workers' direct opposition to unilateral reductions in base rates and unfavourable alterations to bonus structures implemented by platform companies.

The 2022 strike, hampered by limited worker solidarity and unity, failed to achieve substantial outcomes beyond short-term bonus adjustments. In contrast, the 2024 blackout fostered an environment conducive to negotiation, offering a five-day grace period that drew governmental and political attention, ultimately leading to policy actions, including the establishment of the Malaysian Gig Economy Commission (SEGiM) under the Prime Minister's Office. Additional outcomes included telecommunication companies initiating data support programmes and governmental deliberations on potential social security policies for gig workers. Nevertheless, platform companies retained their revised base tariffs and refrained from meeting workers' primary demands.

Whilst certain groups, such as selected drivers for AirAsia Ride, currently benefit from employment models providing fixed salaries and social security protections, the sustainability and broader applicability of such models in substantially improving gig workers' conditions remain contingent upon future institutional reforms (Uchiyama et al., 2025).

6.4 Critics of On-Demand App Gig Work for Youths

In recent years, many countries have witnessed a decline in traditional, stable employment and a notable increase in the proportion of young people engaging in gig work. This trend emerges at the intersection of structural labour market transformations and the widespread expansion of higher education, with Australia specifically reporting a significant decline in full-time employment among young people (Churchill et al., 2019). Against this backdrop, platform companies strategically downplay the inherent risks of gig employment through sophisticated marketing campaigns, promoting an idealised image of young, healthy, and physically fit men efficiently navigating urban landscapes (Gregory, 2021).

Significantly, even youths possessing higher education qualifications are increasingly struggling to secure stable employment, thus inevitably resorting to gig work as a temporary income source. While higher education traditionally functioned as a reliable pathway to stable careers, this correlation has weakened considerably in recent years. Indeed, university graduates frequently find employment unrelated to their academic disciplines; paradoxically, individuals with Vocational Education and Training (VET) qualifications sometimes exhibit higher employability in certain sectors (Avis, 2018; Churchill et al., 2019).

Herrmann et al. (2023), in a study involving 1607 gig workers across 14 countries, identified no clear correlation between educational attainment and earnings in gig work, highlighting the limited economic returns of higher education in this domain (Herrmann et al., 2023). Consequently, gig work represents less of a deliberate career choice for young people and more of a manifestation of economic insecurity and a short-term livelihood strategy (Churchill et al., 2019). Despite offering flexibility valued by some workers, gig work frequently exposes young employees to low remuneration, precarious employment conditions, and substandard working environments (MacDonald & Giazitzoglu, 2019; Marrone & Finotto, 2019; Zamponi & Caciagli, 2019). Furthermore, these precarious conditions are exacerbated by broader economic pressures such as escalating higher education costs, insufficient welfare provision, and rising housing prices, which collectively intensify young people's dependence on gig employment (O'Keeffe et al., 2022).

Young gig workers, particularly those engaged in delivery services, operate within extremely hazardous working conditions. A survey conducted in London revealed that many delivery workers frequently encounter road accidents, with 42% experiencing vehicle damage and 10% sustaining injuries (Christie & Ward, 2019). Employers frequently pressure two-wheeled delivery workers, particularly those aged 17–24, to operate in adverse weather conditions, increasing risky behaviours such as driving while fatigued, speeding, and using mobile phones during rides.

Moreover, the precarity inherent in gig work significantly impedes the long-term career development of young individuals. Such employment often traps young people in cycles of poorly remunerated and unstable jobs, limiting skill development opportunities and diminishing prospects for secure employment (Churchill et al., 2019; MacDonald & Giazitzoglu, 2019). In India, food delivery workers encounter compounded vulnerabilities linked to caste discrimination and social exclusion, intensifying their economic and social precarity (Banerjee, 2024). In Sweden, Adermon and Hensvik (2022) evaluated the efficacy of gig work experience in transitioning to conventional employment. They observed limited advantages for young individuals of Swedish descent, though still inferior to traditional employment experience. Conversely, Arab minority youths derived no discernible benefit from gig experience during job searches, indicating that gig work does not effectively serve as a stepping-stone to conventional employment for ethnic minorities (Adermon & Hensvik, 2022).

Additionally, concerns have emerged regarding government policies encouraging unemployed youths into gig work, potentially immobilising them in low-wage, insecure employment and exacerbating overall labour market instability (Goods et al., 2019). Although such policies often privilege formal employment, they impose further economic burdens upon young individuals (O'Keeffe et al., 2022). Consequently, young gig workers increasingly resort to individualistic coping strategies and collectively mobilise for improved conditions, leveraging both digital platforms and face-to-face solidarity to advocate for their interests (Avagianou et al., 2024).

In Malaysia, gig work similarly represents a critical employment sector for youth; however, targeted research remains scarce. While gig employment offers flexible opportunities for university students and unemployed youths (Uchiyama et al., 2022; Yusof et al., 2022), it continues to lack comprehensive labour protections and social security, thereby perpetuating employment instability (Razak et al., 2023). Abd Samad et al. (2023) emphasise the necessity for Malaysian higher education institutions to design educational frameworks accommodating diverse employment forms, both formal and informal. Policy interventions at the governmental level are thus essential to achieving sustainable youth employment outcomes (Abd Samad et al., 2023).

6.5 Methodology

This study aims to contribute to a comprehensive discussion on the employment of young on-demand app-based gig workers through a case study of Malaysia. Specifically, it conducts a qualitative analysis of the overarching employment-related challenges faced by gig workers engaged in e-hailing and online food delivery (OFD) in Malaysia, identifying the issues they encounter and potential solutions. As highlighted in previous research, gig workers are exposed to various risks, including a lack of social protection, precarious working conditions, and vulnerable contractual arrangements.

This study focuses particularly on young gig workers, examining their perspectives on employment, their perceptions of work, and the necessity of social security, thereby exploring the nature and practice of employment from a youth-centred perspective. The study builds upon Uchiyama et al. (2022), which provided a preliminary analysis of the situation of gig workers in Malaysia. Expanding on this foundation, the present research seeks to generalise these findings by incorporating young workers' perspectives and situating them within the broader Malaysian context. Prior to administering the main survey questions, basic demographic data were collected, including gender, age, work duration, daily working hours, monthly income, and employment status (part-time or full-time). Table 6.2 summarises the four key employment challenges faced by gig workers on online platforms, alongside their future concerns and aspirations.

In accordance with qualitative research methodology, this study conducted semi-structured interviews with e-hailing and OFD gig workers across Malaysia (McIntosh & Morse, 2015). The selection criteria for participants were as follows. First, they had to be actively working on either the Grab or FoodPanda platforms in Malaysia. Second, to focus on younger workers, the study restricted participation to individuals aged between 18 and 35. Third, participants were required to have completed the mandatory platform training and to be actively working at the time of the study. Hence, those who had previously worked in the sector or were still

Table 6.2 Key employment challenges for on-demand gig workers

Section	Segment	Details	References
1	Independent contractor or employee	Gig workers' status; the details of the contract; the concordance of needs for gig workers	Erlich (2021), Koutsimpogiorgos et al. (2020), Prassl and Risak (2017), De Stefano and Aloisi (2018), Sprague (2015), Chen et al. (2019), Todolí-Signes (2017), Christie and Ward (2019)
2	Gig worker behaviour	Freedom of working hours and acceptance of gig work requests; setting minimum task performance; restrictions on account creation and working for competitors; prohibition of business expansion; freedom of dissemination of information; labour union; and freedom of discussing the issues with other drivers and deliverers	Hawley (2018), Todolí-Signes (2017), Minter (2017), Vallas and Schor (2020), Bulian (2021), Montgomery and Baglioni (2021), Umer (2021), Uchiyama et al. (2022)
3	Gig worker social protection	Adequate minimum wage; long working hours; appropriate criteria for the minimum wage and working hours; coverage of benefits such as overtime payment, unemployment or sickness benefits and insurance; recognition of minimum labour standards	Donovan et al. (2016), Aranguiz and Bednarowicz (2018), Todolí-Signes (2017), Hawley (2018), Prassl and Risak (2016), Harpur and Blanck (2020)
4	Interaction between gig worker and consumer	Customer behaviour to gig workers; communication with consumers; gig workers' perspective about how much consumers understand their situations; financial incentives such as tips; mutual evaluation	Healy et al. (2017, 2020), Scully-Russ and Torraco (2020), Belanche et al. (2021), Smith et al. (2021), Uchiyama et al. (2023)
5	Future challenges and prospects	Whether gig work can be considered decent work, productive work, a good job with equal pay for work of equal value; the need for actions from the Malaysian government, gig workers, platforms, and customers, and potential contribution	Roy and Shrivastava (2020), Heeks et al. (2021), Blustein et al. (2023), Song et al. (2025), Uchiyama et al. (2025)

Source: Authors

undergoing training were excluded. It is worth noting that globally, OFD riders are predominantly male (Aguilera et al., 2022; Benvegnù & Kampouri, 2021; Useche et al., 2024). While this study does not explicitly control for gender proportions, gender information was recorded as part of the demographic data collection.

As a general rule, interviews were conducted in person at a location convenient for the participants (e.g., in a cafe, at home, or in their vehicles for e-hailing drivers). However, considering participants' circumstances, alternative formats were also employed, including online interviews via Zoom, Microsoft Teams and telephone interviews using WhatsApp's recording function.

Participants were recruited using three primary methods. First, social media and email were utilised to invite participation after explaining the study's objectives. Second, direct approaches were made to Grab drivers and FoodPanda riders during their work shifts to request their participation. Third, a snowball sampling technique was employed, allowing new participants to be recruited through referrals from existing ones (Goodman, 1961).

The interviews were primarily conducted in English by the author. However, for participants with limited proficiency in English, a native Malay-speaking research assistant, who was a master's student at the University of Malaya, provided real-time interpretation. To facilitate a smooth interview process, scripts for interview questions were prepared in both English and Malay. However, to ensure accuracy, interviews in English or Malay without an interpreter were only conducted when real-time interpretation was available, except in cases where WhatsApp's recording function was used. Upon completion of the interview, participants were compensated with either 5 Malaysian Ringgit (MYR) (approx. 1 USD) in cash or an in-app tip.

Initially, the estimated interview duration ranged from 30 to 90 minutes. However, preliminary research indicated that the actual duration was between 30 and 45 minutes. Given that extended interviews can increase participant fatigue and reduce engagement, this study structured the interviews into five thematic sections, each lasting approximately 5–10 minutes. Each section covered a distinct topic, and participants were not required to respond to all sections. This flexible design aimed to minimise respondent burden while maximising the perceived value of the 5MYR incentive.

Participants willing to engage in longer interviews were permitted to cover multiple sections, but the total interview duration was restricted to a maximum of 45 minutes. Regardless of their level of participation, all respondents were required to answer basic demographic questions. Interviews were recorded, and where necessary, key statements were documented through note-taking. The interviews were approved by the Research Ethics Committee, and data were collected between May 2022 and March 2023. For ease of reference, the following coding system was applied to the interview data: Grab drivers were assigned the code I(G)k, and FoodPanda riders were assigned I(F)k, where k represents the participant's unique identifier. The overall data collection process is illustrated in Fig. 6.2.

The semi-structured interview data were analysed using a four-phase thematic analysis approach: (i) transcription of recordings, (ii) open coding, (iii) axial coding, and (iv) selective coding and mapping. This approach is widely adopted in empirical research (Basukie et al., 2020; Cheng et al., 2018). Thematic analysis enables an in-depth examination of a dataset by identifying and exploring patterns within the data (Braun & Clarke, 2006; Douglas et al., 2009). The methodological flexibility of

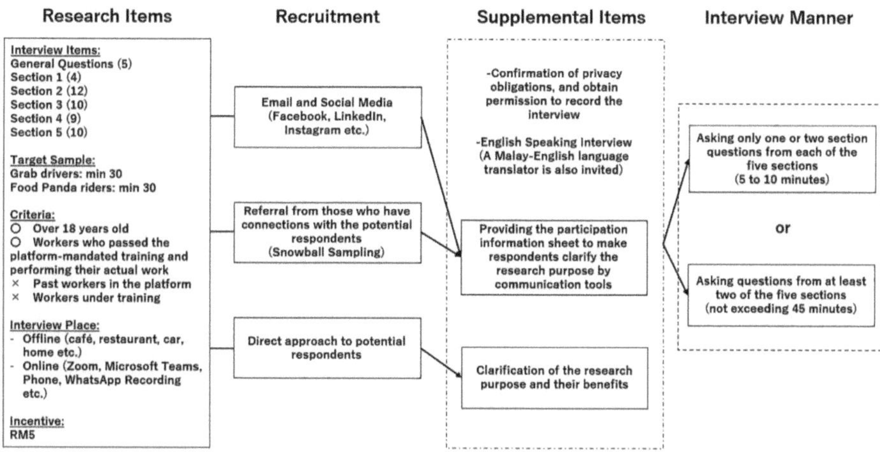

Fig. 6.2 Data collection procedure. Source: Authors

thematic analysis allows for a nuanced and comprehensive interpretation of qualitative data (Braun & Clarke, 2006). This analytical approach ensures that each segment of the data is coded based on its direct relevance to the research question or its potential to offer meaningful insights into the study's objectives. The demographics of the data collected from each gig worker are described in Tables 6.3 and 6.4. For Grab drivers, semi-structured interview data were obtained from a total of 20 respondents in 8 states of Malaysia. For Foodpanda riders, semi-structured interview data were obtained from a total of 35 respondents from a total of 11 states in Malaysia.

6.6 Findings

A thematic analysis of interview data collected from a total of 55 respondents across 11 states in Malaysia identified 22 subthemes, which were subsequently categorised into five main themes, as illustrated in Fig. 6.3. Through listening to the real voices of young gig workers, which existing research has neglected to capture, the study details the ambiguities of work under platform capitalism, algorithmic domination, the lack of social protection systems, the problems of consumer relations, and their fears and hopes for the future.

Table 6.3 Demographics of respondents (grab driver)

Code (G-(k))	Gender	Age	Full time/ part-time	Daily working hours	Working period	Venue	Working area	Monthly earning (RM)
G-1	Male	31	Part-time	7 hours	1.5 years	Online	Melaka	1000
G-2	Male	29	Full-time	8 hours	5 month	Online	Melaka	2000
G-3	Male	35	Full time	8 hours	1 year	Online	Sabah	2000
G-4	Male	29	Full time	7–8 hours	2 years	Offline	Sabah	1500–2000
G-5	Male	30	Full time	12 hours	2 years	Offline	Sabah	2500
G-6	Female	25	Part-time	4 hours	2 years	Online	Selangor	1000
G-7	Male	23	Full time	8 hours	2 years	Online	Sabah	2000
G-8	Male	39	Full-time	7.5 hours	3 months	Online	Sabah	2000
G-9	Male	25	Full-time	12.5 hours	3 years	Offline	Selangor	4000
G-10	Male	24	Full-time	12 hours	2 years	Offline	Sabah	4500
G-11	Male	30	Part-time	8 hours	4 years	Online	Penang	2000
G-12	Male	21	Part-time	14 hours	6 months	Online	Negeri Sembilan	2000
G-13	Male	22	Part-time	6 hours	1 year	Online	Kuala Lumpur	1000
G-14	Male	22	Part-time	4 hours	2 years	Online	Selangor	500–600
G-15	Male	26	Full-time	7.5 hours	4.4 years	Online	Kuala Lumpur	6000
G-16	Male	30	Part-time	5 hours	2 years	Online	Kuala Lumpur	5000
G-17	Male	31	Full-time	12.5 hours	3 years	Offline	Kuala Lumpur	7000–8000
G-18	Male	35	Full-time	8 hours	3 years	Offline	Kelantan	2800
G-19	Male	32	Full-time	4–5 hours	1 month	Offline	Kuala Lumpur	2000
G-20	Male	28	Full-time	10 hours	2 years	Offline	Kuala Lumpur	8000

Source: Author

Table 6.4 Demographics of respondents (FoodPanda rider)

Code (F-(k))	Gender	Age	Full-time/ part-time	Daily working hours	Working period	Venue	Working area	Monthly earning (RM)
F-1	Male	24	Part-time	10 hours	3 years	Offline	Sabah	3000
F-2	Male	31	Full time	10 hours	2 years	Offline	Sabah	1500
F-3	Male	27	Full time	10 hours	2 years	Offline	Sabah	1500
F-4	Male	30	Part-time	10 hours	1 year and 8 months	Offline	Sabah	2000
F-5	Male	23	Full time	12 hours	3 years	Offline	Sabah	1500
F-6	Male	23	Full time	10 hours	3 years	Offline	Sabah	1200–1500
F-7	Male	23	Full time	8 hours	1 year and 6 months	Offline	Sabah	2000
F-8	Male	24	Part-time	12 hours	2 years	Offline	Sabah	2000
F-9	Female	28	Part-time	3-4 hours	1 year	Online	Kuala Lumpur	800–1000
F-10	Male	25	Full time	5–8 hours	2 years	Online	Kuala Lumpur	1200–1800
F-11	Male	18	Full time	12 hours	3 months	Online	Johor	3000
F-12	Male	22	Full time	12 hours	3 years	Online	Johor	3000–4000
F-13	Male	20	Part-time	4 hours	1 month	Online	Johor	250
F-14	Male	19	Full time	12 hours	5 months	Online	Kedah	4000
F-15	Male	20	Part-time	6 hours	1 year and 4 months	Online	Kedah	1000
F-16	Male	19	Part-time	5–7 hours	1 month	Online	Penang	500
F-17	Male	28	Part-time	6 hours	3 years	Online	Penang	1100
F-18	Male	35	Full time	12 hours	1 year	Online	Perak	3000
F-19	Male	32	Part-time	3 hours	2 years	Online	Sarawak	300
F-20	Male	26	Full time	12 hours	1 year	Online	Perak	3000
F-21	Male	29	Full time	12 hours	3 years and 1 month	Online	Perak	2800–3200
F-22	Male	35	Part-time	10 hours	1 year and 6 months	Online	Perak	2500
F-23	Male	22	Part-time	8 hours	5 months	Online	Kedah	1200
F-24	Male	26	Full time	10 hours	1 year	Online	Pahang	4000
F-25	Male	24	Full time	11 hours	11 months	Online	Kedah	6500

(continued)

Table 6.4 (continued)

Code (F-(k))	Gender	Age	Full-time/ part-time	Daily working hours	Working period	Venue	Working area	Monthly earning (RM)
F-26	Male	23	Part-time	6 hours	2 years	Online	Penang	2500
F-27	Male	25	Part-time	12 hours	1 year and 7 months	Online	Kedah	3000
F-28	Male	24	Full time	8 hours	1 year	Online	Melaka	3500
F-29	Male	26	Full-time	12 hours	2 years	Online	Selangor	4000
F-30	Male	23	Part-time	5 hours	4 months	Offline	Kuala Lumpur	700
F-31	Male	23	Part-time	4 hours	4 years	Online	Kuala Lumpur	1000–2000
F-32	Male	21	Part-time	14 hours	1 year	Online	Selangor	1200
F-33	Male	27	Full-time	8 hours	2 years	Online	Kuala Lumpur	4000
F-34	Male	23	Full-time	10 hours	3 years	Online	Selangor	3000
F-35	Male	22	Part-time	6–7 hours	1 year	Offline	Penang	3000

Source: Authors

6.6.1 *Configuring Flexible Work at the Boundary of Employment and Self-Employment*

Many respondents were strongly attracted to the ability to decide for themselves when and where they work in relation to this type of platform gig work. G-26, who lives in Kuala Lumpur, stated that he could earn RM3000–4000 per month even if he only worked for 3–4 hours every day, while G-28 stated that it was ideal in the short term to save money for his marriage between his main job in finance. Flexibility also reduced the strain on their physical and mental health, as many of them stated that the greatest benefit was being able to decide when to work based on their mood and the demands of the day. On the other hand, the limited customer demand outside of urban areas revealed the need to work strategically to meet demand, as G-6s living in Johor stated that they earn more intensively during periods of high tourist traffic.

The reality was that many respondents were engaged full-time beyond the scope of their secondary (gig-like) employment. Several of them regarded it as a fully established and main source of income to support their families as a means of making a stable livelihood (G-8; G-20). In particular, while ride-hailing imposes obligations such as tax reporting, vehicle maintenance and obtaining a PSV licence, many felt that it was freeing in that they could earn an income independently without being employed by a company. G-4 highlighted the benefits of immediacy, noting

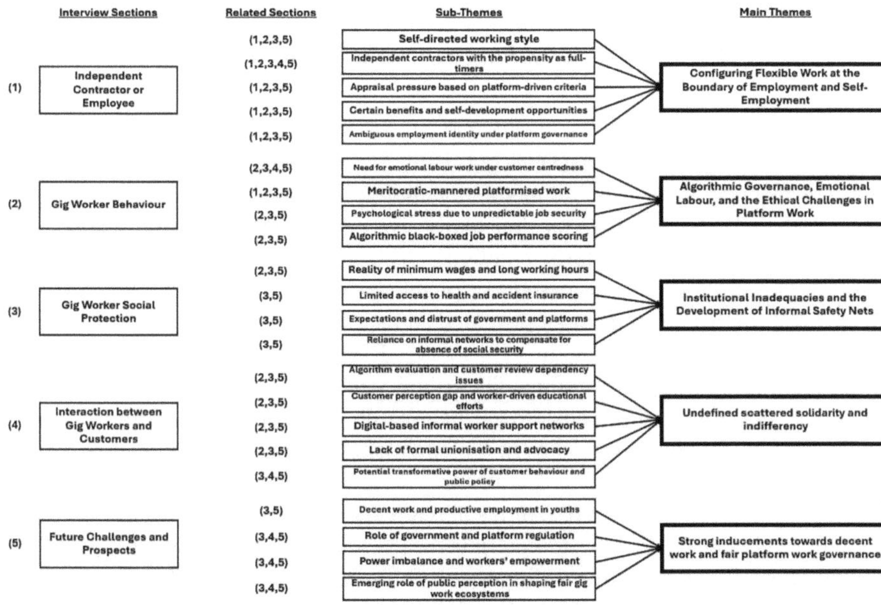

Fig. 6.3 Thematic map. Source: Authors

that in government jobs it takes many years to get a pay rise, whereas drivers can increase their income immediately with effort.

However, the evaluation criteria provided by the platforms put significant pressure on their income directly. Specifically, a five-star rating determines the number of orders for the following week, and some said that once a driver receives a low rating, it is very difficult to regain it (G-9; F-12). Algorithms lacked transparency under the guise of objectivity, and G-2 s stated that there was no place to argue if they were penalised for an unreasonable rating.

Some youth workers perceived a certain degree of personal growth and skill development through platform work, such as improved ability to deal with people and manage risks, and a working attitude in a harsh evaluation environment (G-10; F-19). However, this is left to individual efforts and institutional support, and educational programmes remain lacking. Some defined themselves as ambiguous, neither company employees nor fully self-employed, and were anxious about the absence of rights and protection (G-4; F-25). In particular, the absence of an employment contract and the current situation in which all risks and responsibilities are borne by the self-evolving conflict between freedom and loneliness.

6.6.2 Algorithmic Governance, Emotional Labour, and the Ethical Challenges in Platform Work

The interviews shed light on the complex reality of algorithmic governance as experienced by young Malaysian gig workers. Drivers and riders consistently reported that the system of ratings and rankings imposed by the platform had a direct and immediate impact on their daily lives and income. Several respondents stated that they had to perform emotional labour to maintain high ratings, often beyond what would be considered reasonable professional conduct. For instance, G-11 noted that when a customer provided an incorrect delivery location or made an abrupt change of pick-up location, drivers were forced to adjust without complaining about the fear of a negative rating. The need to always be less frustrated and more courteous, regardless of the customer's behaviour, was a recurring theme.

The root of these pressures lies in the opaqueness of the algorithmic assessment. F-15 described the frustrating experience of receiving automatic and uninformative responses from the platform to queries about a sudden drop in rating. Furthermore, the consequences of low customer ratings are reported to be severe beyond the mutual rating framework. According to the G-9, a single unfavourable rating results in a phone call from the platform, demanding an explanation. In some cases, it was reported that a whole week's work assignment could be halved or an account suspended, which can lead to significant financial hardship (G-3, F-7).

Interestingly, not all respondents were uniformly negative about this platform management system, with some drivers feeling that they use it only as a tool. G-16 and F-21 stated that we are not working under compulsion for the platform, but under freedom and of our own free will. A minority see algorithmic management as a tool that, together with their own will, provides them with clear goals and opportunities to optimise their earnings. However, they also acknowledge that such optimisation often requires significant emotional suppression and strategic self-presentation.

In addition, the dual pressures of competition and ambiguity raise serious ethical issues. Workers are forced to be constantly hyper-vigilant as they adapt to invisible rules. The lack of transparency regarding evaluation criteria and compensation decisions, coupled with the emotional burden and the one-sided nature of algorithmic authority, reveals a structural imbalance in the platform-worker relationship that has been brought to the attention of regulators.

6.6.3 Institutional Inadequacies and the Development of Informal Safety Nets

Many drivers, especially food delivery riders, report cases where they work more than 10 hours a day and still do not reach RM100. This is particularly the case in rural provinces such as Johor and Kedah, where demand is unstable and working from morning till night is generally not profitable enough on some days. Except during the peak season, many respondents stated that the extra income generated by extended working hours is also limited, leading to mental and physical fatigue.

Further problems include the obligation to take out medical insurance and the lack of accident compensation. Voluntary enrolment in SOCSO, a voluntary insurance scheme, is not widespread, and several respondents identified cases where they did not receive compensation. The current situation highlights that hazard preparedness is very weak, as many are unaware of the existence of the compensation scheme or feel that it is practically non-functional due to the cumbersome application process. Furthermore, many of them obtain information on social security and benefits from informal networks rather than formal network channels. In particular, a culture of mutual support among workers has developed on WhatsApp groups and Facebook. While these provide psychological security, they are channels that are limited in resolving their social risks (G-3; F-2).

Respondents also expressed a background of government indifference towards improving conditions for platform workers and distrust of platforms. In fact, platforms change conditions for their own convenience, and clear explanations for this are not well shared, nor are they empowered to officially protest about the improvements. This has resulted in a resistance movement among food delivery riders, particularly in the Klang Valley region, including Kuala Lumpur.

6.6.4 *Undefined Scattered Solidarity and Indifference*

The interview results reveal how the platform's evaluation system promotes competition between workers, which in turn weakens solidarity. G-4 stated that if they lose their rating, they immediately lose their income, which diminishes their sense of camaraderie, indicating the reality of increasing isolation in a competitive environment. This situation is an example of the lack of resistance due to the difficulty of commodification and collectivisation of workers, which is embodied under platform capitalism (Woodcock, 2021).

Drivers also repeatedly express distrust of customer rating systems. F-6 complained that customers need to have a flexible understanding of delivery delays because of traffic congestion and the restaurant's own circumstances, while G-5 also criticised the platform for reflecting one-sided complaints and low ratings from the customer side directly to the driver.

These testimonies indicate that the lack of sufficient opportunities to refute or challenge unfair evaluations on the platform, as well as the lack of customer education and awareness-raising, are serious problems for the drivers.

In addition, the lack of organisation and representation was also highlighted as an issue, with F-3 stating that information is shared through social media groups and other means, but on a small scale and not institutionalised. F-2 stated that they feel representation and organisation are needed, but do not know how to do it. Thus, it was clearly indicated that institutional structural barriers exist, as drivers themselves are aware of the need for an institutional framework and representation, but are unable to take concrete action.

6.6.5 *Strong Inducements Towards Decent Work and Fair Platform Work Governance*

Many young gig workers have a strong preference for decent work with a stable income, a fair and predictable remuneration package and security for the future. However, several respondents (F-1, F-2, F-21) expressed concerns that, although the work allows for short-term income generation, the inherently unstable nature of their earnings makes it extremely difficult to plan for major life events such as marriage or purchasing a home, with securing loans described as particularly challenging. On the other hand, concerns about long-term career paths and lack of retirement security are commonly manifested, although there are also younger people who choose gig work as a basis for their livelihoods. Interestingly, the same occupational type also enjoys a certain popularity among the older retired population, and differences in positioning according to life stage were also observed.

Expectations of and demands for institutional arrangements from the government and platform companies are extremely strong. Unilateral changes to contract conditions and remuneration schemes by platform companies were seen by many respondents as a serious problem, with many calling for active government involvement as a corrective measure. Specifically, there is a strong demand for policy responses to fill the gaps in the current system, such as the application of a minimum wage system, mandatory social insurance, and the development of automatic enrolment schemes for pension and medical insurance. Recently, there have been growing expectations for the provision of social protection and the empowerment of domestic gig workers through initiatives such as the planned establishment of the Malaysian Gig Economy Commission (SEGiM). However, its full implementation remains under discussion (Malay Mail, 2025).

There are also very deep-rooted grievances about sudden and opaque changes in terms and conditions by the platforms, which workers are unable to reject for fear of a low reputation and impact on competition for customers. There is an increasing academic and policy focus on the necessity of granting bargaining rights, alongside enhancing transparency and accountability on the part of platforms, to rectify the pronounced power asymmetry between platforms and workers. Concurrently, the imperative for institutionalised forms of worker representation and support for collective organisation has become progressively apparent.

Furthermore, a lack of public consumer understanding of gig work remains a major challenge. Accounts from the field highlight that gig workers are placed under considerable pressure due to consumers' tendencies to pursue excessively cheap and convenient services. Moreover, it was noted that customers frequently assign low ratings without understanding the underlying causes of delays or unforeseen issues, further exacerbating the challenges faced by workers. These findings highlight the importance of educational interventions and consumer awareness-raising to promote social understanding of platform work and strongly suggest the need for society as a whole to share the realities and challenges of gig work faced by young people.

6.7 Discussion

This study details the impact of platform labour precariousness and institutional inadequacies on workers through semi-structured interviews with young on-demand gig workers in Malaysia. Particularly in the Southeast Asian region, where social security is inadequate among platform workers, and platform domination of the market and power imbalances are significant. The findings contribute to five arguments and specific policy recommendations for platform regulation and the formation of comprehensive informal labour policies (Chalermpong et al., 2025; Uchiyama et al., 2024).

First, while young gig workers were attracted to short-term income generation and flexible working, they were under constant psychological and financial pressure under the influence of the platform's algorithmic management and evaluation system. They emphasised the isolation caused by competition due to the fear that if they lost their reputation, they would immediately lose orders and income as well. Severely, respondents mentioned that once they receive a low evaluation, they receive significantly fewer orders the following week, making it difficult to recover. While several previous studies have highlighted that this one-sided monitoring and management regime under platform capitalism amplifies their mental strain (Cram et al., 2022; Kinowska & Sienkiewicz, 2023), this is not the case in Malaysia, and it is confirmed to be true in the context of young people as well.

Second, the lack of social security and difficulties in planning for the future cause serious concerns for young gig workers. Having chosen gig work to make ends meet and save money, they described extreme difficulty in taking out loans when looking ahead to life events such as buying a house, getting married and raising children, a reality that is far from long-term career and livelihood stability. Their challenges in making loans and credit cards are issues that have not been discussed much in previous research. However, an increasing number of people who use gig work as a secondary income are taking out small loans, and this source of income is important as collateral in case other businesses fail (Barrios et al., 2022). This study suggests that amongst the levels of perceptions in gig workers, relatively low-end gig work, including food delivery and ride-hailing, is less likely to gain social status and is distinct from skills-based gig freelance work. Even if a loan is available, particularly for younger people with less credit history and income, they may be disadvantaged by high interest rates and other disadvantages (Buchak, 2024). This aspect consequently discourages them from continuing these jobs as a long-term vision.

Thirdly, the inadequacy of the institutional framework also underscores that workers themselves face a lack of organisation and representation. While gig workers make effective use of messaging app groups as informal, small-scale channels for sharing information, most are acutely aware of the need for collective representation and organisation as a form of resistance against platform power, yet they lack the means and knowledge to achieve this. The role of social media in facilitating the organisation of gig workers has been observed in numerous countries (Jabagi et al., 2019; Mieruch & McFarlane, 2023; Wood et al., 2019). Messaging app groups have become vital alternative workplace spaces, functioning as sites for exchanging practical advice, providing mutual assistance in emergencies, deciphering and responding to algorithmic management, and onboarding new workers (Vilasís-Pamos et al., 2024). Despite this awareness, most drivers are unable to take concrete steps towards collective organisation due to structural barriers and insufficient access to information.

Notably, two food delivery workers' collective actions in 2022 and 2024 were largely orchestrated via Facebook posts and banners disseminated on social networking platforms, which played a pivotal role in organising protests within the Klang Valley region, including Kuala Lumpur. These actions were spearheaded by active members of the Persatuan Penghantar P-Hailing Malaysia association. However, the influence of such efforts remains limited, as the majority of drivers and rural riders not affiliated with such associations continued working and largely disregarded the strike actions (Uchiyama et al., 2024).

Uchiyama et al. (2025) highlight significant contrasts in the organisation of platform workers between Western countries and Asia. As Cini et al. (2022) demonstrate, in Italy and the United Kingdom, gig workers have built solidarity through self-organised collectives and grassroots unions rather than relying on traditional labour unions. In Italy, in particular, a cultural legacy of student and social movements has fostered a community-based solidarity culture that underpins mobilisation and collective resistance (Cini et al., 2022). In contrast, Uchiyama et al. (2025) observe that in Malaysia, organising efforts have been far more limited, shaped by a cultural and political environment in which collective resistance has historically been suppressed.

Fourth, the lack of understanding and one-sidedness of evaluation on the part of consumers is also a significant source of stress for gig workers. In previous studies, consumers showed empathy and appreciation for the situations faced by gig workers through their interactions with them, while in economic terms, consumers were willing to pay more to gig workers (Healy et al., 2020; Smith et al., 2021). On the other hand, actual actions differed from the above responses. In the context of delivery work, a persistent challenge lies in the structural unfairness whereby delays caused by traffic congestion or store-related issues are nonetheless attributed entirely to drivers. Customers often assign low ratings without distinguishing between factors beyond the driver's control, and such dissatisfaction is directly reflected in drivers' performance evaluations. This disconnect highlights a fundamental asymmetry in platform rating systems, placing disproportionate responsibility and reputational risk on individual workers. This situation highlights the need for consumer education and awareness-raising activities (Uchiyama et al., 2023).

Fifth, there are strong expectations for policy responses and platform regulation. Drivers regard unilateral changes to contract terms and conditions and revision of remuneration schemes by platform companies as a serious problem and call for government intervention. In particular, the application of minimum wages and the design of systems such as mandatory social insurance schemes and auto-enrolment schemes are identified as pressing issues.

The plan to establish the SEGiM (Malaysian Gig Economy Commission) was prompted by the 2024 Grab Blackout and reflects these voices on the ground, but at present, it has not yet operated substantively. In this respect, the Asian region, including Malaysia, could learn institutional design from the experiences of Western countries. For example, in Spain, legislation has led to the formal employment of gig workers, while in France, Belgium and Italy, individual recognition and exploration continue through judicial decisions and administrative measures. In the UK, recognition as an "employee" on a case-by-case basis has been the norm, with only limited rights guarantees (Defossez, 2022). However, in October 2024, the EU formally adopted the Platform Work Directive with the agreement of the European Commission and the European Parliament, incorporating three points into national regulations by Member States: the presumption of an employment relationship, the obligation of transparency in algorithm management and the extension of collective bargaining rights to the self-employed, obliged platform operators to comply with them (European Union, 2024). The development of such a regulatory system serves to clarify the responsibilities and rights of both platform operators and workers by sorting out the structural complexities surrounding platform labour and resolving institutional ambiguities. Creating an environment in which young people, especially those who aspire to flexible working, can choose gig work as part of their career development is essential for the diversification of the labour market in modern society. Clarifying and improving the transparency of institutional design, which comprehensively incorporates the above issues, is an important issue that needs to be urgently addressed to build a sustainable and decent platform labour market.

6.8 Conclusion

This study examines the challenges in youth employment and career development by identifying the employment status and institutional inadequacies of young on-demand gig-workers in Malaysia. Although many young people choose gig work due to its attractiveness for flexibility and short-term income, the reality is that they are exposed to long working hours, unstable income, lack of social security and unilateral control by the platform. In particular, over-reliance on algorithmic evaluation creates a psychological burden and fear of reduced income and reinforces feelings of isolation and uncertainty about the future through competition. Of particular importance is the development of an environment in which gig work is positioned as a sustainable career option for young people, rather than a temporary earner. Currently, it is evident that a lack of credit and income stability is a barrier to life events such as home acquisition, marriage and child rearing, making it difficult to design a long-term lifestyle. This goes beyond mere labour problems and is a serious factor hindering the social independence and human resource development of young people. Lack of organisation and representation is also a major challenge. Information sharing through social networking and messaging apps is functioning to a limited extent, but in the absence of institutional support and a framework for collective bargaining, many young people remain frustrated but unable to take action. In order for young gig workers to form their professional identity and build their careers autonomously, it is essential to develop institutions such as presumption of employment relationships, transparency in algorithm management and granting collective bargaining rights to the self-employed, as stipulated by the Platform Work Directive. In line with the EU's approach, in Malaysia and other ASEAN countries, there is also an urgent need to develop institutions that position these jobs not merely as a means of economic growth, but as future-oriented employment for young people. This study demonstrates the need to reconstruct gig work as sustainable employment for young people and recommends policy formation based on the three pillars of labour protection, platform regulation and social awareness building. Achieving a working environment where young people can enjoy freedom and flexibility while ensuring stability and dignity is the key to the healthy development of the modern labour market and social inclusion.

References

Abd Samad, K., Abd Rahman, N. H., Ismail, S., & Marmaya, N. H. (2023). Is the well-being of gig workers in Malaysia better? The reality of pain and gain. *International Review of Applied Economics, 37*(4), 518–531.

Adams, A., Freedman, J., & Prassl, J. (2018). Rethinking legal taxonomies for the gig economy. *Oxford Review of Economic Policy, 34*(3), 475–494. https://doi.org/10.1093/oxrep/gry006

Adermon, A., & Hensvik, L. (2022). Gig-jobs: Stepping stones or dead ends? *Labour Economics, 76*, 102171.

Aguilera, A., Dablanc, L., Krier, C., & Louvet, N. (2022). Platform-based food delivery in Paris before and during the pandemic: Profile, motivations and mobility patterns of couriers. *European Transport Research Review, 14*(1), 45.

Aranguiz, A., & Bednarowicz, B. (2018). Adapt or perish: Recent developments on social protection in the EU under a gig deal of pressure. *European Labour Law Journal, 9*(4), 329–345.

Asohan, A. (2012). *Digital Malaysia details out … finally!* Digital News Asia. https://www.digitalnewsasia.com/digital_economy/digital-malaysia-details-out-finally

Avagianou, A., Chatzichristos, G., Herod, A., & Gialis, S. (2024). Precarity and agency in youthspaces of work: The case of food delivery platform workers in Athens, Greece. *Environment and Planning A: Economy and Space, 57.*

Avis, J. (2018). Socio-technical imaginary of the fourth industrial revolution and its implications for vocational education and training: A literature review. *Journal of Vocational Education & Training, 70*(3), 337–363.

Banerjee, D. (2024). Caste, gig-economy, and youth: The resurgence of a new age caste politics in urban Gujarat. *South Asian History and Culture, 15*(2), 231–246.

Bank Negara Malaysia. (2020, November 2). *Improving the financial health of gig workers with innovative financial solutions*. https://www.bnm.gov.my/-/improving-the-financial-health-of-gig-workers-with-innovative-financial-solutions

Barrios, J. M., Hochberg, Y. V., & Yi, H. (2022). Launching with a parachute: The gig economy and new business formation. *Journal of Financial Economics, 144*(1), 22–43.

Basukie, J., Wang, Y., & Li, S. (2020). Big data governance and algorithmic management in sharing economy platforms: A case of ridesharing in emerging markets. *Technological Forecasting and Social Change, 161*, 120310. https://doi.org/10.1016/j.techfore.2020.120310

Belanche, D., Casaló, L. V., Flavián, C., & Pérez-Rueda, A. (2021). The role of customers in the gig economy: how perceptions of working conditions and service quality influence the use and recommendation of food delivery services. *Service Business, 15*(1), 45–75.

Benvegnù, C., & Kampouri, N. (2021). "Platformization" beyond the point of production: Reproductive labour and gender roles in the ride-hailing and food-delivery sectors. *South Atlantic Quarterly, 120*(4), 733–747.

Blustein, D. L., Allan, B. A., Davila, A., Smith, C. M., Gordon, M., Wu, X., et al. (2023). Profiles of decent work and precarious work: Exploring macro-level predictors and mental health outcomes. *Journal of Career Assessment, 31*(3), 423–441.

Braun, V., & Clarke, V. (2006). Using thematic analysis in psychology. *Qualitative Research in Psychology, 3*(2), 77–101. https://doi.org/10.1191/1478088706qp063oa

Buchak, G. (2024). Financing the gig economy. *The Journal of Finance, 79*(1), 219–256.

Bulian, L. (2021). The gig is up: Who does gig economy actually benefit? *Interdisciplinary Description of Complex Systems: INDECS, 19*(1), 106–119.

Chalermpong, S., Ratanawaraha, A., & Uchiyama, Y. (2025). *Informal and shared mobility - Status, challenges, and opportunities in Southeast Asia*. Volvo Research and Educational Foundations.

Chen, A., Yuan, C. W., Ma, N. F., Hsu, C. Y., & Hanrahan, B. V. (2019, May). Navigating ride-sharing regulations: How regulations changed the'gig'of ride-sharing for drivers in Taiwan. In *Proceedings of the 2019 CHI conference on human factors in computing systems* (pp. 1–12).

Cheng, X., Fu, S., & de Vreede, G.-J. (2018). A mixed-method investigation of sharing economy-driven car-hailing services: Online and offline perspectives. *International Journal of Information Management, 41*, 57–64. https://doi.org/10.1016/j.ijinfomgt.2018.03.005

Christie, N., & Ward, H. (2019). The health and safety risks for people who drive for work in the gig economy. *Journal of Transport & Health, 13*, 115–127. https://doi.org/10.1016/j.jth.2019.02.007

Churchill, B., Ravn, S., & Craig, L. (2019). Gendered and generational inequalities in the gig economy era. *Journal of Sociology, 55*(4), 627–636. https://doi.org/10.1177/1440783319893754

Cini, L., Maccarrone, V., & Tassinari, A. (2022). With or without U(nions)? Understanding the diversity of gig workers' organising practices in Italy and the UK. *European Journal of Industrial Relations, 28*(3), 341–362. https://doi.org/10.1177/09596801211052531

Cram, W. A., Wiener, M., Tarafdar, M., & Benlian, A. (2022). Examining the impact of algorithmic control on Uber drivers' technostress. *Journal of Management Information Systems, 39*(2), 426–453.

De Groen, W., Maselli, I., & Fabo, B. (2016). *The digital market for local services: A one-night stand for workers? An example from the on-demand economy. An example from the on-demand economy (April 4, 2016)*. CEPS Special Report(133). https://ssrn.com/abstract=2766220

De Stefano, V., & Aloisi, A. (2018). *European legal framework for digital labour platforms*. European Commission, Joint Research Centre. https://hdl.handle.net/1814/60772

Defossez, D. (2022). The employment status of food delivery riders in Europe and the UK: Self-employed or worker? *Maastricht Journal of European and Comparative Law, 29*(1), 25–46.

Department of Statistics Malaysia. (2022). *Graduates statistics 2021*. https://www.dosm.gov.my/v1/index.php?r=column/cthemeByCat&cat=476&bul_id=N0w0QU95YklKRDFoQWhSV3F6N3NHQT09&menu_id=Tm8zcnRjdVRNWWlpWjRlbmtlaDk1UT09

Department of Statistics Malaysia. (2025a, February 10). *[4Q 2024] Labour force.* https://open.dosm.gov.my/publications/labour_qtr_2024-q4

Department of Statistics Malaysia. (2025b, February 10). *[Dec 2024] labour force.* OpenDOSM. https://open.dosm.gov.my/publications/labour_month_2024-12

Donovan, S. A., Bradley, D. H., & Shimabukuro, J. O. (2016). *What does the gig economy mean for workers?*

Douglas, H. A., Hamilton, R. J., & Grubs, R. E. (2009). The effect of BRCA gene testing on family relationships: A thematic analysis of qualitative interviews. *Journal of Genetic Counselling, 18*(5), 418–435. https://doi.org/10.1007/s10897-009-9232-1

Economic Planning Unit. (2021). *Malaysia digital economy blueprint.* https://www.epu.gov.my/sites/default/files/2021-02/malaysia-digital-economy-blueprint.pdf

Erlich, M. (2021). Misclassification in construction: The original gig economy. *ILR Review, 74*(5), 1202–1230.

European Council. (2024, October 16). *EU rules on platform work.* https://www.consilium.europa.eu/en/policies/platform-work-eu/#workers

European Union. (2024, November 11). *Directive (EU) 2024/2831 of the European Parliament and of the Council of 23 October 2024 on improving working conditions in platform work.* https://eur-lex.europa.eu/eli/dir/2024/2831/oj

Free Malaysia Today. (2023, February 17). *98% of delivery riders are 30 or under, says the statistics dept.* https://www.freemalaysiatoday.com/category/nation/2023/02/17/98-of-delivery-riders-are-30-or-under-says-statistics-dept/

Fu, S. (2019). Rethinking digital labour for development. *The Public Sphere: Journal of Public Policy, 7*(1).

Furuoka, F., Uchiyama, Y., Lim, B., Pazim, K. H., Aruchunan, M. E., Paidi, R., Nikitina, L., Jingyi, L., & Omar, S. A. (2022). An effect of the COVID-19 pandemic on the gig economy in Malaysia: An application of "tragedy of the commons". *Istanbul International Modern Scientific Research Congress - III*, 923–935.

Gandhi, A., Budiardjo, E. K., & Sucahyo, Y. G. (2019). Developing the maturity model for gig economy business processes. In *2019 IEEE 9th symposium on computer applications & industrial electronics (ISCAIE).*

Goodman, L. A. (1961). Snowball sampling. *The Annals of Mathematical Statistics, 32*, 148–170.

Goods, C., Veen, A., & Barratt, T. (2019). "Is your gig any good?" Analysing job quality in the Australian platform-based food-delivery sector. *Journal of Industrial Relations, 61*(4), 502–527. https://doi.org/10.1177/0022185618817069

Graham, M., Hjorth, I., & Lehdonvirta, V. (2017). Digital labour and development: Impacts of global digital labour platforms and the gig economy on worker livelihoods. *Transfer: European Review of Labour and Research, 23*(2), 135–162. https://doi.org/10.1177/1024258916687250

Gregory, K. (2021). 'My life is more valuable than this': Understanding risk among on-demand food couriers in Edinburgh. *Work, Employment and Society, 35*(2), 316–331. https://doi.org/10.1177/0950017020969593

Harpur, P., & Blanck, P. (2020). Gig workers with disabilities: opportunities, challenges, and regulatory response. *Journal of Occupational Rehabilitation, 30*(4), 511–520.

Harun, N., Ali, N. M., & Khan, N. L. M. A. (2020). An experimental measure of Malaysia's gig workers using the labour force survey. *Statistical Journal of the IAOS, 36*(4), 969–977. https://doi.org/10.3233/SJI-200749

Hawley, A. J. (2018). Regulating labour platforms, the data deficit. *European Journal of Government and Economics (EJGE), 7*(1), 5–23.

Healy, J., Nicholson, D., & Pekarek, A. (2017). Should we take the gig economy seriously? *Labour & Industry: A Journal of the Social and Economic Relations of Work, 27*(3), 232–248.

Healy, J., & Pekarek, A. (2024). The triangular relationship in platform gig work: Consumers, platform beneficence and worker vulnerability. *New Technology, Work and Employment*, 1–20. https://doi.org/10.1111/ntwe.12310

Healy, J., Pekarek, A., & Vromen, A. (2020). Sceptics or supporters? Consumers' views of work in the gig economy. *New Technology, Work and Employment, 35*(1), 1–19. https://doi.org/10.1111/ntwe.12157

Heeks, R., Graham, M., Mungai, P., Van Belle, J. P., & Woodcock, J. (2021). Systematic evaluation of gig work against decent work standards: The development and application of the fairwork framework. *The Information Society, 37*(5), 267–286.

Herrmann, A. M., Zaal, P. M., Chappin, M. M., Schemmann, B., & Lühmann, A. (2023). "We don't need no (higher) education" - How the gig economy challenges the education-income paradigm. *Technological Forecasting and Social Change, 186*, 122136.

Jabagi, N., Croteau, A.-M., Audebrand, L. K., & Marsan, J. (2019). Gig-workers' motivation: Thinking beyond carrots and sticks. *Journal of Managerial Psychology, 34*(4), 192–213.

Jarrahi, M. H., Sutherland, W., Nelson, S. B., & Sawyer, S. (2020, April 01). Platformic management, boundary resources for gig work, and worker autonomy. *Computer Supported Cooperative Work (CSCW), 29*(1), 153–189. https://doi.org/10.1007/s10606-019-09368-7

Kalleberg, A. L., & Dunn, M. (2016). Good jobs, bad jobs in the gig economy. *LERA for Libraries, 20*(1–2).

Kassi, O., & Lehdonvirta, V. (2018). Online labour index: Measuring the online gig economy for policy and research. *Technological Forecasting and Social Change, 137*, 241–248. https://doi.org/10.1016/j.techfore.2018.07.056

Koutsimpogiorgos, N., Van Slageren, J., Herrmann, A. M., & Frenken, K. (2020). Conceptualizing the gig economy and its regulatory problems. *Policy & Internet, 12*(4), 525–545.

Kinowska, H., & Sienkiewicz, Ł. J. (2023). Influence of algorithmic management practices on workplace well-being–evidence from European organisations. *Information Technology & People, 36*(8), 21–42.

Kost, D., Fieseler, C., & Wong, S. I. (2020). Boundaryless careers in the gig economy: An oxymoron? *Human Resource Management Journal, 30*(1), 100–113. https://doi.org/10.1111/1748-8583.12265

Lim, I. (2021, March 31). *Protect Malaysia's gig workers and ensure no monopolies are possible through legal loopholes, PKR youth chief tells govt*. Malay Mail. https://www.malaymail.com/news/malaysia/2021/03/31/protect-malaysias-gig-workers-and-ensure-no-monopolies-possible-through-leg/1962618

MacDonald, R., & Giazitzoglu, A. (2019). Youth, enterprise and precarity: Or, what is, and what is wrong with, the 'gig economy'? *Journal of Sociology, 55*(4), 724–740.

Malay Mail. (2023, July 17). *Socso CEO: Gig economy operators' reluctance makes it hard to improve social security for workers*. https://www.malaymail.com/news/malaysia/2023/07/17/socso-ceo-gig-economy-operators-reluctance-makes-it-hard-to-improve-social-security-for-workers/80234

Malay Mail. (2025, March 20). *SEGiM is the right regulatory mechanism for our gig economy — Nurhidayah Abdullah*. https://www.malaymail.com/news/what-you-think/2025/03/20/segim-is-the-right-regulatory-mechanism-for-our-gig-economy-nurhidayah-abdullah/170165

Marrone, M., & Finotto, V. (2019). Challenging goliath: Informal unionism and digital platforms in the food delivery sector. The case of riders Union Bologna. *Partecipazione e conflitto, 12*, 691–716.

McIntosh, M. J., & Morse, J. M. (2015). Situating and constructing diversity in semi-structured interviews. *Global Qualitative Nursing Research, 2*, 2333393615597674. https://doi.org/10.1177/2333393615597674

Mieruch, Y., & McFarlane, D. (2023). Gig economy riders on social media in Thailand: Contested identities and emergent civil society organisations. *VOLUNTAS: International Journal of Voluntary and Nonprofit Organisations, 34*(6), 1232–1242.

Ministry of Manpower. (2024, December 17). *Commencement of the platform workers act from 1 January 2025*. https://www.mom.gov.sg/newsroom/press-releases/2024/1217-commencement-of-platform-workers-act-from-1-jan-2025

Ministry of Transport Malaysia. (2023). *e-Hailing services*. https://www.mot.gov.my/en/land/infrastructure/e-hailing-services
Minter, K. (2017). Negotiating labour standards in the gig economy: Airtasker and Unions New South Wales. *The Economic and Labour Relations Review, 28*(3), 438–454.
Montgomery, T., & Baglioni, S. (2021). Defining the gig economy: platform capitalism and the reinvention of precarious work. *International Journal of Sociology and Social Policy, 41*(9/10), 1012–1025.
Ng, A., Tan, Z. G., & Mahadeva, M. (2017). *An uneven future? An exploration of the future of work in Malaysia* [discussion paper].
Prassl, J., & Risak, M. (2017). The legal protection of crowdworkers: Four avenues for workers' rights in the virtual realm. In P. Meil & V. Kirov (Eds.), *Policy implications of virtual work* (pp. 273–295). Springer International Publishing. https://doi.org/10.1007/978-3-319-52057-5_11
O'Keeffe, P., Johnson, B., & Daley, K. (2022). Continuing the precedent: Financially disadvantaging young people in "unprecedented" COVID-19 times. *Australian Journal of Social Issues, 57*(1), 70–87.
Radzi, M. S. N. M., Bidin, A., Musa, M. K., & Hamid, N. A. (2022). Protecting gig workers' interests in Malaysia through registered association under societies act 1966. *IIUMLJ, 30*, 157–179.
Razak, S. S. A., Wahab, H. A., Jusoh, A., & Ramli, N. (2023). *Young workers on digital platform work: A review of rights and protection in Malaysia*. International Conference on Business and Technology.
Roy, G., & Shrivastava, A. K. (2020). Future of gig economy: opportunities and challenges. *Imi Konnect, 9*(1), 14–27.
Scully-Russ, E., & Torraco, R. (2020). The changing nature and organization of work: An integrative review of the literature. *Human Resource Development Review, 19*(1), 66–93.
Smith, B., Goods, C., Barratt, T., & Veen, A. (2021). Consumer 'app-etite'for workers' rights in the Australian 'gig'economy. *Journal of Choice Modelling, 38*, 100254.
Song, F., Lamb, D., & Soltanzadeh, K. (2025). What happens when the gig is up? The relationship between gig work histories and future career prospects. *British Journal of Industrial Relations, 63*, 525–537. https://doi.org/10.1111/bjir.12875
Sprague, R. (2015). Worker (Mis)Classification in the sharing economy: Trying to fit square pegs into round holes. *ABA Journal of Labor & Employment Law, 31*(1), 53–76. https://www.jstor.org/stable/26410781
Stewart, A., & Stanford, J. (2017). Regulating work in the gig economy: What are the options? *Economic and Labour Relations Review, 28*(3), 420–437. https://doi.org/10.1177/1035304617722461
The Star. (2023, September 18). *Why school leavers would rather join the gig economy*. https://www.thestar.com.my/news/nation/2023/09/18/why-school-leavers-rather-join-the-gig-economy
Todolí-Signes, A. (2017). The 'gig economy': employee, self-employed or the need for a special employment regulation? *Transfer: European Review of Labour Research, 23*(2), 193–205.
Tran, M., & Sokas, R. K. (2017). The gig economy and contingent work: An occupational health assessment. *Journal of Occupational and Environmental Medicine, 59*, e63–e66.
Uchiyama, Y., & Furuoka, F. (2024). Characteristics of the market structure: On-demand app gig economy in ASEAN. *JATI-Journal of Southeast Asian Studies, 29*(1), 1–26.
Umer, H. (2021). Illusory freedom of physical platform workers: Insights from Uber eats in Japan. *The Economic and Labour Relations Review, 32*(3), 437–452.
Uchiyama, Y., Furuoka, F., & Akhir, M. N. M. (2022). Gig workers, social protection and labour market inequality: Lessons from Malaysia. *Jurnal Ekonomi Malaysia, 56*(3), 165–184.
Uchiyama, Y., Furuoka, F., Lim, B., Pazim, K. H., & Li, J. (2023). Value creation, consumers' active intervention and workers' working conditions: A new conceptual framework for the gig economy. *Journal Kinabalu, 29*, 143–171.

Uchiyama, Y., Furuoka, F., & Omar, S. A. (2024). The rise and contestation of platform capitalism: Evidence from two food delivery blackouts in Malaysia. *Journal of Industrial Relations*. https://doi.org/10.1177/00221856241294107

Uchiyama, Y., Omar, S. A., Furuoka, F., Nikitina, L., Pazim, K. H., & Lim, B. (2025). Malaysian university students' understanding and perceptions of the gig economy. *Institutions and Economies, 17*(2), 121–142.

UNCTAD. (2020, September 20). *How a gig economy start-up is driving the fourth industrial revolution in Malaysia*. https://unctad.org/news/how-gig-economy-start-driving-fourth-industrial-revolution-malaysia

Useche, S. A., Robayo, S., & Orozco-Fontalvo, M. (2024). The hidden cost of your 'too fast food': Stress-related factors and fatigue predict food delivery riders' occupational crashes. *International Journal of Occupational Safety and Ergonomics, 30*(3), 825–834.

Vallas, S. P. (2019). Platform capitalism: What's at stake for workers? *New Labour Forum, 28*(1), 48–59. https://doi.org/10.1177/1095796018817059

Vallas, S., & Schor, J. B. (2020). What do platforms do? Understanding the gig economy. *Annual Review of Sociology, 46*(1), 273–294.

Vilasís-Pamos, J., Pires, F., Grohmann, R., & Fernandes Araujo, W. (2024). Social media and platform work: Stories, practices, and workers' organisation. *Convergence, 30*(1), 410–427.

Wood, D. M., & Monahan, T. (2019). Platform surveillance. *Surveillance & Society, 17*(1/2), 1–6.

Wood, A. J., Graham, M., Lehdonvirta, V., & Hjorth, I. (2019). Good gig, bad gig: Autonomy and algorithmic control in the global gig economy. *Work Employment and Society, 33*(1), 56–75. https://doi.org/10.1177/0950017018785616

Woodcock, J. (2021). Digital workerism, a framework. In *The fight against platform capitalism* (pp. 11–26). University of Westminster Press. https://doi.org/10.2307/j.ctv1ktbdrm.5

Yee, X. Y. (2022, August 28). *ASM tasked to find solutions to address the issue of SPM holders not furthering their studies*. The Star. https://www.thestar.com.my/news/nation/2022/08/28/asm-tasked-to-find-solutions-to-address-issue-of-spm-holders-not-furthering-their-studies

Yusof, A. B. M., Arshad, M. M., & Ismail, I. A. (2022). Positive youth development through the gig economy among food panda delivery Services in Malacca, Malaysia. *International Journal of Academic Research in Business and Social Sciences, 12*(14), 303–323.

Zakaria, I. (2020, November 16). *Making 'gig work' work in Malaysia*. Malay Mail. https://www.malaymail.com/news/what-you-think/2020/11/16/making-gig-work-work-in-malaysia-izwan-zakaria/1922956

Zamponi, L., & Caciagli, C. (2019). Labour activism and social movement unionism in the gig economy. Food delivery workers' struggles in Italy. *Partecipazione e conflitto, 12*(3), 819–844.

Chapter 7
Conclusion

This concluding chapter synthesises the empirical findings from Chaps. 3–6 and details the theoretical contributions of the study, which are rooted in three theoretical perspectives: the Law of One Unemployment Rate (LOUR), the two-sector search model for young workers, and platform capitalism. The chapter discusses how the empirical findings deepen our understanding of these three theoretical frameworks and underscores their practical significance. Based on the empirical evidence, the chapter recommends two active labour market policies to address high youth unemployment: job search assistance and employment subsidies. It also proposes a "neo-apprenticeship" framework grounded in a holistic taxonomy for knowledge and skill acquisition that synthesises Kajita's classification of educational goals and Nonaka's theory of knowledge creation. The proposed framework aims to address institutional gaps in capability formation and foster a more productive and dynamic society.

7.1 Summary of Empirical Findings

This book comprises four analytical chapters, from Chaps. 3–6. The first two analytical chapters, namely Chaps. 3 and 4, examine the validity of the "Law of One Unemployment Rate" (LOUR). Chapter 3 used several advanced statistical methods to investigate the validity of the first assumption of the LOUR. Table 3.11 in Chap. 3 summarises the findings from the empirical analysis to examine the "uniformity" of unemployment patterns. The findings can be summarised into three interesting facts on the pattern of different unemployment rates. Firstly, six statistical tests out of eight tests indicated the stationarity of the unemployment rate for workers aged 25–34, 35–44, 45–54 and55–64. Secondly, if the 5 per cent significance level is used, five statistical tests indicated the stationarity of unemployment rates for young workers with and without disabilities aged 20–24. However, if the 10 per cent significance level is applied, unemployment rates of young workers

Y. Uchiyama, F. Furuoka, *Youth and Employment*,
https://doi.org/10.1007/978-981-95-3257-5_7

with disabilities cannot be considered a stationary process. Thirdly, if the 10 per cent significance level is used, unemployment rates of teenage workers with and without disabilities could be considered a unit root process.

Chapter 4 also used several statistical methods to investigate the validity of the second assumption of the LOUR. Table 4.5 in Chapter 4 summarises the empirical findings on the "non-persistence" of the age unemployment gap. The findings can be summarised into three interesting facts on the convergence of the age unemployment gap. Firstly, three out of four statistical tests indicated the convergence of the age unemployment gaps between teenage workers without disabilities aged 16–19 and three demographic groups: lower prime-aged workers without disabilities aged 25–34, upper prime-aged workers without disabilities aged 45–54 and older workers without disabilities aged 55–64. Secondly, two statistical tests indicated the convergence of the age unemployment gap between teenage workers without disabilities aged 16–19 and middle prime-age workers without disabilities aged 34–44. Thirdly, findings indicated that there is no convergence in the remaining twelve age unemployment gaps.

Chapter 5 reveals the reality of freelancing and cloud work in Southeast Asia and its implications for employment through semi-structured interviews with nine high-end youth gig workers based in Bangkok, Thailand. The survey participants ranged from language teachers and designers to accountants and policy advisors, all of whom were engaged in high-skilled work facilitated by digital technology. Many participants valued flexibility and autonomy as key benefits, with some viewing gig work as a temporary income source and others as a means of long-term career development. The latter group particularly focused on internalising skills through practice and integrating multi-disciplinary careers without relying on institutional frameworks. On the other hand, performance-based evaluations and isolated work environments created psychological stress and occupational loneliness, and the lack of social support threatened the sustainability of employment. Additionally, institutional barriers such as family responsibilities and access barriers to the formal employment market were highlighted, with these types of working styles functioning as a coping mechanism for structural constraints. This chapter empirically demonstrates that even highly skilled youth workers in the digital economy find themselves in non-institutional career settings that simultaneously embody both freedom and vulnerability.

Chapter 6 shows the structural realities and institutional vulnerabilities of on-demand gig work through semi-structured interviews with 55 youth workers (aged 18–35) engaged in ride-hailing and food delivery across Malaysia. Most participants turned to platform work for flexible time management and immediate income amidst limited access to regular employment. While such jobs appear to offer autonomy, they are marked by algorithmic control, opaque pay systems, long hours, and exclusion from social protection. Income instability, self-funded healthcare and insurance, and responsibility for vehicle upkeep significantly eroded economic security. Perceptions of gig work varied from a temporary measure to a flexible long-term career, yet concerns over future security remained consistent across both views. Continued engagement in platform work failed to deliver the compensation or benefits of standard employment, highlighting entrenched career discontinuity. Participants exhibited a high degree of platform dependency, constantly responding to app notifications and incentive fluctuations. Daily variation in workload and earnings made long-term planning unfeasible. The solitary and dispersed nature of the work limited social solidarity, reinforcing information asymmetries and weak bargaining power. The 2022 and 2024 strikes marked emerging collective resistance to wage cuts and algorithmic control. Although the 2024 protest attracted public attention, it failed to prompt regulatory reform, leaving the platform's dominant structure intact. Ultimately, this chapter underscores that, while on-demand gig work is framed as flexible employment, it entrenches precarious conditions within a broader landscape of institutional neglect.

7.2 Theoretical Contribution

The main theoretical foundation for the first two analytical chapters, from Chaps. 3 and 4, is the Law of One Unemployment Rate (LOUR). Chapter 3 empirically tested the first assumption of the LOUR which posits "uniformity" in the patterns of unemployment rates among different demographic groups. The findings indicated that the unemployment rates of older workers aged 25–64 exhibit a mean-reversion propensity. Conversely, the unemployment rates of teenage workers aged 16–19 did now show this mean-reversion propensity. These facts imply a lack of "uniformity" among different unemployment rates. In other words, the empirical analysis in Chap. 3 offered empirical evidence for the violation of the first assumption of the LOUR.

Chapter 4 empirically tested the second assumption of the LOUR, which posits "non-persistence" in the age unemployment gap. The age unemployment gap is defined as the difference in the unemployment rate between young workers and older workers. The age unemployment gap is the difference in unemployment rates between young workers aged 16–24 and older workers aged 25–64. The empirical findings overwhelmingly indicated no convergence in the age unemployment gaps. This means that the age unemployment gap between young workers and older workers persists. This finding also appears to to violate the second assumption of the LOUR.

Chapter 1 introduced another interesting theoretical perspective, which is known as the two-sector search model for young workers. The basic assumption of this two-sector model, expressed in inequation (1.2) in Chapter 1, is that the root cause of the high unemployment rate is the higher job destruction rate for young workers aged 16–24 compared to older workers aged 25–64. This assumption could be reinterpreted as the "procyclical" assumption for young workers. In other words, under this "procyclical" assumption, the younger worker would lose their employment earlier compared with the older workers. In fact, the findings in Table 4.2 in Furuoka (2024a) confirmed the "procyclical" assumption for workers with disabilities. In other words, the findings indicated that workers with disabilities lose their employment earlier than all workers, regardless of whether they have disabilities. However, the findings in Table 3.5 in Chap. 3 of this book indicate that young workers and older workers lose their employment at the same time. This suggests that the statistical analysis in that chapter offered empirical evidence to violate the "procyclical" assumption for young workers.

This study aims to theoretically elucidate the new restructuring process of labour organisation in the Global South by focusing on platform work and gig work, which are trending forms of employment that young people are actively engaging in, in response to the theoretical challenges of platform capitalism and institutional exclusion. As outlined in Chap. 2, this book is grounded in platform capitalism theory, while also connecting it with literature on regulatory capitalism and labour market fluidity surrounding institutional exclusion and inclusion. This framework captures the simultaneity of institutional embedding and deviation in platform labour.

The analysis in Chap. 5 reveals that even freelance and cloud work, which are formally considered high-skilled and autonomous, structurally hinder long-term career development due to the lack of social protection and connection to regular employment. In particular, participants were autonomously reconstructing their skills and internalising their expertise outside the institutional framework, but this process was unstable and prone to isolation, revealing that the fluidity provided by platforms coexists with career discontinuity. This provides a new counter-perspective to conventional discussions on human capital and vocational education, highlighting how 'expertise,' 'professionalism,' and 'autonomy' are constructed in an incomplete manner within non-institutional labour spaces.

Additionally, Chap. 6 demonstrated that institutional exclusion is equally severe in platform labour that does not depend on skills, and that the platform's labour control in urban spaces significantly hinders the construction of social capital. The food delivery rider strikes in 2022 and 2024 particularly illustrate how gig work is becoming politicised and how collective action is beginning to take shape in Southeast Asia, despite the region's generally weak worker organisation. At the same time, these actions underscore both the possibilities and limitations of normative agency in challenging platform dominance. A common theme emerging from both chapters is that conventional gig work does not simply mean the flexibilisation of labour forms, but rather fundamentally reconfigures young people's career development and the social recognition of labour within institutional vacuums. In other words, gig work functions not only as an expression of freedom and preference but also as a forced choice arising at the intersection of institutional constraints and platform structures.

This perspective suggests that when considering platform labour in the Global South, it is essential to adopt a multi-layered perspective that encompasses institutional inclusion/exclusion, social recognition, and self-identity formation, rather than focusing solely on economic rationality or the circulation of skills. This book attempts to theoretically reposition the intersection of youth employment and platform capitalism from this perspective, contributing to restoring geographical and structural balance in existing platform labour research, which has been biased toward the Global North.

7.3 Practical Significance

The first two analytical chapters indicated that young people, especially teenage workers with disabilities aged 16–19, tend to suffer from a prolonged period of unemployment. Chapter 3 demonstrated that the unemployment rates of young workers are considered a unit root process. By contrast, unemployment rates of older workers could be considered as a stationary process. This implies that unemployment of older workers would have a mean-reversion propensity, but the unemployment rate of young people lacks this crucial propensity. Chapter 4 indicated that the difference between their unemployment rates and the unemployment rates of prime-aged workers would not converge. In other words, the age unemployment gap would be persistent for a longer period of time. These two analytical chapters offered clear empirical proof of the labour market failure that resulted in young people facing a longer period of joblessness than older workers.

Policymakers should address two aspects of this market failure regarding youth unemployment. Firstly, they should recognise that young unemployment rates are not a stationary process. In other words, the unemployment rates of young people would not decline to a lower level after the end of the economic downturn. Policymakers would need to take appropriate active labour market policy (ALMP) measures to stimulate employment opportunities for young people. Secondly, they should also know that the difference between the unemployment rates of young people and the unemployment rates of older people would be persistent. Policymakers may need to implement effective ALMP measures to narrow down the age unemployment gap.

However, the question remains: What would be an appropriate and effective measure to reduce the high level of youth unemployment? The two-sector search model for young workers in Appendix 2 of Chap. 1 of this book, together with Furuoka's (2024b) study on the disability–employment relationship, suggests that job search assistance could be an effective tool for reducing the youth unemployment rate. Figures 6.7 and 6.8 in Furuoka (2024b) show that job search assistance would shift the job creation (JC) curve to the right. At the same time, job search assistance would also shift the wage-setting (WS) curve to the right. From this simultaneous rightward movement of the JC and WS curves, it can be inferred that the vacancy–unemployment ratio would be reduced and youth unemployment rates would decline. Furthermore, Appendix 2 of Chap. 1 this book and Furuoka's (2024b) study suggest that wage subsidies could be considered another effective tool for reducing the youth unemployment rate. From Figs. 6.5 and 6.6 in Furuoka (2024b), it is suggested that wage subsidies would shift the JC curve to the right, which could contribute to decreasing the vacancy–unemployment ratio and reducing youth unemployment rates.

This study conducted qualitative research on youth gig workers in Thailand and Malaysia within the Southeast Asian context, revealing the profound impact of shifting employment structures and institutional voids under the platform economy on young people's career development. Chapter 5 focuses on high-skilled gig work, while Chap. 6 examines youths engaged in on-demand delivery and driving services. Regardless of job type, the study empirically confirms that employment instability in exchange for flexibility, exclusion from institutional protections and career discontinuity are consistent challenges faced by workers. These findings should be reinterpreted not merely as diversification of the labour market but as structural institutional failure toward youths. For inexperienced youths, the expansion of gig work provides flexible employment opportunities outside traditional full-time employment, but it also signifies a transition to "institutionally unprotected employment" where conventional support mechanisms such as social insurance, vocational training, compensation systems, and labour organisations are unable to respond. This chapter derives the following four practical implications to address these institutional gaps.

First, the effective introduction of minimum wage standards and wage guarantee systems is essential. While high-skilled gig workers may appear to have wages linked to their skills, in reality, they lack pricing power due to algorithms and market fluctuations, while on-demand gig workers are fully dependent on the platform. In response to this situation, the establishment of an institutional framework that ensures a minimum level of economic stability is essential for supporting the long-term career development of youths. Relevant references for institutional design include Singapore's Platform Workers Bill, implemented in January 2025, the United Kingdom's third legal category of "worker", and the provisions concerning remuneration transparency and contractual protection outlined in the European Union's Platform Work Directive.

Second, the expansion of social security systems is required. Under the current system, gig workers are excluded from access to health insurance, pensions, and employment insurance as independent contractors who are not employees. For youths at the early stages of their careers, such institutional exclusion poses significant risks to future income security and long-term life planning. Singapore's pioneering legal protections for intermediate worker categories offer a potential model for broader application across Asia.

Third, it is essential to promote the redistribution of digital skills education and vocational training in order to address regional and income-based disparities. The spread of platforms in the digital economy seemed to overcome geographical limitations on labour. However, in reality, freelance and crowd work are concentrated in urban areas, and youths in rural areas and low-income groups are at a disadvantage in terms of educational opportunities and market access. For example, in Thailand, there is an overwhelming gap in education and income between Bangkok and provincial cities, which has a significant impact on youths' career choices. Therefore, the development of intermediate support organisations in rural areas and the expansion of community-based vocational training are essential for distributing the benefits of platform work more widely.

Fourth, it is necessary to strengthen grassroots support through professional associations and labour unions in order to address information asymmetries and enhance workers' bargaining power. The delivery worker strikes in 2022 and 2024, discussed in Chap. 6, were the beginning of countermeasures against platform domination, but they have not yet become institutionalised. In Asia, compared to Europe and the United States, the foundations for organisation and collective bargaining are weak, and information gaps and lack of bargaining power are structurally entrenched (Uchiyama & Furuoka, 2025). Therefore, it is imperative for governments, NGOs, and academic institutions to collaborate in building institutional frameworks that support the self-organisation of gig workers and enhance their bargaining power. Moreover, alternative governance models such as platform cooperativism or the concept of social common capital may also offer promising pathways for fostering more democratic and inclusive forms of platform labour organisation (Uchiyama, 2025a, 2025b).

This book visualises the structural vulnerabilities inherent in the employment of youths in the digital economy and presents specific policy recommendations for complementing and reforming it. To make the freedom of employment for young people truly meaningful, comprehensive institutional reforms and career support for youths are indispensable, and the findings could serve as a catalyst for the reconstruction of employment policies, particularly in the Global South.

7.4 The Way Forward: Towards a Productive and Dynamic Society

The problems that young people currently face in the labour market are the persistence of high youth unemployment and the rise of precarious work as a result of the deindustrialisation process. As the Fordist mass employment that absorbed youth into the labour force has effectively ended with the structural transformation from manufacturing to the service sector, young people have no choice but to seek employment opportunities in gig work or precarious work (Furlong, 2016; MacDonald, 2016; Roberts, 2016). As Chap. 2 pointed out, the precariousness faced by young workers is internalised in platform capitalism, which is a new form of exploitation mechanism in the contemporary economic system. To be more specific, the platform owners accumulate their capital and wealth by playing an intermediate role in the digital space. This foregrounds two issues. Firstly, the current education system does not prepare young people for this structural change and transformation of the economic system. The lack of appropriate preparation puts young people in an even more "precarious" situation. Secondly, an alternative 'sponge' or gig work does not provide sufficient training opportunities for young workers to update their skills and knowledge (MacDonald, 2016; Roberts, 2016).

In this context, the current study suggests introducing a "neo-apprenticeship" scheme in order to provide more decent work and employment opportunities for young people. This scheme can be defined as a work-based and 'learning-by-doing' type of lifelong learning process (Ahmadi & Marandi, 2014; Ryan, 1998). The new form of apprenticeship could be part of vocational education or technical and vocational education and training (TVET), combining on-the-job training in the

Table 7.1 Trajectory of the progression path in the neo-apprenticeship

Phases	Opening	Showing	Awakening	Entering
Mode	Preparation	Socialisation	Externalisation Combination Internalisation	Application Creation
Knowledge management	Systemisation of personal tacit knowledge	Tacit to tacit	Tacit to tacit, through explicit knowledge	Commercialisation of new knowledge to create value
Neo-apprenticeship scheme	Life-value setting and job search	*Nova lernanto*	*Funkcianta spertulo*	*Valorkreinto*

Source: Authors

firm with off-the-job training in the school (Bills et al., 2016; Skrobanek, 2016). There are also critics of this system. For instance, Parsons (1990) noted that achieving a synthesis of on-the-job and off-the-job training can be difficult because the two types of training take place in different locations and contexts. However, this form of apprenticeship places greater emphasis on on-the-job training in the workplace by placing the off-the-job training at schools as a preparatory stage.

The trajectory of the progression path in this neo-apprenticeship is summarised in Table 7.1. As discussed in Chap. 2, it is based on the synthesis of Kajita's classification of educational goals and Nonaka's theory of knowledge creation (Kajita, 2014; Nonaka, 1991). This synthesis provides a taxonomy for holistic knowledge and skill acquisition. In particular, this taxonomy is based on the four phases of socialisation, externalisation, combination, and internalisation (SECI) in the knowledge management model (Nonaka & Takeuchi, 1995). The first phase, the "opening", is the pre-SECI stage, where young people prepare for future employment opportunities. In this stage, it is important that young people systematise their personal tacit knowledge gained from previous experiences. As Becerril-Montekio et al. (2016) emphasised, this process of systematising personal tacit knowledge is important for prioritisation. In this preparatory phase, young people are encouraged to contemplate and understand their own goals and preferences. In other words, the systematisation of personal tacit knowledge helps them to identify and prioritise the core values and beliefs that will guide their decisions regarding future career perspectives.

Despite its preparatory nature, the "opening" phase is crucial because, in contemporary society, firms serve as the primary storehouses of knowledge and skills. It would therefore be difficult, if not impossible, for young people to fully develop their innate potential without joining a firm. Accordingly, it is imperative that firms "open" their doors and allow young people to join their organisations. In addition, there is a need to ensure a match between young people's aspirations and firms' expectations. From the perspective of labour market intervention, policymakers may need to consider creating job-search assistance mechanisms to help young people find suitable employment. As discussed in Chap. 4, in 1998, the British government launched a bold initiative for youth employment known as the New Deal for Young

People (NDYP). Under this initiative, the government implemented the "gateway" program, through which unemployed youth received job-search assistance and other forms of guidance for six months (Gregg, 2001; Olle, 2022). Other countries could consider implementing a "gateway" program tailored to their particular contexts.

The second phase, the "showing", initiates the SECI process or the "socialisation" mode of knowledge management. In this mode, young people become novice learners, or the *nova lernanto* in Esperanto, while receiving on-the-job training (OJT) in a firm. It is important that firms provide meaningful learning by systematically and comprehensively "showing" and sharing their accumulated knowledge and information with the *nova lernanto*. In this process, mentors' primary function is to guide the *nova lernanto*. As Nonaka (1991) clearly articulated, young people need to work closely with their mentors in the OJT program. This is because they may not be able to gain valuable and useful knowledge and skills through the use of language alone; imitation and practice are crucial elements in this phase. In other words, human language serves as a good conduit for sharing theoretical information, but it may fail to transmit tacit and implicit practical knowledge. Spoken and written language often cannot fully capture the embedded emotions and nuanced details ingrained in human interaction in the workplace. Therefore, socialisation or shared experience between mentors and novice learners is crucial in this stage. The creation of tacit knowledge during mentor–mentee interactions and shared experiences can be identified as "socialisation" (Nonaka, 1991). From the perspective of labour market intervention, policymakers may consider creating wage-subsidy schemes and subsidised employment programs to assist young people in gaining work experience and appropriate OJT opportunities in the workplace. For example, in 2010, the Jordanian government introduced the wage subsidy program targeting young women, known as the "New Opportunities for Women" (NOW) program. Under this initiative, the government offered wage subsidies and sponsored training programs for young female university graduates for six months (Kluve et al., 2017).

The third phase, the "awakening", is the core stage of the SECI process. In this stage, the "externalisation–combination–internalisation" mode of knowledge management occurs: young people gain expertise in a specific area through various forms of learning and practice in the workplace. In the process of transformation from a *novula lernanto* into an operational specialist or *funkcianta spertulo* in Esperanto, three distinct knowledge management modes are identified. Namely, conversion of tacit knowledge into explicit knowledge (i.e., the externalisation mode), conversion of explicit knowledge into new explicit knowledge (i.e., the combination mode), and the conversion of explicit knowledge into tacit knowledge (i.e., the internalisation mode). In the transformation from a novice to a specialist, learners need to 'awaken' to the true nature of knowledge acquisition and management so that they become autonomous agents and specialists (*funkcianta spertulo*) who can create new knowledge independently, without assistance or guidance from others.

First, in the externalisation mode, metaphors play a crucial role in reconciling contradictory ideas into a simple expression in the creative process of knowledge conversion (Nonaka, 1991).

Metaphors are often used to explain complex and intangible ideas through more vivid and familiar images. For example, in the *Lotus Sutra*, the Buddha used the metaphor of the lotus flower as a skilful means, or *upaya* in Sanskrit, to explain the simultaneity of cause and effect. In daily life, a cause takes place first, and an effect follows. However, the Buddha revealed that the cause of carrying out various meritorious practices and the effect of attaining Buddhahood can occur simultaneously. This idea may appear counterintuitive. Therefore, the Buddha used the metaphor of a lotus flower, which bears fruit (i.e., the effect) before it blooms (i.e., the cause), to elucidate the simultaneity of practice and the attainment of Buddhahood (Ikeda et al., 2000). Similarly, some creative ideas and innovative concepts may appear to a novice or learner to be counterintuitive and contradictory in nature. During the externalisation process, apparent contradictions within new ideas are resolved through the use of metaphor. In other words, these contradictions are resolved through systematic comparison or analogy (Nonaka, 1991). Second, in the combination mode, new explicit knowledge is created by combining, sorting, and recontextualising existing explicit knowledge held by individual workers in the firm (Nonaka, 1991). Third, in the internalisation mode, action plays a crucial role in creating new tacit knowledge: through the repetitive processes of "trial and error" and the experiential practice of "learning by doing," explicit knowledge is transformed into a new form of tacit knowledge (Nonaka, 1991).

The final phase, the "entering", is the post-SECI stage in which *novula lernanto* is transformed into a value creator or *valorkreinto* in Esperanto via *funkcianta spertulo*. There is a need to differentiate the *funkcianta spertulo* from the *valorkreinto*. The former has acquired all the necessary knowledge and skills to create new knowledge through the four modes of socialisation, externalisation, combination, and internalisation. On the other hand, the latter is able to apply this new knowledge to create value for the firm. The difference between the two can be elucidated by Marx's theory on the two-fold characteristics of commodities, namely 'use-value' and 'exchange value', and Kojin Karatani's reinterpretation of these concepts (Karatani, 2020). Marx employed the Hegelian dialectic of two antithetical processes to explain the conversion of commodities into money. He captured the dynamic interplay of the "sale" and the "purchase" in two separate circuits: the *commodity circuit* or the process of "selling in order to buy", and the *money circuit* or the process of "buying in order to sell". In the former circuit, producers create a product that may have a "use-value" or qualitative utility for consumption. However, they need to sell these products to obtain money. In this first metamorphosis, or the *salto mortale* of the commodity, the commodity needs to manifest its "exchange-value" or the quantitative relation among commodities (Marx, 1986; Vidal, 2019; Furuoka, 2024c).[1] Based on Marx's emphasis on the transient and accidental nature of

[1] In this commodity circuit $C_1 - M - C_2$, the first commodity (C_1) is transformed into the second commodity (C_2) at the end of the economic transaction. There are two producers involved in this transaction: the first producer (P_1), who produces linen (L), and the second producer (P_2), who produces coats (C). Both producers want to sell their products. However, in isolation, without exchange, these products may not have any tangible value, as producers could only create

"exchange-value", Karatani claims there is an arbitrary relationship between the qualitative worth of a commodity (i.e., use-value) and its quantitative worth (i.e., exchange-value) in economic transactions. He draws an analogy with the arbitrary association between the physical form of language or phoneme (i.e., signifier) and the conceptual form of language or meaning (i.e., signified) in linguistic communication (Karatani, 2020). This theoretical interpretation can be used to examine the uniqueness of the *valorkreinto* in the progression path.

More precisely, a *funkcianta spertulo* may possess all the necessary skills and knowledge for creating products with qualitative usefulness. However, *funkcianta spertulo* may lack the specific knowledge required to create products with quantitative exchangeability. In contrast, the *valorkreinto* has expertise and confidence, and dares to "enter" the real world of business to earn money, as they are equipped with knowledge and skills in management, sales, marketing, and finance. These practical skills enable them to navigate and thrive in the competitive business environment. Thus, the *valorkreinto* possesses the wisdom and knowledge to manifest a commodity's exchange-value (i.e., signified) in a differential relation where use-value functions as the signifier. Without business acumen, newly acquired knowledge may not directly contribute to creating monetary value within the firm. Hence, a host of valuable inventions and newly gained knowledge cannot be commercialised (Grimaldi, 2009). In other words, the *valorkreinto* is a value-creator who can commercialise new knowledge and ideas, transforming them into realised monetary value in the market.

In short, the end of Fordist mass employment has led to the emergence of youth unemployment as a grave social issue. In this era of deindustrialisation, the gig economy has drawn attention for its "labour-absorbing" power to provide necessary employment opportunities for young people. Despite these high expectations, this solution is only a second-best choice due to the lack of sufficient training, learning, and career development opportunities for gig workers (Matriano et al., 2025). In the search for a better solution to youth unemployment in this century (Avent, 2016), firms are expected to offer more decent employment with better learning opportunities to address this urgent challenge in the labour market. This book has suggested that firms, as modern storehouses of knowledge, may consider providing new youth

"potential" value in isolation. These potential values could be lost if nobody wishes to buy the products. In other words, a fundamental contradiction in this transaction lies in the nature of the commodity itself. From the standpoint of the "seller," the product may not have use-value. At the same time, it may be seen as a commodity with use-value for the "buyer." Thus, money plays a mediating role, resolving this contradiction and creating a unity or a realised value in which the qualitative use-value of one product is expressed in the qualitative use-value of another product. For example, 20 yards of linen is exchanged for one coat. In this value-form analysis, the quantitative and proportional worth of the two commodities ($20L = C$) is considered their "exchange-value". In this process, the first metamorphosis ($C_1 - M$) is the transformation from the particular (i.e., commodity) to the universal (i.e., money), while the second metamorphosis ($M - C_2$) is the transformation from the universal (i.e., money) to the particular (i.e., commodity). In this sense, the second transformation is easier than the first (Marx, 1986; Harvey, 2017, 2018; Furuoka, 2024c).

training programs, such as the “neo-apprenticeship” scheme, which is based on the synthesis of Kajita’s theory of educational goals in education research (Kajita, 2014) and Nonaka’s theory of knowledge creation, specifically the socialisation, externalisation, combination, and internalisation (SECI) in business research (Nonaka, 1991). Among the four main phases of the learning process, namely the “opening”, the “showing”, the “awakening”, and the “entering”, the most important phase, as Kajita (2014) stresses, could be the “opening”, which enables young people to discover their boundless potential and to believe that they can achieve anything. In other words, a key determinant of building a productive and dynamic society may be young people’s faith in themselves and their inherent life force.

References

Ahmadi, S. D., & Marandi, S. S. (2014). Social software in the classroom: The case of wikis for scaffolding. *Procedia, 98*, 100–108.

Avent, R. (2016). *Wealth of humans: Work, power, and status in the twenty-first century*. Macmillan.

Becerril-Montekio, V., Alcalde-Rabanal, J., Darney, B. G., & Orozco-Nunez, E. (2016). Using systematised tacit knowledge to prioritise implementation challenges in existing maternal health programs: Implications for the post-MDG era. *Health Policy and Planning, 31*(8), 1031–1038.

Bills, D. B., Graf, L., & Protsch, P. (2016). Vocationalism. In A. Furlong (Ed.), *Routledge handbook of youth and young adulthood* (pp. 129–136). Routledge.

Furlong, A. (2016). The changing landscape of youth and young adulthood. In A. Furlong (Ed.), *Routledge handbook of youth and young adulthood* (pp. 19–27). Routledge.

Furuoka, F. (2024a). Patterns and convergence of unemployment rate among people with disabilities: Testing the “law of one unemployment rate”. In *Disability and employment: Towards a humanistic economy* (pp. 69–109). Springer Nature Singapore.

Furuoka, F. (2024b). Labour market interventions to reduce the disability unemployment gap. In *Disability and employment: Towards a humanistic economy* (pp. 147–176). Springer Nature Singapore.

Furuoka, F. (2024c). Understanding disability in the context of the labour market and production. In *Disability and employment: Towards a humanistic economy* (pp. 11–34). Springer Nature Singapore.

Gregg, P. (2001). The impact of youth unemployment on adult unemployment in the NCDS. *Economic Journal, 111*(475), 626–653.

Grimaldi, G. (2009). Ideas, errors and the commercialisation of valuable knowledge. *Technology Analysis & Strategic Management, 21*(6), 699–710.

Harvey, D. (2017). *Marx, capital, and madness of economic reason*. Oxford University Press.

Harvey, D. (2018). *A companion to Marx’s capital*. Verso Books.

Ikeda, D., Saito, K., & Endo, T. (2000). *Wisdom of the Lotus Sutra*. World Tribune Publications.

Kajita, E. (2014). “Kai-Ji-Go-Nyu” no kyoiku-shiso to jissenka [Educational philosophy of “Kai-Ji-Go-Nyu” and its application]. *Journal of Humanistic Education, 2*, 1–8.

Karatani, K. (2020). *Marx: Towards the centre of possibility*. Verso Books.

Kluve, J., Puerto, S., Robalino, D., Romero, J. M., Rother, F., Stoterau, J., Weidenkaff, F., & Witte, M. (2017). Interventions to improve the labour market outcomes of youth. *Campbell Systematic Reviews, 12*. https://doi.org/10.4073/csr.2017.12

MacDonald, R. (2016). Precarious work. In A. Furlong (Ed.), *Routledge handbook of youth and young adulthood* (pp. 156–1163). Routledge.

Marx, K. (1986). *Capital: A critique of political economy*. Progress.

Matriano, M. T., Harthi, S., & Matriano, R. (2025). Learning organisations' talent management and gig economy. In M. W. Bari & F. Di Virgilio (Eds.), *Handbook of talent management and learning organisations* (pp. 200–218). CRC Press.

Nonaka, I. (1991). The knowledge-creating company. *Harvard Business Review, 69*(6), 96–104.

Nonaka, I. (1994). A dynamic theory of organisational knowledge creation. *Organisation Science, 5*(1), 14–37.

Nonaka, I., & Takeuchi, H. (1995). *The knowledge-creating company: How Japanese companies create the dynamics of innovation.* Oxford University Press.

Olle, H. (2022). *The new deal for young people (NDYP).* Edge Foundation Paper No. 13.

Parsons, K. (1990). Trainers and tutors in the YTS environment. In Wallace, C. & Cross, M. (eds), *Youth in transition: The sociology of youth and youth policy*, (pp. 73–95). Routledge.

Roberts, K. (2016). Socio-economic reproduction. In A. Furlong (Ed.), *Routledge handbook of youth and young adulthood* (pp. 28–35). Routledge.

Ryan, P. (1998). Is an apprenticeship better? A review of the economic evidence. *Journal of Vocational Education & Training, 50*(2), 289–325.

Skrobanek, J. (2016). Vocational education and training and the transition from school to work: Challenges and dilemmas. In A. Furlong (Ed.), *Routledge handbook of youth and young adulthood* (pp. 137–146). Routledge.

Uchiyama, Y. (2025a). Cosmolocalism against platform capitalism: Evidence from ridesharing. *tripleC: Communication, Capitalism & Critique. Open Access Journal for a Global Sustainable Information Society, 23*(1), 23–39.

Uchiyama, Y. (2025b). Sustainable shared mobility as social common capital: Conceptual framework and case analysis. *Mobilities, 2025*, 1–21.

Uchiyama, Y., & Furuoka, F. (2025). Uberisation and resistance to online food delivery gig work in Asia: Lessons from Malaysia. *Journal of Contemporary Asia*, 1–18.

Vidal, M. (2019). Work and exploitation in capitalism. In M. Vidal, T. Smith, T. Rotta, & P. Prew (Eds.), *Oxford handbook of Karl Marx* (pp. 241–260). Oxford University Press.

MIX
Papier aus verantwortungsvollen Quellen
Paper from responsible sources
FSC® C105338

FSC
www.fsc.org

If you have any concerns about our products,
you can contact us on
ProductSafety@springernature.com

In case Publisher is established outside the EU,
the EU authorized representative is:
Springer Nature Customer Service Center GmbH
Europaplatz 3, 69115 Heidelberg, Germany

Printed by Libri Plureos GmbH
in Hamburg, Germany